Brief Authority

*Excursions of a Common Man
in an Uncommon World*

Brief Authority

Excursions of a Common Man in an Uncommon World

BY

EDWIN F. STANTON

Former Ambassador to Thailand

HARPER & BROTHERS PUBLISHERS NEW YORK

To

JOSIE

Contents

(vii)

Contents

Foreword

Old age is said to be something that happens to someone else. But middle age happens to all of us, and a curious experience it is, a halfway mark, a time for drawing up a balance sheet. In the contemporary jungle through which a man walks, it is a good time to clear the ground so that he can look about and attempt to arrive at some understanding of what has happened to him.

Perhaps it is imprudent for a Foreign Service Officer, one of that frequently castigated group of the country's public servants, to recount the experiences which have befallen him. I am conscious that the story is a plain one and even more plainly told. Nevertheless, it represents an honest effort to give a picture of the ups and down of life in the Foreign Service and some meaning and significance to the whirlpool of events in which I, like many another Foreign Service Officer, have found myself caught. Headlines, beating upon us with our morning coffee, bombard us with facts, but they do not, they cannot by their very nature, convey the inner meaning of events.

Today, with armies mustered, with nation hostile to nation, with internal dissension widening the rifts between peoples inside the boundaries of their own lands, with the threat of The Bomb hanging over the head of civilization, we need, more than ever, to know the meaning of the things that are happening to us. Because only by full understanding will we be able to shape intelligently the future course of events. It is certain that if we do not decide for ourselves, the decision will be made for us.

The setting of my own experiences has been the Far East. Thirty-two years in the Foreign Service. From the time I was a callow but buoyant twenty, I have been a part of the Foreign Service, the members of which are underpaid, overworked, live in the hot spots of international turmoil, and devote all their energies and the best of their intelligence to serving their nation. It is disheartening that for many years these loyal servants were forgotten men, only to be dragged from the darkness of obscurity into the blazing light of publicity, there to be maligned and pilloried. I am proud to have been a Foreign Service Officer, one of that group which, in war and peace—though they have known little peace in the Far East—under pressure or under gunfire, suffering internment in enemy hands as a common experience, represented the United States with, in that ringing phrase which ushered them into the service, "the special trust and confidence" of the President.

Thirty-two years! I can remember with tolerant amusement the twenty-year-old boy setting off on his first assignment, as a student interpreter, for Peiping. Naïve as I was, I did not picture the diplomatic service as an affair of pink teas and formal dress, but neither was I prepared to discover that my first dwelling place was to be a coal bin.

It was part of my experience to be confronted by bandits in Inner Mongolia, by the depredations of Chinese warlords, by famine, flood and cholera; and, during exciting and crowded years, to see Chinese nationalism on the march and the slow, difficult efforts to build a new kind of government, checked midway by war with

Japan. And then after Pearl Harbor, in common with many of my colleagues, I experienced contemporary man's purgatory, internment and confinement. Anyone fatuous enough to pride himself on his knowledge of human nature is likely to have eye-opening experiences in internment. It was both curious and disheartening to watch prominent, solid citizens, both official and nonofficial, disintegrate under the test; to see instances of thievery, temper and talebearing. But there were others, like the "playboy of Shanghai," who devoted themselves to their fellow prisoners and sustained their morale.

With the disaster at Pearl Harbor, my life in China ended. After the war I returned to the Far East and, in time, had the good fortune to become Ambassador to Thailand. This small country, whose name means "free," has had a gallant history marked by a long and magnificent struggle for freedom. It is unfortunate that the chief knowledge of Americans concerning the Thai people is derived from a pleasant musical comedy taken from the book, *Anna and the King of Siam*. Musical comedy has its place but it is entirely misleading to think of Siam, or Thailand, in such terms. Much more representative of the spirit of its people is the fact that Thailand was the first Asian country to send a contingent of troops to Korea to fight beside the troops of the United Nations; that their bravery earned for them the nickname of Little Tigers; that Thailand has given unswerving support to the United Nations; that it did not hesitate to support fully the principle of collective security and was the first to ratify the Manila Pact; and finally, that this little country is our best friend in Southeast Asia.

Perhaps those years of Foreign Service can best be summed up not in terms of power conflicts and violent death, of bombs and machine guns, but in terms of friendships: friendships with men and women of every description, from the teacher who explained to me the tranquil wisdom of Confucius to the Thai taxi driver who expounded protocol; from a haggard peasant woman who had lost everything, home, husband and children, whispering, "Oh, bitter, bitter!" to the girl Queen of Thailand who learned so quickly the rigid etiquette of a formal court; from patient rice farmers to impatient prime ministers, from eager and idealistic young Chinese and Thai dreaming of a better world, to eager and idealistic young Americans holding a similar dream. The words were different but the dream was the same, the vision of Confucius, the wise and learned one, who said, "All within the four seas are brothers."

Brief Authority

1

Special Trust and Confidence

THE young diplomat, wearing pince-nez that gouged deep holes on either side of his nose but on which he insisted because he thought them impressive, took ship from San Francisco, in 1921, on the S.S. *Golden State,* together with shining new matched luggage bought with his last remaining pennies to be in keeping with his new state.

The voyage promised to be pleasant because one supposed the passengers must be commenting to one another, "A young diplomat on his way to Peiping, you know." It was impossible not to feel slightly important, particularly at twenty, though I knew such pleasurable sensations would not have been approved by the venerable Dr. Theobold, principal of the Breeks Memorial School in Ootacamund, south India, where I had acquired my early education. In fact, such unruly emotions would have been incontinently suppressed with a cane in pursuance of the Spartan discipline which molded both mind and character at Breeks.

My frivolous mood dissipated altogether when I recalled that momentous interview, a short time before, with Charles Evans

Hughes, Secretary of State under President Harding, who shook hands with me and wished me well. He was impressive and solemn as he sat working at his papers, his face marked by stern dignity. He scrutinized me intently and then called my attention to a phrase in my commission. I have never forgotten it: "Reposing special trust and confidence in your integrity, prudence and ability." To a young man of twenty, those words were both sober and exhilarating.

They were the culmination of months of strenuous study in preparation for a career in the Foreign Service of the United States, which had been my goal ever since Julean Arnold, on leave from his post as Commercial Attaché of the American Legation in Peiping, had lectured at the University of Southern California.

Foreign Service, Mr. Arnold stressed over and over, meant service. And he quoted that much used and abused phrase: "The Foreign Service is the country's first line of defense." Personally, I prefer to think of it as a bridge of understanding. It seemed to me then, and it seems to me now, that there is no more interesting, vital, challenging job in the world.

I had been assigned to the Peiping Legation as student interpreter with a salary of $1,500 a year. After a rigorous ordeal of examinations, physical, written and oral, covering international and maritime law, United States and European history, economics and languages, I was surprised I ever passed. I still remember facing a severe and solemn board of examiners who asked what appeared to be impossible questions and ended mildly by inquiring whether I could play the guitar.

Up the turgid waters of the Whangpoo River plowed the *Golden State*, scattering hundreds of little sampans and junks right and left. Round the bend of the muddy flats, which stretched on either side, loomed the skyline of Shanghai. Solid impressive buildings, hotels, banks, offices lined the Bund, that broad avenue built by the British and other foreigners living in their concessions.

What struck me most forcibly at first was that ocean of humanity flooding the streets, buying, selling, eating, spitting, and always talking, talking. The clack-clack of countless wooden sandals striking the pavements punctuated the roar of sound. Rickshas drawn by weary men, their faces sometimes completely hidden by huge straw hats, darted in all directions, even threading, incongruously between automobiles and streetcars.

Occasionally, there was an Occidental in this kaleidoscope of Oriental life but he was immediately swallowed up, lost in the crowds. The giant Sikh policemen towered over street intersections, impassive and unmoved by the jostling crowds and the pandemonium of sound.

My ricksha boy kept asking, "Master, you wantchee see pleety Chinese girl?" But I had one pressing job to perform; I had to find the American Consulate in order to borrow enough money to get to Peiping. In government service, in the old days, one always paid one's travel expenses, which later—sometimes months later— were refunded by the Treasury. The harsh fact was I had staked my all on that matched luggage.

When my train fare had been advanced by N. F. Allman, whom I found in the huge shabby old brick building on Soochow Creek, I took the famous Blue Express to Peiping. It was dusk when the train glided past the outer walls of the great city and stopped at Chien Men Station. Above, towered massive forty-foot walls crowned by imposing towers guarding one of the principal entrances into the city. The descriptions of Marco Polo and other famous travelers crowded through my mind but none had completely captured the majesty of those magnificent walls reaching up into the night.

This first impact of the famous Imperial City was never to be forgotten. There was majesty, there was dignity, there was strength, there was severe beauty. There was also pandemonium. Swarms of

(3)

coolies set upon each passenger, seized his baggage and made off with it, gesticulating wildly and shouting at the top of their lungs. Hawkers of food, vendors of a fantastic conglomeration of articles besought the passengers to eat or to buy.

Eager hands clutched at my luggage while I strained my eyes looking for someone from the Legation. Surely it was customary to meet a newly appointed officer. But there was no one. I stepped into a ricksha drawn by a strapping man, far more robust than the puny fellows of Shanghai, took a long, uneven breath and said, "American Legation."

To my delight we headed straight for the towering walls and gate I had seen as we came into the station. They soared up and up, those wonderful walls. We raced along through the poorly lit Chien Men Gate of the Imperial City, made a sharp right turn and drew up before an imposing entrance guarded by two smart United States Marines.

The Legation had closed for the night and one of the marines sent me to the officer of the day, a cherubic fellow who, in turn, suggested a hotel. At this hour, he explained, the senior officers of the Legation would be dressing for dinner.

At the Grand Hotel de Pékin I pulled my chair close to the window. This was China and I was here. My thoughts were a mixture of disappointment, excitement and pleasure, about in the proportions one generally finds in life.

I sat absorbing the feeling of a new land, and little by little the disillusionment of my somewhat flat arrival faded. This was a return to the East for which I had a deep nostalgia, a kind of homecoming, like those in India when I had returned from school high in the Nilgiri Hills, to be met by my father with a hamper loaded with goodies.

The first six years of my life had been spent happily at Kurnool, India, where my father represented the American Baptist Foreign

Mission Society. I remember India, not looking up as most small children do, but looking down from the very top of a great banyan tree which spread its long branches and twisted roots over an immense section of our cool, shady garden, heavy with the fragrance of mango and lime blossoms, and alive with the hum of bees and the flashing green-and-red-winged parakeets.

But this paradise had its snakes. There were scorpions in the dry leaves and cobras in the banyan roots. There were, indeed, cobras everywhere. They coiled among the rocks and ferns. Their favorite haunt was the fernery and the big red pottery water jars in the bathrooms upstairs. Relaxed they were beautiful, aroused deadly, so my father had to shoot them from time to time in the lovely garden surrounding our bungalow. But the Telugus, with whom he worked for forty years, both feared and worshiped them, for the king cobra is an important deity in the Hindu religion and therefore highly regarded.

There was a memorable day when my father was sitting with a group of Telugus, listening, as he did so often, to the outpourings of their troubles, emotional, financial, and spiritual. The conversation broke off as a long glistening shape slid among them, made for Dad's feet and coiled around them, its head resting on his shoe. The king cobra! The Telugus caught their breath in mingled fear and awe. "King Cobra," one of them whispered, "is protecting our holy missionary."

My father, a singularly patient man, sat unmoving and continued to talk, on and on. Eventually the great snake uncoiled and glided away. This signal manifestation of its respect for my father, their counselor and friend, created something of a sensation among the Telugus. They came to him even more frequently, day and night, and he never failed to give them what help he could. They even expected him to cure their physical ills as well as their spiritual ones. The most popular medicine in his cupboard was a painkiller, which burned its way down the patient's gullet and caused almost instant relief for anything from scorpion stings to cholera.

Sitting in my room at the Grand Hotel de Pékin I thought much of my inspiring father, hoping that I too would be able to serve, as he had done, with enthusiasm and optimism in the face of discouragement.

For the time being, the China outside the window faded and I was once more in India. I remembered the world at the top of the banyan tree as a child's world of sheer delight. To climb ever higher and higher, swaying back and forth in the treetop, was exhilarating. To climb a little closer to the sky, to look deep into sapphire blue space was an emotional and spiritual experience. Was God really there? What was He like: stern and terrible in His goodness, or meek and mild?

From down below, mingled with the scent of flowers, came the tantalizing aroma of the spices, herbs and condiments being skillfully blended by our faithful Ayah in a delicious curry. Her voice rose in the old Telugu song:

> Curry in the pot
> Smells so good;
> Pearly white rice
> Fresh as rain.

"Little master," called the old gardener, his joints creaking loudly as he walked, "come down or the spirit of the great tree will be offended."

I slid down from my perch to help my little sister Kathy stitch banana leaves together to make plates for the curry.

A carefree, sunlit life in the garden, with my father's earnest voice reading morning prayers, with Mama singing softly while she strummed her guitar, and Ayah spinning fabulous Telugu tales of heroes and wise men. All this changed when I was sent away to school. First, for a painful year, there was a girl's boarding school to which an unhappy six-year-old, complete with Little Lord Fauntleroy suit and blond curls, was sent in care of older sister, Betty. Then the Spartan life of the Breeks Memorial School where discipline was rigid and the rod ruled us all. Six cuts with a cane was the penalty for incorrect Virgil scanning and twenty or more for misdemeanors and infractions of school rules. Breeks left its mark on both mind and body, but it was a good mark.

It was the memory of the Breeks discipline that sent me to the Legation early the following morning, although the hotel manager assured me that no self-respecting legation opened for official business before ten o'clock. And he was quite right.

In due course, however, I was ushered into a book-lined room and presented to the Legation's Chinese Secretary, Willys R. Peck, a profound scholar of Chinese and one of our Government's most able diplomats. Mr. Peck was also in charge of the student inter-preters, supervising their studies. He was kindness itself, though my heart sank when he broke the news that no word had been received from Washington about my appointment. Did this mean that it had fallen through and that my matched luggage and I would be sent home?

Oh, no, it was not unusual for an officer to arrive weeks ahead of the official announcement. With this reassurance, I listened attentively while he outlined the courses I must study: the Chinese language, Chinese history, China's relations with the United States and other countries, the Government and its economy. He gave me a list of books and of recommended Chinese teachers. And, finally, he introduced me to the senior student interpreter—there were eight of us altogether. "Come to me with any problems that may arise," said Mr. Peck.

The prior arrivals took me in charge, summed up my ignorance at a glance, and before lunch was over they had managed to sell me a polo pony which I could ill afford and which I found later shied at the sight of a polo ball, and persuaded me to engage a houseboy with a villainous disposition and an iniquitous nature.

The student's mess was an enchanting old Chinese temple of historic fame, where, it was told me, one of the Manchu Emperors had committed suicide. The approach was through a circular moon gate. The buildings were laid out in a series of outer and inner courtyards in conventional Chinese architectural style in such a way that one did not lead straight into the next, so there would be no easy entry for obnoxious spirits.

The center building was strikingly handsome, with a great interior hall, the beams of which were lacquered in black and supported by thick vermilion posts. A carved ceiling painted in green and gold was a fine example of Chinese decorative design. The windows were wooden frames covered with paper which admitted the softest light.

"Where," I asked diffidently, "are my quarters?"

My guide, Flavius Josephus Chapman III from Roanoke, Virginia, smiled. "You're going to be just fine," he assured me blandly. "We've cleaned out the coal bin for you."

2

Five Cartloads of Books

IF ONE wishes to be acquainted with the past and the present, he must read five cartloads of books." With this famous proverb the Chinese teacher Chin Te Ming initiated me to the study of the Chinese language and history.

After a few days spent in settling in my coal-bin quarters; learning how to manipulate the perforated kerosene tin that served as a shower in the students' community bathroom; trying to persuade my houseboy Li to perform a few light tasks, which he did with reluctance; and listening with awe to the senior students toss off Chinese sentences like firecrackers, I had been introduced to Chin Ming Te, who was to be my mentor and guide through the labyrinthine maze of written and spoken Chinese.

My tutor, whose name signified Golden and Illustrious Virtue, was a courtly old-style gentleman, who wore a silk gown with a long-sleeved overjacket, and a small skull cap with a button on top. Once an official in the old Manchu imperial court, he had beautiful hands with long tapering fingernails, the hallmark of the scholar.

But to me his most fascinating feature was a single long hair growing from a mole on the chin of his round, benign face.

We set to work, Tutor Chin trying to instill into me the four tones basic to the use of the spoken language, which he repeated endlessly and with infinite patience. Hour after hour, he sat bolt upright and almost immovable, occasionally caressing that long hair with his improbable fingernails.

The first few months must have been incredibly dull for him; certainly they were frustrating for me. And my colleagues deepened my despair by telling of the horrendous mistakes made by using the wrong tone and of the staggering stiffness of the quarterly and yearly examinations, which flunked out most students.

After six months, the tones were no longer impossible and the written characters became fascinating. Tutor Chin also brightened up. He loved to talk of the glories of the past, of the learning and wisdom of Confucius, Mencius, Lao-tzu and other sages. As a Confucionist, he had firm respect for Heaven, the Emperor and the family at a time when revolutionary ideas had undermined old beliefs and customs but had failed to substitute anything of an enduring nature.

Mr. Chin had little use for Sun Yat-sen and the other revolutionaries because they were not rooted in the classics, and the dignity and discipline of the great Confucius. "They value not learning," he said, "but are driven only by a restless urge to change everything."

"Venerable teacher," I asked, "may not change be good for your honorable country?"

"Orderly, reasonable change might be good, indeed; for do not the seasons change, bringing with them the essence of life and death? Change could be good for China. There is much to learn from the West. But many of these men know not what they seek.

They have not sufficient knowledge of the past nor comprehension of things of the West, yet they set themselves up as leaders."

My tutor pointed to the growing number of warloads, the depredations of their troops, the instability of Government, the heavy burden of taxes upon the people.

"Heaven is not pleased," he declared.

So I came to realize the overpowering weight of the past as it affected men of his caste and learning. At the same time, however, I was hearing much of the "new spirit" from a young Chinese student at Tsing Hua University. This spirit, he said, would banish old beliefs and customs and substitute for them what he called "modern nationalistic ideas and policies," which would make China both great and modern. There was, he felt, much virtue in the new techniques of the West. At the same time, being an ardent nationalist, he talked vehemently of the necessity of China liberating herself from the shackles of the great Western powers. His adoration for Sun Yat-sen was equaled only by his contempt for Confucius.

So it was that, at this early stage in my career, I heard much talk about changing China. It was revealing and valuable talk and helped to explain some of the anomalies current in the China of the 1920's. The old conservative spirit embellished with the culture of centuries versus the young restless untutored force existing on nationalism and undigested new ideas. The two were often in serious conflict; between them, they were to determine China's future and her destiny.

I was absorbing Chinese history and culture and ideas through my very pores and at the same time soaking up the atmosphere of Peiping. In the evenings I often lingered at fascinating booths that displayed merchandise of every description, from imperial jade rings to old nails. Each stall was brightly illuminated by lamps or candles with gaily painted horn shades. There were beautiful porcelains, ancient bronzes, gorgeous silks, subtle paintings. "Straight from the hands of thieves," F.J., my mentor and colleague, told me with disillusionment.

At the same time I began to participate in a small way in the official life of the capital. One of the first of these occasions was the splendid reception given by the President of China on New Year's Day, to which members of the diplomatic corps were invited. This invitation threw the students into a tizzy and we went into a huddle over our wardrobes, turning up six dress suits and four top hats. We drew lots for the tails and resolved the shortage of toppers by arranging that after a student had passed down the guard of honor, resplendent in blue and gold uniforms, he would pass his top hat to a Legation messenger, who raced back with it, behind the guards, handed it to the next student, who then made his appearance in full regalia. It worked like a charm.

Those first six months were crowded with work, interest, and new impressions. At the end of that time I timidly tried out my Chinese on a farmer outside the city. En route to the lovely purple Western Hills, studded with interesting old temples, I stopped by the roadside to chat with a Chinese farmer who was resting from his labors, leaning on his long-handled hoe. In my best Chinese, paying particular attention to my tones, I asked about his crops.

He listened politely, looked puzzled, and finally replied in Chinese that he did not speak English. A crestfallen young student tried to comfort himself with the thought that perhaps spoken Chinese of city and country greatly differed, which is actually the case. Frequent trips during the next few months, talks with country folk, muleteers, priests in the temples, and others, brought about a decided improvement in my ability to speak this complicated but amazingly expressive language.

One day, during the summer of 1922, Clifford Pope, a young ichthyologist from the American Museum of Natural History, which was engaged in the fascinating mission of exploring the vast reaches of Outer Mongolia for the missing link between the continents of Asia and North America, asked, "Ed, how would you like to join me on an expedition to the Yellow River region northwest of Peiping?"

Permission had to be sought from my chief, who encouraged the students to travel about in the interior in order to acquire knowledge of local conditions. With his consent, off we went with sleeping bags, a few cans of food, and mountains of scientific gear.

We took the train up through the Western Hills, past stretches of the Great Wall of China, begun in the third century B.C. by the ruthless Emperor who established a police state rivaling those created by Hitler and Stalin. He so loathed scholars that he slew them by the hundreds and burned the Confucian and other classical books.

At the end of the railway, we were still several days' trek from our destination, the great loop which the Yellow River makes as it flows majestically through the Ordos Desert of Inner Mongolia. We spent a day and a night in the town of Kwei Hua Cheng, where my Chinese was taxed as I struggled to understand and be understood among the western Chinese.

I managed to explain to the innkeeper that we needed two carts to proceed west to the Yellow River. Wang beamed and explained that carts were more scarce than jade in his miserable town but they would be found. And dear they were, too. In the end the bandits got them and us as well at the little town of Melodious Frogs, two days' journey from Kwei Hua Cheng.

During the 1920's, bandits constituted a scourge more deadly than the epidemics of typhus or black plague that periodically swept the country. From ancient times China has suffered from bandits, the severity of this kind of plague being a faithful barometer of the country's political and economic condition. The two decades following the overthrow of the Manchu dynasty, in 1911, and the establishment of a republican form of government were twenty years of internal political confusion and dissension in which the Central Government exercised only a modicum of actual authority and the country was at the mercy of ambitious, rapacious warlords. The poor farmer was taxed double, treble, and the end was not yet, for he often had to pay fifty to a hundred years in advance!

The merchant likewise paid taxes of every conceivable kind both to his local warlord and to the Central Government. He paid yet again if he moved his goods from the bailiwick of one warlord into that of another. The country was split and divided into areas of power controlled by these rapacious individuals, who were constantly at war with one another in an attempt to extend their domain and their power. Between the warlords, the bandits, and the ineffectual Central Government, the helpless farmers and merchants suffered acutely. At that time, it looked as though the birth of the new spirit of nationalism had resulted in the opening of Pandora's box, out of which had sprung oppression, injustice, and greed. Hope for a united China had been dimmed.

"But," said Mr. Peck of the Legation, who briefed us on conditions in China, "do not forget that the birth of any new nation is accompanied by travail and chaotic conditions. In the case of the new Chinese Republic, we are witnessing an effort on the part of the country's new leaders, who are imbued by a strong spirit of nationalism, to throw out the traditions and customs of centuries in order to make room for the new. The tragedy is," he added, "that the outpourings of Sun Yat-sen offered as the new ideals are vapid and xenophobic."

So it was a disrupted countryside into which we traveled. As we approached the small mud-walled Village of Melodious Frogs, lying on a fertile plain with the Yellow River to the south and a range of mountains to the north rising sharply into the quiet spaces of the great Mongolian plateau, we observed the dusty cart tracks were choked with people. I asked our cart driver, an amiable ruffian, what was going on. He replied that there was a big fair with much drinking of *Kao liang* (a fiery liquor made from sorghum).

We put up at a small inn just inside the west gate. The place was jammed. There was bedlam, travelers shouting and horses and mules kicking up their hoofs in delight to be out of harness. Innkeeper Tung, the Understanding One, was a big fellow whose rough appearance and stentorian voice belied his name. But he made us welcome in a lordly manner and ushered us into a small room with a floor of mother earth, mud walls, and a raised *kang*, or platform, spread with dirty mats to be used for sitting, sleeping and eating. In winter, the *kang* can be warmed by shoveling hot coals into a cavity underneath.

We unpacked only essentials and strolled into the village square to view the fair. It was now dark and the dancing lights from hundreds of candles and unshaded lamp wicks illuminated the many small booths selling food, vegetables and especially frogs, the delicacy of the town. Mongols from the high plateau rubbed shoulders with Chinese or Kazaks from the far west. We were ravenously hungry and, seated in a food booth, had a superb meal of roast duck and noodles cooked with peanuts, a fine clear soup with floating pigeon eggs, and sweet lotus-seed dessert.

Replete, we returned to the inn to find that there were little friends sharing our hard couch with us. Having on previous trips into the country experienced the voracious appetites of these monsters, we had come armed with insect repellent. After anointing ourselves, we lay down to sleep. But sleep was not to be. From adjoining rooms we could hear all too clearly the shouts of revelers playing a drinking game accompanied by a doggerel verse that increased in volume as the losing players drank their cups of wine. These bursts of sound were interspersed with the steady clack-clack of the mahjong tiles as they were shuffled around.

Shortly after midnight, we managed to doze off but were almost immediately awakened by shouts and the staccato sound of machine-gun fire. The smell of smoke rapidly pervaded our room as the flimsy buildings of the little town began to burn. Innkeeper Tung rushed into our room, his face ashen yellow. On his knees, he begged us to protect him. The Ko Lao Hui bandits had taken the town and were pillaging and killing.

We sat tight, nervously awaiting developments. After a while protests from without were silenced by shots, the bandits invaded the courtyard and then the head bandit, a giant of a man, his eyes bright from opium, appeared in our room. He barked at the followers who had crowded in after him and they hastened to leave.

We offered him tea and cigarettes. He inhaled deeply at a cigarette and explained that he was a *Ta Ko*, or big brother, of the Elder Brothers Society. The Ko Lao Hui was a secret fraternal organization that had existed since the early days of the Manchu dynasty and had opposed the Imperial regime. The bandit chief described with pride and gusto how the organization had killed corrupt Manchu officials and tax collectors, "to sweeten the bitterness of the people."

No doubt, the liquidation of extortionate officials had gained for the Elder Brothers some popularity and considerable notoriety, but it was widely known as a cruel and fierce secret society that had slain tens of thousands of Manchus and not a few foreign missionaries.

Presently the bandit handed me his calling card, which was impressive in size, and asked us to "lend" him our firearms and carts and horses as he had urgent need of them. I told him we had no weapons (having hidden our shotguns and hunting rifles). As for carts and horses, I was afraid that the Honorable Brother would experience trouble and inconvenience if he took them because we were of the American Legation.

His answer was to shout to his men to seize our carts and horses, which they did with despatch and relish. He then opened one of our tins of canned pineapple, pronounced it good, and promised to return our transportation within a day or two.

The next afternoon, my companion and I set out to learn what had happened to a foreign missionary we had been told about. We were appalled at what we saw as we walked through the village. Dead men, women, and children lay sprawled in all attitudes in the streets; houses were in flames. Groups of bandits battered on the doors, tortured the luckless inhabitants to force them to disclose their hidden treasures, and often shot them in cold blood, stripping them of all belongings.

Fortunately, we were not molested and found our missionary, a likable Swedish gentleman. He had been living among the Chinese and Mongols of this remote region for twenty-five years, a lonely and dangerous life. He explained that the Village of Melodious Frogs and others in the general vicinity were repeatedly attacked and looted by the Ko Lao Hui and other groups and that banditry was rampant throughout a wide area in the northwest. The authorities were powerless and, anyhow, they were much too pre-occupied with their intrigues in Peiping to interfere. He himself had been robbed of what little money he had but he served us tea and a few dried biscuits. Our hearts were heavy as we left him but he was not discouraged.

For two days we remained in the village among these scenes of pillage and butchery, wondering how the country people could be so patient in the face of frequent visitations of death and rapine.

An elderly cook at the inn, with kind eyes and a friendly smile, said serenely, "What does death mean to us poor people since Heaven is our friend?"

After much jingling of Mexican dollars, the popular currency in China in those days, we managed to hire two forlorn little donkeys, on which we piled our belongings and set out for a nearby village where Clifford hoped to set up his scientific headquarters. We had not gone five miles when we saw a cloud of dust ahead of us. Gradually there emerged out of it some twenty bandits brandishing rifles and pistols.

"Not again," my companion groaned. "This is really too much!"

They surrounded us and, remembering the fate of the hapless villagers, I thought the game was up. Emulating as far as possible the politeness of the *Ta Ko*, I drew out of my pocket with a flourish that bandit chieftain's calling card and showed it to the man who appeared to be the leader of the group. The Big Brother, I assured him, would be extremely angry if we were molested.

That calling card—surely the most ridiculous weapon ever used against a troop of armed bandits—worked like a charm and the men went off without a word.

For a month we remained in the village where Clifford set up his headquarters and carried on his field work. As soon as word got around that he was willing to pay for reptiles and strange animals, the people for miles around brought in a weird assortment of creatures. For weeks I lived among live and dead specimens and thought I would never get rid of the smell of formaldehyde. We constantly heard of the depredations of our friends the bandits in surrounding villages, but fortunately were not molested again.

We returned to Peiping with an incredible collection of vipers, reptiles, fish and frogs, including some rare specimens, all scientifically mounted, described and preserved, which were later acclaimed in the scientific world. At the slightest opportunity we unloaded our exploits with the bandits on some new arrival and basked in the exclamations, the bated breath, and the looks of admiration.

The approach of final examinations dissipated my rosy dreams of glory but the role of hero had been pleasurable while it lasted. The finals were very stiff, particularly the oral part, which involved interpreting for Mr. Peck, reading and translating at sight difficult Chinese official papers and despatches. Our revered Mr. Peck bore down hard at this time but my trips into the country, added to the patient efforts of my tutor, stood me in good stead.

When I told the Venerable Teacher Chin that I had passed my finals, he replied, "Do not forget there remain four more cartloads of books to study before you can begin to understand the past and the present. The wise man upon passing his examinations understands that he knows nothing."

3

Vice Consul on His Own

WHEN the examinations were successfully over, the American Minister, Dr. Jacob Gould Schurman, summoned me. "Stanton," he said, "you have done creditably in your examinations and I am pleased. I expect," he added with a smile, "you will find it easier in future to translate the Chinese inscriptions on tombstones."

On several occasions he had visited such historic spots as the mausoleums of the Ming and Ching emperors, where he had called upon me to translate the long inscriptions on the stone monuments set among beautiful old pine trees. Trembling in my shoes, because I recognized only one character in ten of the archaic Chinese hieroglyphics, I rattled off translations that, as Mr. Schurman was perfectly aware, I invented for the most part. His only comment at the time was, "Extraordinary, extraordinary."

"Having finished your language studies here, the time has come," he said, "for you to embark on your duties as a consular officer. Consul General Gauss at Mukden has repeatedly requested that a language officer be assigned to his staff, so I am sending you there.

It's an interesting post at the very center of Marshal Chang Tso-lin's Manchurian empire."

Chang Tso-lin had risen spectacularly from bandit chieftain to became a powerful military and political figure who not only ruled most of Manchuria but overshadowed the shaky Central Government residing in Peking.

"The Old Tiger, Chang Tso-lin," Dr. Schurman concluded, "is a power that the Government here must reckon with and his position is also important in relation to the Bolsheviks who are establishing themselves more firmly in eastern Siberia and along China's northern frontiers."

It was November and bleakly cold when I arrived in Mukden, my first post. Under the experienced guidance of my chief, Consul General Gauss, I learned the rudiments of consular work, including where and how to certificate invoices, visas, passports and a host of other papers. For many weeks I lived in mortal fear of placing the wrong stamp on the wrong document or on the wrong part of a document. But my chief was patient and I learned much.

It was political reporting, however, that fascinated me. I had long had visions of writing masterly political reports, which, because of their style and comprehensiveness would earn commendations from the Legation and ultimately the Department of State. Being a neophyte I could scarcely expect to do this at my first post, but it was part of my job to gather information for my chief.

Mukden seemed to be alive with intriguers and intrigues, for not only was it the capital of the "Old Tiger's" Manchurian stronghold, but Japanese and Russian influences and interests were potent elements in the political and economic situation. The Japanese regarded themselves as lords of Manchuria, following on their victories in the Russo-Japanese war, the cession to them of Port Arthur, their virtual control of the Manchurian railways, and the vast industrial and other enterprises which they had established.

Parts of Mukden, like parts of Manchuria, were almost wholly
Japanese and certainly completely dominated by them. The Japanese gave lavish parties at which much *sake*, their rice wine, was
consumed and geishas imported from Japan swayed gracefully as
they waited on the guests.

From the Japanese one heard much talk about the political intrigues of the Chinese, their inefficiency and corruption. At Chinese
official functions one heard about the wicked "dwarf men," as the
Chinese call the Japanese, and their grasping ambitions to seize
control of all of Manchuria. From the "white" Russians who had
fled to China from the terrors of Bolshevik atrocities and a regime
that sought their extermination, we learned of Soviet ambitions in
Manchuria, where Russia had once been the dominating force,
and of Soviet penetration into Outer Mongolia.

Mukden was an absorbing post and the most interesting person
was, of course, Marshal Chang Tso-lin, the Old Tiger, the appella-
tion he had acquired as a dashing, ruthless bandit chieftain. His
sagacity and dominating personality had led many a petty bandit
chief to cast in his lot with him, thus augmenting his strength and
extending the territory under his control until he was undisputed
overlord of the greater part of Manchuria. He then set up his own
government and bestowed upon himself the title of Marshal. In
the winter of 1923, when I was posted at Mukden, he was at peace
with the Central Government but brooked no interference.

I was naturally keen to see the Old Tiger and my chance came
at the grand New Year's reception given by him. He lived in a
magnificent old palace elaborately guarded by soldiers with tommy
guns. Consul General Gauss and I went through courtyard after
courtyard and past innumerable guards until we came to the inner
sanctum. This was a large hall, garishly modernized. But it was
striking. The floor was covered with tiger skins and dozens more

hung on the walls. At the far end on a raised platform draped with the most magnificent tiger skins, sat the Old Tiger himself.

He was a man in his sixties with sharp aquiline features, a thin scraggly mustache and a depressed, grim mouth. He looked tired though it was rumored that he had just had a pipe of opium before the reception. He greeted Mr. Gauss and me cordially and chatted with us for some little time, in sharp contrast to his brief greetings to the Japanese officials who had come to pay their respects. No doubt, this mark of favor was intended to impress the Japanese, and the Old Tiger probably hoped that the United States would prove to be a counterbalance if not deterrent to Japanese ambitions in Manchuria. So I had my glimpse of the Old Tiger before being transferred from Mukden to Kalgan, some hundred and fifty miles northwest of Peiping.

In the spring of 1924, a telegram from the Department of State arrived, saying, "Stanton assigned Kalgan should proceed immediately." I stopped over briefly at Peiping to receive instructions from the Legation, where I learned that I would be in charge, which thrilled me, but the thrill was dampened by reports on the disturbed and dangerous conditions prevailing. It was also explained to me that relations with the local Chinese officials were not of the best because of their persistent efforts to curtail and restrict American business activities, particularly the motor transport business between Kalgan and Urga, the capital city of Mongolia.

Apropos of Mongolia, the Legation wished full and comprehensive reports on political developments in that remote area where the Bolsheviks had not only set up a so-called "People's Government" in an area bordering on Siberia, known as Tannu Tuva, but were egging on the Mongols to throw off the last vestiges of Chinese suzerainty.

"It's a difficult post," the Legation people said and just before I left they added, "Don't forget you are also expected to look after British and Swedish interests, since their countries have no consular representatives in the Kalgan area."

"Vice Consul of the United States of America at Kalgan," read my official calling card in English and Chinese. It sounded fine and I had a plentiful supply printed, knowing that in China the calling card is the diplomat's most useful and effective tool. I was twenty-three years old, somewhat scared at the thought of the duties and responsibilities of the post, which covered an area almost as large as the United States.

To make my official calls, I hired the most elaborate carriage in Kalgan, complete with a solemn-faced driver in a fine flowing gown and two grooms with whisk brooms whose duty it was to clear the way by shouting noisily, "Make way for the great American Vice Consul." The Governor and other provincial officials on whom I called had been appointed by the Peiping Government but actually they were henchmen of the Old Tiger of Manchuria, for at that particular time, his authority extended through most of the provinces bordering on Mongolia.

My official calls had barely been completed when Kalgan was struck by a disastrous flood. The river dividing the town come down with a roar because of unusually heavy spring rains. It burst its banks and spewed death and destruction through the crowded business district. In a matter of hours, the center of town, including the railway station and yards, was a shambles, and thousands found themselves without food or shelter. As though that were not enough, the flood carried horror in its wake in the form of an epidemic of cholera, which decimated the population living in crowded, unsanitary conditions.

Something had to be done. Civic-minded Chinese, acting through benevolent societies and the Chamber of Commerce, asked me to attend a meeting at which a relief committee was to be organized.

I attended gladly and assured them of my support and willingness to seek aid from the American Red Cross. The Governor, who presided, quickly organized a committee and enlisted the aid of the Swedish medical missionary in the fight to halt the epidemic. We all literally rolled up our sleeves and set to work, building shelters, setting up feeding stations and improvising clinics.

A cholera epidemic is a fearsome thing. The dying and the living are alike gripped by the fear of death. I made the rounds with our medical and sanitary teams, whose jobs were to fumigate and inspect the houses, bury the dead, provide food, clothing and shelter. I noticed many houses had long white strips of paper with strange Chinese characters written on them, which were pasted on the front doors.

"Mr. Liu," I said to a member of the team who had left the buying and selling of tea and volunteered for this unpleasant duty, "what is the meaning of these strips of white paper?"

"Those are charms against the epidemic," he replied. "An ancient custom. The characters say that the Three Pure Ones of the Taoist religion have ordered the expulsion of all malignant spirits and demons that are causing the epidemic." He went on to explain that the Chinese have great faith in these written charms and believe that they will protect them from diseases of many kinds. We went into house after house which bore these paper charms, only to find dead or dying within. The power of the Three Pure Ones had proved unavailing.

For the dying not much could be done, but the heroic labors of medical and sanitation committees, who worked day and night amid indescribable conditions of filth and stench, saved thousands of lives. Then the supply of anti-cholera serum ran out. Gloom and despair seized us and fear assumed panic proportions. It was at this dark moment that word was received from the Red Cross in response to my appeal. They had arranged through the Rockefeller Medical

Center at Peiping to send quantities of serum and other medicines as soon as rail communications were restored. But the railway tracks in the vicinity of Kalgan were still under six feet of silt. When I told the relief committee that the American Red Cross was ready and willing to help but the railway must be cleared before such help could reach us, they said the track would be cleared within a week. The committee spread the word and the next morning there was a huge turnout of citizens who dug and shoveled for days.

Out of that nightmare of an emergency was built a bridge of good will that smoothed the way for me as nothing else could have done. The grateful people of Kalgan prepared a scroll of thanks twenty feet in length for the American Red Cross.

With the ravages of flood and disease receding, there was time to look at Kalgan and settle myself in my new quarters. The town was set on a plateau and connected with Peiping by a railway that wound through bare mountains denuded of trees, by the millions who, for centuries, have chopped down everything in their desperate search for firewood and fuel. A few miles to the northeast of the town the surrounding mountains opened into a pass which led to a higher plateau. Beyond were the great rolling plains of Mongolia. Long camel caravans plodded slowly up and down the pass, carrying wool, skins and fine furs from the outer spaces of Mongolia to Kalgan; tea, silks, tobacco and sundry goods from China to Urga, the holy city of Mongolia where a Living Buddha and thirty thousand Lama priests lived in temples patterned after the famous Potala of Lhasa. It was this trade with Mongolia and with the far northwestern provinces of China and Central Asia that made Kalgan an important commercial center.

The town itself was drab and unattractive but the purple coloring of the mountains cast a cloak of beauty over the insipid brownness. It was a frontier town, lashed by cold, blustering winds in winter and choking clouds of dust in early spring, churned up in the wastes of the Gobi Desert. Those dust storms are not easily forgotten. For days, sun, moon, and stars were blotted out by swirling, stinging particles of sand and dust. One peered through the reddish brown gloom, awed by the fearful spectacle and intimidated by its steady seepage through doors, windows, and every crack, as though it were alive. The hair, mouth, eyes, ears and nose were filled with dust. Only dust to breathe.

After a particularly smothering siege of dust, I dined with the manager of a big British firm in Kalgan. For dessert we were served "Peiping dust," a gourmet's delicacy composed of finely powdered and roasted Chinese chestnuts surrounded by candied lotus seeds and topped by whipped cream. One mouthful was all I could swallow for it brought back much too vividly and realistically all the dust I had swallowed for days.

"Tastes like our last dust storm, doesn't it?" said my host in resignation. "But our cook is so proud of it I didn't have the heart to stop him."

A bachelor settling into his first house makes many a lamentable mistake. There was the new rug for the living room and the new curtains, both of which I could ill afford and both of which turned out to be ghastly mistakes. In fact, they ruined an otherwise rather pleasant room. The consular residence was a comfortable bungalow with a fairly large living room looking onto the garden, a small dining room, two bedrooms and bath. The young garden, surrounded by a mud wall, was laid out in formal design but the plantings, particularly the lilacs, were good. In season, I was able to fill the house with fragrant white and purple lilacs. The Chinese who came to call admired everything, but not so the foreign ladies of Kalgan who, I was told privately, said to each other, "That poor bachelor—what horrible taste!"

The American community though small was sprinkled with a

number of rough diamonds. They were the men who had pioneered the motor transport service from Kalgan to Urga, 750 miles to the north. There were no roads, but during the summer months, the trucks, once having gained the rolling steppes of Mongolia, raced along at a fast clip. It proved to be a lucrative business and it was not long before the local Chinese officials and merchants set up rival transport services. The competition was fierce. Discriminatory rules and regulations were imposed in increasing number by the Chinese, driving some Americans out of business.

It being an important part of my duties to protect American business interests, I called often on the local Governor to protest against such regulations. My relations with the Governor were cordial as a result of our joint labors on the relief committee during the flood but, as he himself and his friends were also engaged in this rewarding business, he did not give me much satisfaction. The new regulations, he told me, did not contravene the treaties between the United States and China; on the contrary, they actually gave protection to the merchants of my country. The Governor, in short, was past master at polite prevarications, and having, in accordance with custom, paid a very substantial sum for his appointment as Governor, he was intent on relining his pockets as speedily as possible.

Troubles with the Governor and other local officials were soon overshadowed, however, by the Bolshevik cloud which loomed over the Mongolian horizon. I commenced to receive reports from Americans and Chinese who traded with the Mongols that the Bolsheviks were bringing increasing pressure to bear on the Mongolian princes to cease business with the Chinese and foreigners. In July, 1921, the Mongols proclaimed Outer Mongolia an independent republic and were more tightly drawn into the expanding orbit of Soviet power. The Soviets provided aid, advice, and trade. To the Mongols, who longed for complete independence from Chinese rule, which had done little to win the friendship of these proud, nomadic people, formerly the masters of all China and central Asia, the Bolshevik pressure and propaganda were both appealing and irresistible.

Bolshevik influence spread steadily and one could foresee that the Chinese would be driven from Mongolia and trade terminated between that country and China. I remember well a long talk with a prominent Mongolian prince who spoke Chinese and, indeed, had a certain liking for the Chinese. He said that the Mongols did not particularly like or trust the Russians but that they were less disliked than the Chinese, who for years had treated the Mongols like dogs.

"We know we can expect nothing good from the Chinese," said the prince, "but these new Russians, they promise much."

Promises, I reminded him, might be empty words.

There was no dullness in the work at Kalgan. Even the daily routine had its brighter moments. There were the requests from business concerns in the United States inquiring about the possibility of selling patented diapers for babies and brushless shaving cream for male adults. In reply, I pointed out that for three thousand years Chinese babies had not felt the need of diapers and had found a neat slit in the seat of the pants quite adequate, and that the market for brushless shaving cream was likewise poor because Chinese men seldom need to shave.

Then there were requests for postage stamps and general information. But the inquiries calling for the greatest resourcefulness were those asking for an authentic brick or stone from the Great Wall of China. Since nearly a thousand miles of the Great Wall ran through the Kalgan consular district, one could not ignore such requests. On the other hand, the Great Wall was a day's journey away and I hardly felt justified in leaving my post to collect bricks to satisfy the collector's zeal of my compatriots. I turned the problem over to a bright young Chinese clerk in the Consulate.

Next day he appeared, beaming, with half a dozen large bricks. "From the Great Wall of China, Honorable Vice Consul."

I commended him for his initiative but expressed some doubt that the bricks had actually come from the Great Wall. He smiled. "Honorable Sir, there is an old brick kiln just beyond the consulate compound."

Much of my time was taken up with the protection of British and Swedish interests. British oil, tobacco, and cold-storage companies did extensive business in the Kalgan consular district, and they were always running into trouble with the local warlords or bandits. On one occasion, a British cold-storage firm, which had bought 100,000 sheep in Mongolia and was herding them down by easy stages, ran afoul of a local warlord whose troops seized the sheep and drove them off to his bailiwick, close to the Yellow River.

The matter required negotiation. Arrived at his headquarters to pay my respects, I was received with great politeness and offered ceremonial tea. The warlord and I discussed every sort of subject except sheep. When the time came to leave, I remarked that I had heard, but could not believe it was true, that some of his troops had in error seized 100,000 sheep belonging to a British firm. I emphasized that this story had caused serious concern to the British Legation in Peiping. Blandly and politely, he assured me that the story had no foundation in fact and that he made a particular point of protecting foreign lives and property.

We agreed, smiling, that the rumor was false. Then I suggested, since this was the case, that he issue the necessary orders to his troops and thus facilitate the onward journey of the sheep. He asked me to assure the British Legation that all would be well. And it was.

4

A Neophyte Among the Warlords

A FEW months later, my friend the Governor, who was also the Kalgan warlord, was having dinner with me at the Consulate. He liked to come to admire the view overlooking the valley and beyond drab Kalgan, the colorful mountains. He used to say that "the Consulate air was safe air." No doubt he was right, judging by the reports one heard of intrigues and liquidations occurring from time to time among his followers.

On this occasion he told me that serious trouble was brewing between the Old Tiger and General Feng Yu-hsiang, known to foreigners as the "Christian General," because of his reported conversion to the Christian faith earlier in his career. However, he had succumbed to the violence and intrigue which characterized the political life of the times and the only vestige of his religion was his delight in having his soldiers sing Christian hymns.

General Feng Yu-hsiang had given sporadic support to the principal military and political figure in North China, Marshal Wu Pei-fu, in the latter's efforts to drive the forces of Marshal Chang

Tso-lin from North China back into Manchuria. It now appeared that the "Christian General" was seeking to establish his own empire in north and northwestern China.

He seized Peiping while his erstwhile ally Marshal Wu Pei-fu was engaged along the coast above Tientsin against Marshal Chang Tso-lin's forces. He drove out the young Manchu Emperor who had been residing in Peiping as a "ward" of the Government, and then decided to expand and consolidate his position by pushing up the railway toward Kalgan. The Peiping-Suiyan Railway leading to Kalgan and the adjoining countryside was, for weeks, the scene of seesaw engagements between the contending forces. While the gladiators slugged it out, the people suffered. Kalgan was cut off. Martial law was declared in the town, the merchants began closing their stores and an ominous tension pervaded the air.

Suddenly, the forces of the Christian General broke through and were at the outskirts of the town. I was working in the office, a small building adjoining the residence, when the gateman came running in and jabbered that a big fight was about to take place right around the Consulate. I dashed out to look. Sure enough, the mountainside above the Consulate was black with Feng Yu-hsiang's cavalry. They commenced to charge down the hill.

At that instant there broke out a shattering chatter from the machine guns that, without my knowledge, had been set up by the Governor's forces in the old brick kiln about fifty yards from our garden wall. The firing was so heavy that a breeze of whining bullets enveloped the compound and much of the garden was churned up. I looked to see what had happened to some friends who had been playing tennis. They were, very sensibly, lying flat on their faces, for all the world like the card gardeners in *Alice in Wonderland*.

At the first lull in the fighting, I made my way cautiously to the brick kiln and pointed out to the officer in charge of the machine-gun post that the property his troops were firing into and over was the American Consulate. He apologized, shouted orders to his troops to move, and then continued the battle.

It was soon evident that the Governor's forces could not hold the town. They began to withdraw, looting and pillaging as they went. Billowing clouds of smoke told the story. Then word came that some Americans living in the town were being molested and were in danger. The effort to reach them through the burning, looting, shooting rabble of troops was a nightmare.

By much talk, great good fortune and the liberal use of my calling cards, I was able to bring this little group to the Consulate, where they and other members of the American community spent the night. We organized watches and all that wild night kept turning away from the Consulate's gate soldiers brandishing guns.

As dawn broke we could clearly see thousands of troops bivouacked on the slopes of the surrounding mountains. They lifted their voices exultantly in the hymn, "Onward, Christian Soldiers!"

For the next few weeks there was much shooting of "traitors," issuing of proclamations, and requisitioning of money and supplies from the populace. It had happened to the people of Kalgan many times before but now it was done to the accompaniment of Christian hymns. A friend of mine, head of the Chamber of Commerce in Kalgan, came to see me a week or two after the "new lords" had taken over. He spoke of the demands made on the merchants for money and commented, "They take as well as they sing."

Being confronted by new *de facto* masters, who rapidly pushed their troops further west along the railway, it was necessary for me to meet them and endeavor to ensure adequate protection for foreign lives and property. I therefore called on Marshal Feng, who had his headquarters in an old dilapidated school building. All was Spartan simplicity and the Marshal was plainly dressed in a simple cotton uniform without any insignia. He was tall and benign of countenance, but his eyes were hard and shrewd.

He listened impassively to my request that American, British, and Swedish lives and property be fully protected and replied that his troops were well disciplined and would not molest the people. I said the troops of such a famous leader could not be undisciplined but pressed, nevertheless, for the issuance of a proclamation and orders that would prevent any incidents or misunderstandings. He finally agreed. I came to know the Christian General fairly well and to realize that his simplicity cloaked a tremendous ambition and that his relatively well-equipped and disciplined army of nearly two hundred thousand men represented a potent military and political force in north China.

Life in Kalgan settled down but the merchants who had groaned under the taxes levied by the Old Tiger's regime groaned even louder—in private—over the multitude of taxes imposed by Marshal Feng in the name of education, public improvements, and good works. It was even rumored by the Chinese merchants of Kalgan that Marshal Feng was "inclined," as they put it, toward the Communists. This was denied by the missionaries who were tutoring Marshal Feng and his wife, a former YWCA secretary. However, Red Russian advisers began to appear at his headquarters in Kalgan and military supplies came in mysteriously from the far north. Early in 1926, Marshal Feng went off to Moscow to study "military strategy," so the merchants seemed to be right.

On the whole, it was a depressing period, except for the comings and goings of the scientific expedition of the American Museum of Natural History, under the leadership of Roy Chapman Andrews. The search for the missing link between life on the continents of Asia and North America, in which the expedition was engaged, was a thrilling objective. It was my duty and pleasure to make all necessary arrangements with the Chinese authorities of Kalgan and elsewhere in the Kalgan consular district and to smooth out any difficulties that might arise.

I remember being aroused in the middle of the night by one of the expedition's men in charge of transport, who told me the military had seized all the expedition's camels.

"They are loading them this minute at the railway station to ship them west. If they leave Kalgan we will never see them again and, as you know, it's virtually impossible to obtain fresh camels in time for the start of the expedition."

Sleepy-eyed, I went with him to the station. He was right. Bellowing and protesting, the camels were being loaded onto the train. We finally found the officer in charge, who had made himself comfortable in a goods wagon and was pensively smoking a cigarette when I appeared. He invited me into the wagon and offered tea and cigarettes. I protested strenuously against the seizure of the camels. He replied that orders from the chief of staff called categorically for fifty camels to be delivered to troops further west and that these were the only camels he could find.

He added mildly, "Please think of my great difficulty."

"I am indeed thinking of your difficulty," I said, "and how much more serious it will be for you tomorrow when I tell your great General Feng that fifty camels of the expedition for which he has issued a protecting permit have been seized by his troops."

"Ai ya," said the young officer, "does our great General Feng protect these camels?"

"Yes, indeed. They are very special camels and protected by a special pass."

"Release them! Release them instantly," he shouted to his men.

I returned to bed, pleased that the expedition's work would not be hindered for lack of camels.

The westward march of Marshal Feng's troops during the next twelve months resulted in hard times for the people and virtual cessation of trade, for taxes were staggering and all trade was regulated and controlled by his subordinates. His troops reached the city of Tatungfu, some seventy-five miles west of Kalgan, where they laid siege to the city and in doing so clashed with General Yen Hsi-shan, the powerful warlord of the province of Shanhsi. The siege dragged on for two months as the city was stoutly defended.

The word trickled out that conditions inside were frightful, that the inhabitants were starving, that an epidemic was sweeping the city, and that thirty-one British and Swedish missionaries were being held and could not get out. I passed on these reports to our Legation, which was presently requested by the British and Swedish Governments to authorize me to proceed to Tatungfu and negotiate the release of their nationals.

I set off for Tatungfu accompanied by a fabulous Swede, popularly known as "Duke Larsen of Mongolia," because of his great knowledge of the Mongolian language, princes and people, which had made him an authority on that part of the world. Originally, Larsen had come to China for the British and Foreign Bible Society but his unique knowledge in time made him a consultant and adviser to the Peiping Government on Mongolian affairs.

On my arrival at Tatungfu, I called on General Han Fu-chu, one of the principal lieutenants of the Christian General, whose troops were besieging the city. Our first discussion, held at his headquarters, a requisitioned school, was punctuated by the rattle of machine-gun fire and the boom of artillery. The general was a mild-appearing, soft-spoken man who had a reputation as an intellectual and a scholar. He was proud of his calligraphy, that esoteric art by which Chinese characters are written in flowing lines expressing the writer's inner urge for graceful form and sensitive meaning. He pointed to some of the scrolls hanging on the walls of his sparsely furnished room and, to the harsh and discordant sound of battle,

launched into a dissertation on the relative merits of famous callig-
raphists of the Sung and Ming dynasties.

I listened attentively, having learned the value of the polite attitude in China; also, the General's little lecture was extremely interesting. But at a suitable pause I brought up my mission, emphasizing strongly the concern felt by the governments of Great
Britain, Sweden and the United States for the safety and welfare of
the British and Swedish nationals in the besieged city.

"I have been ordered," I said, "to negotiate with you and with
the general defending the city for the evacuation of these foreign
nationals."

General Han explained that his troops had captured the outer
wall of the city and were in process of breaching the inner wall, a
massive thirty-foot structure. I pressed him to agree to a six-hour
ceasefire to make possible the evacuation of the missionaries. After
some argument, he agreed, but said he doubted whether his "be-
nighted" opponent defending the city would do so.

The next step was to persuade the defending General Fu Tso-yi
to take the same step. I prepared a strong but flowery official letter
which through a devious channel was smuggled into the city. Next
day, General Fu answered politely that he was responsible for the
safety of these foreign nationals and his concern for them was so
great he could not let them fall into the hands of the "bandits" attacking the city.

The issue was fairly joined. It required days of negotiation by
letter to convince General Fu that responsibility for the safety of
this little group, after they left the city walls, would be mine. Finally,
he agreed to a six-hour truce but insisted that the city gates could
not be opened to permit the exit of the missionaries.

"I will arrange for their descent over the city walls," he added.

This sounded both uncomfortable and hazardous but, having

gained his consent to a ceasefire, it seemed wise not to quibble over methods of exit.

At the agreed time, Duke Larsen and I, both looking pale and wan, started across the "no man's land" between the outer and inner walls, while thousands of Chinese soldiers watched. When we were halfway across, there was a heavy burst of machine-gun fire. Bullets whistled over our heads and smashed into the wall ahead of us with a sickening crack. Obviously, the arrangements had broken down.

"Back!" I yelled to Larsen.

Once within General Han's lines I shouted for the officer responsible for the truce arrangements and roundly berated him. A threat to report him to General Han caused him to beg for half an hour in which, he said, he personally would deliver orders to his men and see to it that there was no further trouble. Duke Larsen and I waited and worried, fearing that, in the interim, the other side would resume hostilities. But, in precisely half an hour, the officer was back and assured us that this time all would be well.

Again we started off, with even greater nervousness than we had felt on our first attempt. We reached the foot of the great wall and peered up. A cheery British voice hailed us, "I say, are you there?"

A Chinese officer appeared on the parapet and explained that the foreigners would be lowered over the wall in gunny sacks. I protested and demanded ladders. He countered that they had no ladders; anyhow, the missionaries were willing to make the descent by gunny sack. So, in gunny sacks they came, bumping down the face of the wall. All thirty-one were finally on the ground, including two sick.

Mission accomplished, I reported to the Legation.

A few months later, leave was granted me and I took advantage of the opportunity to visit my parents, who were still in India. The trip, made by slow freighter, took all my savings because in those days the Government's appropriations were not sufficient to cover the cost of home-leave transportation except in emergency cases. Wonderful to be reunited with the family again, even if briefly.

As I left Kalgan to go on leave I looked around at the crowd of friends who had gathered at the railway station to say good-by. I felt such a lump in my throat that I could not speak to them.

"You are a sentimental fool," I told myself.

5

The Tinder Box

EVERYTHING had gone wrong on that hot and dusty day in the summer of 1927 when I arrived at my new post, Tsinan, capital of Shantung province. The train was nearly twenty-four hours late because of military operations along the line. All night long I had been attacked by little bedfellows, which had come to rest in the train cushions after leaping replete from some resplendent Chinese general. To top the rest, I had lost my luggage, including those matched and once splendid pieces, now battered by time and rough handling. Still they had held all my wardrobe and to arrive at a new post without my clothes was a minor catastrophe. While clothes do not make a diplomat, they are an indispensable adjunct.

Harvey Milbourne, the consular colleague whom I was relieving, heard my tribulations with philosophy. "Oh, well," he said, "you were lucky to get through at all. The last train," he added calmly, "was blown up."

The situation at Tsinan, as he outlined it, made the blowing up of a train seem like a trifle. Some reporters likened it to a "tinder box,"

All China was in a ferment because a restless, revolutionary spirit had gripped the country and nationalism was on the march. And at Tsinan it was confronted by the ambitions of Imperial Japan.

The hero of that revolutionary movement is commonly regarded as being Sun Yat-sen, although for years he was a hero *in absentia*, and better known as a political exile in the United States, Europe and Japan than in China itself. Born in the year 1866, he had attempted as a young man to stage uprisings in Canton and elsewhere in South China, all of which proved to be unsuccessful.

Ironically enough, the explosion which was to set in motion the forces that resulted in the abdication of power by the once mighty Manchu Empire and the establishment of a republic was the result of pure accident. On the night of October 9, 1911, a fanatical revolutionary in Hankow, up the Yangtze River, was tinkering with a crude bomb which unexpectedly exploded. At that time Sun Yat-sen was in Denver, Colorado, fifteen thousand miles away.

For a brief period he tasted glory when he returned to China in January, 1912, and was named provisional president of the new Government. Then he was whirled and buffeted about by the turmoil and strife which plunged the country into civil war during the ensuing fifteen years. The sad fact was that the revolutionary leaders were weak and they were at odds. In the north, the dominating influence was the warlords, who had little use for Sun Yat-sen or the other leaders of the south, except insofar as they might further their own tireless ambitions. In the south, the situation was even more confused by the repeated efforts of Sun Yat-sen, now the head of the Southern Government, now a political exile, to seize control of Canton and become the dominant figure. It was February, 1923, when he again returned to Canton, with the aid of mercenary troops from the southern provinces of Yunnan and Kwangsi. Even then his position was far from secure, while his administration was marked by excesses and corruption.

In Russia, the new leaders were quick to see that the revolutionary movement in China and the chaotic conditions prevailing there offered rich opportunities to extend Communism to that vast country and its five hundred million people. In September, 1920, by a dramatic stroke of diplomacy, they proposed to cancel all pre-revolutionary treaties and to restore to China everything that had been seized from her by the Tsarist Government; to establish economic relations on the basis of most-favored-nation treatment; to relinquish extraterritorial rights; and to sign a special agreement regarding the use of the Chinese Eastern Railway in Manchuria.

This sudden and shrewd diplomatic move caused jubilation among the Chinese and consternation among the Western powers. It was promptly followed by another bold stroke. A joint statement was signed by Dr. Sun and M. Joffee, the Soviet envoy to China, in January, 1923, in which the latter declared that Dr. Sun could count on the support of the U. S. S. R. in his efforts to achieve national unification and full national independence. A few months later, Comrade Michael Borodin arrived in Canton from Moscow to give the promised "support," and became the apostle of those doctrines and techniques which ultimately delivered China into the hands of the Reds.

Five days after his arrival in Canton, Borodin explained his plan, which called for the "immediate organization of a provisional national committee consisting of twenty-one members of the Kuomintang [Chinese revolutionary party], Communists, members of the Association of Socialist Youth and of workmen's unions under the chairmanship of Dr. Sun."

To fellow Communists Borodin said frankly, "In the press I spoke of the Kuomintang, but to us it means that I was speaking of the increase, in the end, of the influence of the Communist party."

Liberally supplied with funds and weapons Borodin proceeded to carry out the sinister plans of Moscow to communize China by gaining control of the movement for national independence. A young and promising officer, Chiang Kai-shek, together with other officers and troops, was trained and armed. The forging of this military weapon was accompanied by relentless efforts to infiltrate the Kuomintang party with Communists and to gain control over students and laborers, particularly in the large industrial cities of Shanghai and Hankow.

As the shadow of the red flag more closely enveloped Dr. Sun, during the latter part of 1924, a welter of intrigue and treachery in north China resulted in the ousting of warlord Wu Pei-fu. A triumvirate, consisting of Marshal Tuan Ch'i-jui; Marshal Chang Tso-lin, the Old Tiger of Manchuria; and Marshal Feng Yu-hsiang, the Christian General, invited Dr. Sun to come to Peiping to confer with them. When he arrived in December, he was a very sick man. He was taken to the Rockefeller Hospital, where it was discovered that he was suffering from cancer of the liver in an advanced stage.

During his last hours, while he lay in a semiconscious state, his supporters were intriguing among themselves. They pressed the dying man to sign a number of papers. One of these was his "'Testament," which enjoins his followers to continue the revolutionary struggle for national liberty and international equality. Another was a letter of "fraternal greeting" to Soviet comrades.

He died on March 12, 1925. Thus passed away a revolutionary who was sparked by the stirring concept of an independent China, a great China. In his zeal to win freedom for his country from what he termed the throttling hands of foreign imperialism and the "unequal treaties," he turned to the U.S.S.R., an utterly ruthless imperialistic power. The growth of Communism, which eventually led to the delivering up of all China to the Reds, is one of the most tragic chapters in the history of the Chinese people.

There was an interlude, however, in which hope was high that the new spirit of nationalism might indeed prove to be the cohesive force necessary to unify China and to give her that measure of good and enlightened government needed to ensure peace and prosperity for her sorely tried people. It was a stormy and often a bloody period, marked initially by the dominion of Borodin and other Soviet advisers over the Southern Government and the Kuomintang, and the organization and training of a sizable army for the purpose of overthrowing the northern government established in Peiping.

In the latter part of 1926, the southern forces, including not only the divisions trained by Soviet advisers and commanded by General Chiang Kai-shek, but motley troops from other southern provinces, reached the middle Yangtze River. They seized the three great industrial cities of Wuchang, Hanyang and Hankow, which straddle the wide and swiftly flowing river. The Red elements in the Nationalist forces set up a regime that indulged in an orgy of Communism and took intense satisfaction in forcing the British Government to give up its concession in Hankow.

Early in 1927, the Nationalist forces commenced to move down river on Nanking and Shanghai. The northern armies melted before the Nationalist propaganda and the skillful Communist tactics of infiltration and subversion. When Nanking fell in March there were wanton killing and pillaging, tragic attacks on foreign consular representatives and missionaries, some of whom escaped under the protecting barrage of gunfire laid down by foreign gunboats in the Yangtze River.

A stream of refugee mission workers poured into Shanghai. Their tales of atrocities committed by the southern troops, stirred up by Red political agents, were fearful. The foreign powers and their nationals in the International Settlement and the French concession braced themselves for similar excesses. The northern troops who were supposed to guard Shanghai vanished, for the Communist agents in the city had done their work well. Thousands of Communists, like beetles, emerged from dark and secret recesses and systematically organized students, laborers and the "toiling masses" into shouting, chanting columns who demanded death for reactionary traitors and the "running dogs of the imperialists."

For a time the Communists, who had been organized by Chou En-lai, now the Foreign Minister of the Red regime in Peiping, were in control of the Chinese-administered section of the city. The International Settlement would also have fallen if it had not been guarded by foreign troops and the gunmen of the king of the Shanghai underworld. The latter, who in his declining years yearned for respectability, lived in a magnificent mansion in the French concession. From his headquarters he let loose his thugs against the Reds in the native city, causing such havoc in their ranks that their hour of triumph was brief.

When General Chiang Kai-shek arrived in Shanghai, it was apparent to him that the Communists had made far-reaching plans to seize and hold Shanghai. He had already learned of the Communists' efforts to infiltrate the Kuomintang and gain control of the party. He and the more conservative elements in the Kuomintang decided the time had come to expel the Communists and to deport all Soviet advisers from China. The execution of these orders was accompanied by the letting of much Communist blood at Shanghai, Canton and Hankow and the fall of the Communist-dominated regime at Hankow. None the less, the hard core of the Communist organization remained in Kiangsi and other provinces, where it became the implacable foe of Chiang Kai-shek and those in the Kuomintang who were responsible for these drastic measures.

As though it were not enough for warlord to be pitted against warlord, and Nationalist against Soviet-supported Communist, the Japanese began to take a hand. As a result of their military successes, the Nationalist armies planned to continue the campaign against the northern armies and to capture Peiping. But problems arising from difficulties with the Communists and of establishing a firm government at Nanking caused the temporary suspension of the campaign. Nevertheless the declared intention of the Nationalists to gain control of north China caused the Japanese to move swiftly, to "protect their nationals," as they described it. They dispatched several thousand infantry and cavalry to the provinces of Shantung in the summer of 1927. No one believed this well-worn diplomatic explanation. There was a buzz of speculation as to the real motives of the Japanese Government and whether Chinese and Japanese troops would clash, if and when the former arrived in Tsinan.

This was the "tinder box" when I reached Tsinan in the summer of 1927.

6

Caught in the Crossfire

I RUBBED my eyes when I saw the well-built Consulate residence and office set in a pleasant garden, having expected the usual shabby quarters. The building was in the modern section of Tsinan where German and Japanese influence were evident in the orderly arrangement of broad streets and sturdy buildings and residences.

According to the number one houseboy, the green tiles in the bathroom had come all the way from Belgium, and when a bath had rid me of my nocturnal friends I was restored to equanimity.

At lunch my colleague said that Li, the gentlemen's tailor, would be glad to whip up some summer suits. This he did, a few days later, but the fit and design were distinctly his own creation and bore no resemblance to the garments worn by the handsome and impeccably dressed gentlemen appearing in his soiled and much-thumbed catalog. Furthermore, they were not cheap. And so commenced a new but familiar series of installment payments, made slowly and erratically, as my salary was only $2,500 a year, with no allowances for official entertainment. At such times I longed fervently to be the local manager of one of the large American companies operating in China, who were receiving three times my salary plus various allowances.

Next day we started the round of our official calls. The first visit was to the Chinese Commissioner for Foreign Affairs, a rather sad little wisp of a man with a few stray, discolored teeth. From him we extracted as much information as possible, since we were concerned over the explosive nature of the situation. He was worried both by the Japanese troops who had poured into Shantung province and by the "bandit" nationalist troops who were attempting to push north along the railway, which ran through Tsinan to Peiping.

I asked him to arrange for me to call on the Governor, Warlord Chang Tsung-chang, who controlled the province. A few days later an appointment was made and I met the Governor, a giant of a man with a heavy face and great powerful hands. He was said to have started as a wharf coolie, loading cargo at the port of Vladivostok, drifted into the more lucrative life of a petty gangster, and later become a bandit chieftain in Manchuria. As such his fame spread and he came to the notice of Marshal Chang Tso-lin, the Old Tiger of Manchuria, who placed him in his personal bodyguard, perhaps because of his great size and physical strength.

As the star of the Old Tiger rose, this loyal henchman followed in his wake, rewarded for his faithfulness by being made Governor of the Province of Shantung. He had a reputation for harsh and corrupt administration and the heaviest of heavy hands in the collection of taxes from distracted merchants and farmers, who were ground between human rapaciousness and the calamities of flood and famine that frequently swept the province.

Governor Chang had augmented his army by recruiting farmer boys and bandits. He had, as well, a mercenary force of several thousand White Russians who had been picked up in Manchuria. This "White Russian brigade" acted as a personal bodyguard and manned several improvised armored trains. The Governor had also drawn into his service a number of colorful figures. One of these was, by his own account, a French count who had been an ace pilot in the First World War. His mission was said to be the training of an air force for the Governor. Most of his time, however, seemed to be spent at the Tsinan Club, where he daily fascinated the ladies of the foreign community with tales of his heroic exploits and with his insinuating and captivating manners, while the husbands played billiards or rolled dice for drinks.

The Governor, too, had a taste for the ladies and for choice cognac. During that first interview and, indeed, during all subsequent ones, he tossed off glasses of cognac, but he managed to ask some shrewd questions about the attitude of the United States toward the Nationalists, the Japanese and his chief, the Old Tiger. He assured me that he was on friendly terms with all the foreign Consuls, even the Japanese, and forthwith invited me to his next party for the foreign community. This was quite an affair, including all the prettiest ladies from General Chang's own harem, on whom he had thoughtfully pinned numbers so that his guests might be able to identify them. He was in a most convivial mood and insisted that his guests dance with each numbered lady.

Such social distractions seemed to underscore rather than dispel the atmosphere of tension that hung over the city. The air was thick with rumors, and the foreign community was apprehensive at the thought of the Nationalists advancing on Tsinan, and wondered if the anti-foreign incidents which had occurred at Nanking were a foretaste of what might be expected. In mounting uneasiness we observed the bellicose and provocative statements issued by the Japanese, even by friendly mild-mannered Consul General Nishida who occasionally would sing ancient Japanese lullabies when among friends.

The air was electric with the inevitability of a clash between the

Nationalists and the Japanese, because the former sought to free China from foreign domination, particularly that of the Japanese, and the latter were consumed by visions of an Imperial Japan ruling over a mighty empire embracing China, Southeast Asia and most of the southwest Pacific.

In the spring of 1928, events began to hasten toward the inevitable. The Nationalists resumed their attacks on the northern armies, aided by the defection of the forces of the Christian General, which were noted for the rapidity with which they changed sides. The Japanese promptly rushed troops back to Tsinan and began to build barbed-wire barricades with sand-bagged gun emplacements around those areas of the city in which most of the Japanese were living.

It was obvious to my colleague, Ernest Price, and myself that the presence of Japanese troops was bound to provoke undisciplined elements in the advancing Nationalist armies to shoot. We did what we could to prepare the American community, which consisted of a few businessmen and a group of twenty or thirty American doctors and professors working at a fine Presbyterian institution known as the Cheloo University and Medical College. There were many anxious consultations with the consular representatives of other nations, although we found our Japanese colleague less and less accessible.

An uneasy calm descended over the city between the arrival of the vanguards of the Nationalist armies of General Chiang Kai-shek and the hasty departure of General Chang Tsung-chang. The latter, much to our relief, retreated in good order, the retreat covered by an armored train manned by his White Russian guards. The latter sang lustily as the train pulled out, the singing mellowing, as the vodka bottle passed around, into a nostalgic chant for Mother Russia and the homes they had once known.

And then, on May 3, 1928, shots rang out. Isolated at first, the firing spread like a swift-running flood until it silenced all other sounds. The crash of rifles was punctuated by the angry clatter of machine guns, by the thump, thump of the mortars.

"This is it!" Price and I took a deep breath and set in motion the plans we had made to warn Americans to keep off the streets. We tried frantically to get reliable news as to what was happening but our consular colleagues knew no more than we did and we could not reach the Japanese Consul General at all.

Meager scraps of news came from Chinese running past the Consulate, fleeing from the battle. The Chinese, they said, were trying to drive the Japanese from their barricaded areas. Fighting was bitter, they said. Both sides kill with the knife, they said, and made graphic gestures as though thrusting with a bayonet. So much shooting, they said. Many people killed.

While Price and I were wondering what we could do, we found ourselves in the middle of a brisk engagement taking place on the street in front of the consulate. Japanese soldiers were firing from behind telephone poles, dragging sandbags along with them. Further up the street the Chinese were firing back. A Japanese soldier was hit. Blood gushed from his head wound. He fell sideways with a thud and sprawled grotesquely. The fighting seesawed, back and forth, up and down the street.

The Consulate was caught in the crossfire and, as more and more bullets smacked into the walls, Price and I found it expedient to stretch gracefully on the floor or behind a convenient sofa. Not until the following day did the Japanese clear the street in front of the Consulate, which brought about an immediate improvement in our appetites.

For several days the fighting raged around the Japanese areas, with the Chinese pouring in a continuous and heavy fire and pinning down the defending Japanese troops. When reinforcements arrived, the Japanese took the offensive, forced the Chinese to withdraw into the walled city, stormed the walls and subdued Chinese resistance in bloody street battles.

In view of the savage nature of the fighting and the atrocities that were being committed by both sides, the foreign Consuls decided to evacuate their nationals and arrange for safe conduct by train from Tsinan to the port of Tsingtao. To accomplish this we had to move back and forth through the fighting zones, an exciting and hazardous undertaking. Without the aid of the liaison officers of the Japanese military it would have been impossible for us to pass through their lines, but all went well. Women, children and elderly men were safely placed aboard the international train.

Daily contact with Japanese military officers during these negotiations gave me an insight into their thinking. Their fanatical belief in the destiny of Japan was constantly manifested. Indeed, their frankness, especially after a number of cups of *sake*, was disconcerting and ominous. Yet they were eager to cover these ambitious plans with a cloak of legality while moving steadily along a course of expanding imperialism which seized on any pretext.

With the evacuation of the majority of our citizens we were relieved of our greatest concern, but we returned to face the uncertainty and ill will generated by this clash between Nationalist forces of China and those of Imperial Japan. The main body of the Nationalist forces had not joined in the hostilities. In fact, they sought to avoid a full-scale engagement. Chiang Kai-shek, according to our Chinese friends, repeatedly ordered his troops to break off the engagement. He was not anxious to antagonize the Japanese. He knew of their desire to seize Shantung and was troubled by a warning issued to him and to Marshal Chang Tso-lin that the Imperial Government would not tolerate any disturbance of the peace in Manchuria. Moreover, General Chiang desired to complete the northern campaign and occupy Peiping.

But because the Japanese wanted, as their military men put it grimly, "to teach the Chinese a lesson," the fighting continued for almost ten days. The total number of casualties rose to several thousands, the civilian population suffering heavily from wanton acts of the combatants.

I saw huddled groups of homeless, their faces haggard with the terror of their experiences, tightly clutching the poor remnants of their belongings tied in haphazard bundles, bewildered and dazed by the disaster that had struck them. One of these tragic victims told me:

"We lived next door to a Japanese family. They were killed by our Chinese soldiers *but I do not know why*. Then came the fierce Japanese who blamed me and my family. I told them that I was a poor carpenter, that I had lived side by side, at peace with Matsui. *Ai ya.* They did not believe. They shot my little ones, burned me with cigarette butts, beat me with their guns, took my wife away, burned down my little shop. Heaven has deserted me," he wailed.

But I do not know why. That was the leitmotif of the noncombatant. Indeed, it was almost impossible to discover the "why" of the Tsinan Incident, except that the ingredients had been there. When the fighting subsided and it was possible to move about the city, Ernest Price and I sought to gather and sift all available information in order to present a comprehensive and reliable report to Washington. The Chinese and Japanese versions of the incident varied greatly. We searched for the facts.

In spite of conflicting claims we found that the hands of neither side were clean with respect to the commission of atrocities. There was no reliable evidence as to who had fired the first shot. Our findings, set down in telegrams and written reports in our best departmental style, were rewarded with an impersonal and brief commendation. The reports written by Ernest Price were so excellent that I thought they should have been accorded warmer praise. However, in the Foreign Service one learns that much is expected but praise is sparingly given.

With the end of the Tsinan Incident, new orders took me to Canton. En route, I got a brief glimpse of teeming, luxurious Shanghai. Having just emerged from the clash at Tsinan, it was interesting to see that Shanghai appeared to have forgotten its own recent blood bath. As before, it was intent on the endless buying and selling of goods of all descriptions.

A small British coastal steamer, neat and orderly, its officers dressing for dinner every night although there were only a half-dozen first-class passengers, took me from Shanghai to Hong Kong. I had not seen this British colony and jewel in the imperial crown for ten years. Out of the South China Sea it appeared one morning, cloaked in a green and purple mantle, with wisps of fleecy white clouds veiling its peak. It rose from its waterfront, alive with ocean liners and thousands of little sampans, in orderly tiers of well-built business buildings housing commercial concerns of every known nationality trading round the world. Above and up to the peak were the fine residences of British officialdom and wealthy merchants who made fortunes and brought in much revenue because Hong Kong was the finest port in the Far East with no customs duties to pay and every conceivable facility to encourage shipping and trade. At night myriad lights twinkled up and down its slopes, giving the little island a touch of unreality, denied by its absorption in mercantile pursuits.

Canton, which we reached next day, is approached by the winding, sluggish Pearl River. How the Scotch captain was able to navigate his ship through the thousands of sampans was a miracle.

"We have to be cautious," he explained. "If we hit one of these cockleshells or they hit us, there'll be the divil to pay." Anti-British boycotts or demonstrations, he said, were often caused by the swamping of a sampan by a British river steamer. "And there," he pointed out, "is Shameen where you'll find the United States Consulate."

I saw a tiny little island almost floating on the river. The buildings were so spick and span, the streets so straight and clean, the lawns and little park so green, that it looked for all the world like a freshly painted toy. On closer inspection, however, it was evident that time and the humid climate had effected ravages on some of these Victorian structures. A notable example was the genteel but shabby building that housed the United States Consulate General and quite a number of the staff.

To our friends abroad it has always seemed a major mystery that the richest country on earth rents the shabbiest buildings to house its representatives. This particular building was of really ancient vintage, on which neither the landlord nor the United States Government was willing to spend a penny. Offices had to be improvised, so some of the staff perched on the verandah, dispensing visas, certifying invoices, and registering citizens, while a cloud of mosquitoes hung around tormentingly. But the staff was a particularly nice cheerful group, which sensibly made fun of the hard work in the face of dripping humidity, pests and cramped quarters.

The Consul General assigned me to the task of supervising the visa section of the office, one of the busiest departments because of the large numbers of Chinese merchants who desired to visit the United States on business. This job called for the detective powers of Sherlock Holmes and the judgment of Solomon. So eager were the merchants to get to the United States, so rigid were the immigration regulations, that novel methods were constantly being devised to hoodwink the unwary consular officer.

The complicated Immigration Laws of those days required that a merchant desiring to visit the United States must produce evidence that he was a man of substance and would not become a public charge while in the United States. The most ingenious methods were devised for establishing financial substance. Letters flowed into the Consulate, guaranteeing the financial wealth of the applicants. These letters, couched in flowery language, extolled the virtues of the applicant's father, grandfather and great great grandfather; dilated on the applicant's own heavenly merits, including his financial and business successes; and concluded by a solemn oath made in the name of the spirits of the writer's venerable ancestors that he would guarantee the applicant.

Getting at the actual facts of the case was where the Sherlock Holmes techniques came in. In one such case I made what I believed to be an unexpected descent on the business address of an applicant named Li. It seemed to be a prosperous little shop selling hardware of all descriptions. Mr. Li himself was there, welcomed me with a smile, sat me down at a handsome blackwood table and plied me with scented tea and cigarettes. To all the questions about his gross and net income, his taxes and so forth he had prompt replies.

Then I asked to inspect his books, which he produced, and so impressively clean and neat and fresh were they that the ink was barely dry on most of the pages. I called for his accountant. At this point Mr. Li went into a huddle with several men in the store. At length he came back, beaming no longer.

The store, he admitted, did not belong to him. He had rented it to make an impression on the Consulate and had hired an accountant to write up a fine set of books for our inspection. The men who had provided his glowing affidavits were either dead or had not even a nodding acquaintance with him.

"Mr. Li," I suggested, "America is too far away for you. Why don't you settle for a trip to Hong Kong instead?"

He smiled and apologized for taking up my time. At least it had been a good try.

While I was doing my detective work I was settling down on Shameen which, over the years, had been turned by the British and other foreigners residing on the island into a comfortable business and residential area. It was, for us, a well-ordered life, but Shameen was surrounded by poverty. The island was encircled by thousands of little sampans on which Chinese families lived, worked and died. After a hectic day in the office we used to stroll along the short road that followed the rim of the island. Then we would lean over the parapet and watch sampan life, which never lost its fascination for me.

The sampans, which were not more than sixteen feet in length, were covered at one end with old matting to form a sort of shelter. This was the private quarters for the family, where they slept, cooked and stored their few belongings.

There was one family in particular I came to know well. When I strolled past at dusk the mother would be cooking the evening meal in a red earthenware pot. I could smell the rice and the dried fish. There were usually a few greens and a few red peppers. The baby, lying in a crudely made rope hammock, would be wailing. Three other children, scarcely more than babies, howled and pulled at the mother's trousers. She was a young woman, but already old with childbearing and hard labor. She kept pushing the babies automatically away from the rice pot. She stirred, cooked and pushed as she kept up a steady stream of talk directed toward and sometimes against her husband. He sat with a cigarette dangling between his lips, a thin, tired man bowed down by the daily struggle for existence and life forces he could not control.

Whenever I came to this spot I found Ah Kwak's sampan tied up there. After a time I was recognized as a friend. The youngsters became enthusiastic about the hard candy I brought them, although at first they had been dubious as they had never tasted it. One evening, they invited me aboard the sampan to share their evening meal. I had picked up only a few Cantonese phrases and they could not understand my northern Chinese, but we managed without much conversation, for there was plenty of good will and plenty of laughter. Most of the latter was occasioned by my handling of chopsticks, which the mother had cleaned for me by casually dipping them in the dirty Pearl River and then wiping them on her soiled trousers.

I was sorry to leave these friendly people when I was sent back to Tsinan, where I was impressed, as I have been so often, by the speed with which cities and people bandage up the wounds of war. Gaping holes in the buildings had been repaired, new huts had been pierced together out of matting and old kerosene tins. How the Chinese would manage without old kerosene tins is hard to imagine. A tin of kerosene provides not only oil for their small lamps but the tin itself is used for cooking, storage of grain and roofing for huts. This is one Western product which has been a boon to the Chinese population.

There was a new set of Chinese officials in the provincial government, who had been appointed by the Nationalist Government at Nanking. The Japanese were still there in full force. The Chinese insisted that the Japanese withdraw their forces from Shantung before they would consider the sweeping guarantees and compensation demanded by the Japanese in connection with the Tsinan Incident. The Japanese were equally adamant.

Both sides laid their cases before the League of Nations, but that august body was not able to compose the differences between the two governments. Behind the scenes, the Western powers and their representatives in Tsinan worked quietly to keep the negotiations going and to urge both parties to make concessions. Progress was slow but eventually an agreement was reached, guarantees were given, and Japanese troops commenced to withdraw in May, 1929, a year after the incident.

The urge to get away from international bickering and intrigue became compelling. What I needed was, as the Thai say, to "clean my mind." What better, here in this province of his birth, than to turn to the Doctrine of the Mean, in which the great sage Confucius summed up, two thousand years ago, the moral and spiritual truth which he believed should guide both rulers and the people.

"The power of spiritual forces in the universe," he said, "how active it is everywhere. Invisible to the eyes and impalpable to the senses, it is inherent in all things, and nothing can escape its operation. Like the rush of mighty waters, the presence of unseen powers is felt, sometimes above us, sometimes around us."

Certainly such tranquil wisdom had been lost to sight during the tumultuous months at Tsinan. So I went to the little walled city called Ch'u Fu in southwestern Shantung. Many of its inhabitants bear the surname of the Sage, Kung, and regard themselves as his lineal descendants, as did the magistrate of the district, to whom I had an introduction. Stately and dignified, he was also learned in the life and teachings of Confucius.

Accompanied by Magistrate Kung, I visited the Confucian temple, its yellow tiled roofs glittering in the brilliant sunlight. We passed through several spacious courtyards enclosed by stucco walls of a faded vermilion. In the inner courtyard, paved with marble slabs, stood the Great Hall, a thing of beauty, its gracefully tapering golden roofs rising into the blue heaven and supported by slim white marble columns entwined with dragons. The ceiling, of exquisitely carved and painted wood, soared high above us. There was quiet, simplicity, dignity. At the far end was an immense stone statue of the illustrious sage, compelling in its majesty. Before it the magistrate prostrated himself. For over two thousand years the moral maxims and social ethics of Confucius had guided both the people and their rulers.

From this Great Hall the turmoil of man's struggle to enhance his ego and achieve his ambitions was excluded. There was no room here for intrigue, no room for clashing ambition; neither time nor space for my own personal hopes, which seemed petty and trivial as I looked at the grave but kindly face of a thinker who taught the three moral qualities of wisdom, compassion and courage. How tragic that China's new leaders had decreed against a blending of this ancient but ageless wisdom with the young, vibrant spirit of nationalism.

As I stood there with Magistrate Kung, I looked about the Great Hall once again. The calmness and peace of great wisdom flooded through me like a cleansing, healing stream.

7

Shanghai—Testing Ground

Hot roasted chestnuts!" cried the chestnut vendor. "Tasty varnished chickens," shouted the seller of poultry. "Virtuous cure-all tiger bones," sang the wandering apothecary.

These and a thousand other street cries filled the streets and *hutungs*, or small lanes, of Peiping. Vendors carrying their wares strung on sturdy bamboo poles trotted from door to door or set themselves up for daily business on some particular street well known as a shopping center. There was the medicine man gravely dispensing the dust of dragon bones; the fortuneteller reading his cabalistic charts and horoscopes; the letter writer looking learned with his long fingernails and the steel-rimmed glasses, without lenses. The barber plucked hair from his customers' forehead and cheeks by skillfully twisting two pieces of thread over the skin; the seller of foods draped his food stand with the grotesque and ghastly corpses of chickens, ducks, dogs and cats, but nevertheless the foods and sauces smelled delicious. Dotted along the street were numberless smart city gentlemen who gracefully presided over a variety of games of chance and took away the country yokels' money.

There is no city quite like Peiping. When I was assigned to the Legation as Second Secretary in the summer of 1930, I was as pleased and puffed up as though I had been made Secretary of State. Into this capital city of emperors had flowed the products of the culture of centuries, including the finest in paintings, silks, porcelains, jewels and lacquerware. The Imperial Palace in the Forbidden City, the Temple of Heaven, the Summer Palace, are architectural gems of glittering tiles laid in diminishing tapered tiers, tall vermilion columns, ornately carved, painted ceilings, white marble terraces surrounded by balustrades richly carved with dragons and pomegranates. The writings and sayings, poems and essays of China's most noted philosophers, historians, poets and novelists, provided an intellectual feast. It was a city whose inspiring sights, discordant sounds and pungent smells combined to produce a fascination that cast a spell over all visitors and residents.

And when the duties and pleasures of the enchanting city of Peiping brought weariness, one could escape to the Western Hills, which loomed, purple and inviting, a short distance from the city. By day they stood out sharply against the blue of the sky, turning to a dark purple as the setting sun fell behind them in a glowing mass.

I found the hills and temples nestled in their purple folds serenely peaceful. Their very names suggest peace and contemplative calm: the Temple of the Sleeping Buddha, the Temple of Spiritual Light, the Temple of Exalted Heaven. Wonderfully restful it was to sit on the terrace of a favorite temple, with F. J., or Lucile Swan, a sculptress of charm and sensitivity. Far to the left one saw the Summer Palace, the Jade Fountain Pagoda, the Black Dragon Pool. In front of us stretched the broad level plains, shimmering in the heat and the dust of the afternoon sun. Those golden hues turned to rose and melted into deep purple as night fell. The sound of a temple gong and the low chanting of the priests faintly stirred the evening quiet.

With all this to enjoy I was delighted to be back in Peiping; delighted, too, with my new quarters in the picturesque San Kuan Miao where, as a student, I had been assigned to the coal bin. But now my sitting room, which had been one of the main halls of the old temple, was spacious and colorful, the rafters of the steep gabled roof being supported by handsome red lacquer pillars. The doors were richly carved with dragons and flowers, the windows covered with a transparent paper glued to wooden frames of the meander pattern. A small dining room, bedroom and guest bedroom, together with servants' quarters and kitchen, completed my domain.

There was some government furniture but it was shabby and it sagged. Within the limits of my slender salary I did what I could to spruce things up, and bought one or two Chinese tapestry hangings. These, with a table or two of gold and black lacquer, had to suffice.

The Minister, Nelson T. Johnson, assigned me to the Chinese section where incoming and outgoing despatches to and from the Chinese Government were translated. This was putting to practical use the previous years of study but it taxed one's knowledge to the utmost because so many English phrases have no exact counterpart in Chinese. Subtle shades of meaning trip the unwary.

In the translation department I discovered Flavius Josephus Chapman III, with whom I had become fast friends during our student days. It was a pleasure to work with him and also to hear about his latest escapades. He had erratic, impish qualities that endeared him to some and baffled others, but of his excellent knowledge and command of the Chinese language, both written and spoken, there was no doubt. His love of pranks found its outlet in the playing of practical jokes on our Legation's sedate and protocol-minded chief of chancery or executive officer.

As an aftermath of the famous Sacco-Vanzetti case, our Embassies and Legations received a warning circular, alerting them to be on the lookout for bombs or explosives sent through the mail. In Peiping this duty fell on the chief of chancery, who opened all mail and marked it for action. One morning the chief sat down at his desk with mail piled high before him. He picked up a package and, with consternation, heard a tick, tick, tick. A time bomb! He yelled for the marine guard, who came at the double.

"It sounds like a bomb," he said, thrusting the package into the hands of the astonished guard. "Destroy it!"

The guard blanched at finding himself the custodian of a live bomb. He ran with it to the officer of the day, who called out the guard. With the latter at attention, the package was dumped into a large bucket of water. It still went tick, tick, tick.

In desperation, the young officer ordered the guard to pick up the bucket and rush it to a remote part of the great wall surrounding the city of Peiping. They rushed. They dumped it over the wall. Forty feet below the package hit the ground and broke open. Out rolled an old, battered alarm clock still valiantly ticking. It was one of F. J.'s practical jokes. His popularity with the chief of chancery declined noticeably.

After seeing only a single facet of the complicated political scene from my station at Tsinan, it was exciting and instructive to be at the center of things, with reports and telegrams pouring daily into the Legation from our consular offices all over China. One could see the political situation developing throughout the country, with the spirit of nationalism striving to change the old, to crush its enemies, to establish itself as the dominant political force, to rid itself of "foreign imperialism," and to unify the country. This spirit had driven the Nationalist forces from Canton to Peiping, which was occupied in June, 1928, with the assistance of two northern generals who had changed sides. In the face of this combine the Old Tiger had withdrawn his troops from Peiping to Manchuria. On the way, a mysterious bomb had wrecked his train and ended the days of the old general. He had been succeeded by his son, Chang Hsueh-liang, who came out in support of the Nationalist Government. With these events the northern campaign had ended, giving the Nationalist Government the prestige that it sorely needed and the right to demand recognition by the foreign powers, which had been duly accorded.

The new Government had decided to make Nanking its capital. It was hard beset. Problems of administration, of finance, of taxation, of trade, of famine, of party organization and discipline had to be met and solved. In its struggle to cope with these difficulties the Nationalists became increasingly authoritarian in practice. However, they chose to call it "the period of political tutelage," in conformity with the teachings of Dr. Sun Yat-sen, who had advocated three stages in the evolution of government for the young republic.

Worst of all, they had failed to achieve the unity that was so essential to them, as political and personal factors combined against them. In the south, warlords and hostile elements had sought to assert their independence by linking themselves with the hard core of the Communist group which had set up "soviets" in the southern provinces of Kiangsi, Fukien and Kwangtung. Under the political leadership of Mao Tse-tung and the wily military tactics of Chu Teh, the Communists had grown in strength. Generalissimo Chiang Kai-shek sent several military expeditions against his erstwhile Communist colleagues in the years 1930-1931, which were not only unsuccessful but resulted in thousands of casualties and the loss of valuable military equipment to the Communist forces.

The international relations of the new Government were equally pressing and complicated. The impetus behind the national revolution had been the strong determination of the Chinese people to get rid of foreign imperialism, controls, concessions and dictation. There was a universal desire to abolish the "unequal treaties," and to see China a sovereign and independent nation.

Although the Government's initial statements had been lacking in tact and liberally sprinkled with threats and warnings, the United States and other powers realized that China would not be denied her just and burning desire for complete independence. Washington had shown wisdom and taken the initiative by instructing our able minister, J. V. A. MacMurray, to commence negotiations with the Nationalist Government regarding tariff autonomy. On July 25, 1928, the United States had entered into a treaty with the new Government of China, abrogating the provisions of all former treaties, which had denied to China full tariff autonomy. This was of signal importance to the Nationalist Government because it indicated the intention of the United States to proceed as rapidly as possible to give China full sovereign rights not only with respect to tariff autonomy but other treaty limitations.

Daily reports on all these complex matters were prepared at the Legation and sent to Washington, together with recommendations for action or changes in the implementation of policy. A pressing concern was to find a solution to the problem of extraterritorial rights, which had been acquired by the foreign powers, including the United States, some eighty years previously and had been written into the first treaties concluded with China. The Chinese were demanding the abolition of these rights, providing for the trial of foreign nationals by their own authorities, which they felt was an infringement of sovereignty.

Duties were heavy but tremendously interesting. At the same time, diplomatic life in Peiping was studded with social activities, which were sometimes very pleasant. Dinner parties were sprinkled with the bores, the brilliant and the beauties, with the bores holding forth at many affairs. Some took their entertaining with humorless seriousness, delving into rules of protocol, slaving over seating plans, laying snares to entrap visiting lions to their tables.

Protocol being easier to master than good talk they devised recipes for perpetual conversation. One such method was the alphabetical system. "A" was for the American Legation and the peculiarities of its staff. "B" was the boring Mr. So & So. "C" was for club activities. "D" was for dangerous trips into the interior with heroic exploits. And so on through as much of the alphabet as might be necessary to sustain conversation through a long dinner. But not all dinners were such stodgy affairs. At many one could talk with eminent scholars, scientists and medical men, with cultivated and knowledgeable diplomats, with writers, artists and musicians, or with Chinese and Mongolian princesses.

I remember a dinner party at the British Legation at which I was seated beside a Chinese lady whose delicately shaped oval face was a classic example of Chinese beauty. She did not, it appeared, favor the new Government's effort to overthrow the traditions of the past.

"But don't you approve of the more dominant and vital role played by women in your country?" I asked.

She smiled faintly. "They have always been dominant. There is an old Chinese story of two husbands caught by their wives in the act of planning to run away. The husbands, belabored by a torrent of words, ran to the nearest magistrate. At his gate they sounded the drum used for dire emergencies. The magistrate came rushing out, shouting, 'What's the trouble? What's the trouble?' They told him.

"Meantime, their wives had sent word to the magistrate's wife. When the magistrate led the two men into his courtroom he saw with consternation that his wife was seated in his official chair. By this time the wives had arrived.

" 'What is the complaint?' asked the magistrate's wife.

" 'Disobedient husbands, your ladyship,' answered the wives.

" 'Two hundred blows each,' she ordered.

"When the blows had been duly administered, the magistrate's wife said, 'And now it is ordered by the court that you carry your wives home on your backs.' She then turned to the magistrate. 'If you were not an official appointed by the Imperial Court, I would order two hundred blows for you. Be more submissive in future.'

"So you see," my dinner partner concluded with a graceful gesture of her exquisite hands, "we women were not without power, even in the old days."

Nor can I forget that it was at a diplomatic dinner party that I caught the gleam of turquoise green across a big formal Legation drawing room. Then I saw the girl, a bright particular star, flashing eyes, a cloud of jet-black hair, a face alive with vivacity and charm. Her name was Josephine.

Minister Johnson spent much of his time at Nanking, where delicate negotiations were in progress. I accompanied him as assistant and general handyman. It was my duty to buy tickets, arrange transportation and official functions, read and summarize his voluminous memoranda, and help in the drafting of telegrams and despatches. For long hours I decoded telegrams when code clerks were not available and licked stamps.

We spent months at a time in Nanking. The Minister worked closely with Sir Miles Lampson, the British Minister, on the question of extraterritoriality. The team work was good and agreement was reached on point after point with Dr. C. T. Wang, the Chinese Minister for Foreign Affairs. The latter, who had been educated in the United States, was one of the shrewdest and ablest foreign ministers that China ever had.

Nanking was undergoing a transformation to make it the fitting seat of the new Government. While it was not beautiful, the green of the rice fields surrounded the old walls like an emerald carpet. In the distance rose Purple Mountain, a fitting resting place for the remains of Sun Yat-sen, the revolutionary leader. Within the city most of the population lived in cramped and rather miserable quarters because of the steady increase in their numbers, occasioned by the influx of officials and merchants. Quarters for foreign consular and diplomatic staffs were equally crowded and particularly so for American personnel.

For years, the United States Government had had at Nanking an old decrepit building that was the delight of white ants and other termites. From time to time, portions sagged and collapsed and might or might not be repaired, depending on whether funds were forthcoming from Washington. Into it were squeezed living quarters for the Consul General and his family and the offices of the Consulate General, which overflowed onto the verandahs of the old building. When the Minister and his staff came down from Peiping, supercompression took place. Literally every inch of space was occupied and bulged with ministers, consul generals, consuls, diplomatic secretaries, ordinary secretaries and the Chinese staff, the latter being the most important members of the establishment.

The summer months were fierce and dripping. The mosquitoes were unrelenting. The bath water, which came from the mighty Yangtze River flowing directly in front of the city, was muddy and for some reason very scarce. (The local inhabitants said the water mains were full of eels.) The electric current was a feeble glimmer by night and insufficient by day to turn an electric fan or operate a refrigerator. To cool off we used to go aboard the small American gunboat anchored in the river. The steel decks of the little craft were burning hot but the drinks, at least, were cold.

And then, on September 18, 1931, came the day that electrified the Nationalist Government and the people of China. The Japanese struck in Manchuria, their troops occupied Mukden and clashed with the troops of Chang Hsueh-liang. In a few months they occupied all strategic points and Manchuria was lost to China. The people were stunned. So were the great powers. China in desperation laid the "Manchurian Incident" before the League of Nations in the hope that a wrong would be righted and justice done.

(69)

Prolonged and angry wrangling ensued, and eventually a Commission was appointed to investigate the "incident." The League's recommendations availed nothing. Japan remained in control of Manchuria for she had embarked on the plan of expansion and conquest that ultimately was to plunge her into war with the United States.

Japan's action in Manchuria touched off a wave of anti-Japanese sentiment. The feeling was especially intense in Shanghai, where strikes and boycotts were organized. The leaders of Japan did not seem to gauge the strength of this sentiment, perhaps because they had grown so accustomed to anti-Japanese slogans. However, the extent of the boycott should have served as a warning of the bitterness which swept the country. The explosion which occurred in Shanghai fourteen months later was inevitable.

In January, 1932, some two thousand Japanese marines and gunmen, or *ronin*, moved into the densely populated section of the Chinese quarter of Shanghai known as Chapei. They did not meet much resistance until they approached the railway station, which was defended by units of the 19th Route Army of the Nationalist forces. In a sharp engagement, the Japanese were thrown back with heavy losses. Their astonishment and chagrin were almost ludicrous. I remember a Japanese consular officer saying to me, "But they dared to fight against our Imperial marines!"

They did indeed, and so furiously did they defend every foot of territory that the Japanese marines, to their humiliation, had to call on the Japanese army to come to their assistance. It required eighty thousand Japanese troops, planes, tanks and naval units to bring the military phase of the "Shanghai Incident" to a close. Even so, the 19th Route Army was not defeated but withdrew on orders to positions about twenty miles from Shanghai as a result of mediation efforts made by the British and American governments to bring about a cessation of hostilities.

Although the actual fighting lasted only thirty days it was indescribably savage, from street to street, house to house, trench to trench. Overhead, Japanese planes droned daily, dropping bombs indiscriminately upon the Chinese section of the city, which went up in flames. The massacre of civilian Chinese was appalling, many of them being rounded up and, on the pretext that they were snipers, shot or used as human targets for bayonet practice. A British member of the Shanghai Municipal Police Force told me that he had seen the most tragic and lamentable sights: women and children who had been bayoneted to death, lying in a singed heap among the charred remnants of their little stores; babies wailing among corpses for their mothers; while hundreds of street dogs gnawed at the dead. Over the city hung the stench of death.

Among the Japanese I had many friends and I could not help wondering what their inner thoughts might be. Did they believe that Japan's destiny should be achieved, regardless of the cost in human life and suffering? Did they approve of the wanton massacre of civilians? As sensitive, intelligent persons they must have been shocked, or were their finer instincts transcended by the burning vision of Japan's imperial destiny?

The net result of this holocaust of fire and blood in Shanghai was to spread among the Chinese people a feeling of strength and unity. "We fought the dwarf men well at Shanghai," one said to me, "even though they had many planes and battleships." He added, "We are stronger now." Certainly, in a spiritual sense, as well as psychological, this was true. Thousands of Chinese from all parts of the country contributed money, food and clothes to their troops who had fought so courageously at Shanghai. The Chinese people toughened under the flames roaring through their homes, and that toughened spirit enabled them to endure the long bitter years ahead.

It was in a glum, despondent mood that I returned with the

Minister from Shanghai to Peiping. I was depressed by what I had seen, but Peiping seemed untouched by the recent tragic events in Shanghai. At a dinner party I tried to tell something of what I had seen to my partner.

"How frightfully interesting," she replied, "but have you heard about dowager Mrs. Chalfonte Quimple at the Yardleys' party? Well, my dear, it seems she went into a perfect fury when she saw the seating arrangement. And what do you suppose she did? During cocktails she slipped into the dining room and rearranged the seating cards so that she sat on the left of the British Minister.

"When we went in to dinner there was the most utter confusion. The guests could not find their places and went round and round the table. Mr. Yardley fell into a rage with his wife and called her a stupid fool. The only person who was calm and collected was Mrs. Chalfonte Quimple, who said to the British Minister, 'How too delightful to be sitting next to you.'

"He is no fool," my dinner partner raced on. "He guessed that she was responsible. He drawled, 'Do you enjoy these childish pranks, Mrs. Chalfonte Quimple?'"

8

Diplomat as Detective

A VAST mass of turgid brown water, the Yangtze River, swirling, eddying, moving ceaselessly, flowed by the windows of the United States Consulate General at Hankow. I was fascinated at the spectacle and awed by the thought that this great river had been flowing for millions of years, cutting steep gorges through solid rock a hundred feet in depth, depositing millions of tons of fertile sediment through the heart of China. It was the giver of life to millions and equally the careless destroyer in times of flood.

This day, in the summer of 1932, just after I had arrived in Hankow to take up a new assignment, the river was alive with big and little craft. White river steamers, which plied between Shanghai and Hankow, reflected the hot sun. Snorting tugs pulled long strings of heavily laden barges. Everywhere were thousands of little sampans darting about the river like water beetles. Some were right in front of the Consulate, which was on the river bank. It seemed incredible that the thin, emaciated man, whose every rib was plainly visible and whose face under his enormous straw hat was drawn

with fatigue, could possibly propel his sampan filled high with heavy
sacks of grain, against the swiftly moving river. One long oar, set
into a forked stick near the rear of the boat, was his only means
of propulsion. This he manipulated with a forceful but deft push
and twist of arms and body.

Just beyond, a young woman skillfully maneuvered her sampan
against the current. Between anchored boats, she stopped to sell
sticky sweetmeats and condiments. On looking more closely I saw
that many of the sampans, including the little ferries, were navi-
gated by women and young girls. The latter, slim in their dark
blue cotton jackets and trousers, laughed and chattered, perhaps
conscious of the graceful picture they made as they rhythmically
pushed their oars, or perhaps merely glad to be young. The older
women pushed listlessly, endlessly, pausing only to tie back a strand
of hair blown across their tired faces, continuing the weary labor
that was necessary to earn a few bowls of rice for themselves and
their children. The river was a panorama of man's struggle to wrest
a living from this swiftly running current, which resembled the
short span of his life but, in its ceaseless flow, was timeless.

I took one look at the United States Consulate General. Indu-
bitably, this was another ancient building, a "has been" on which
neither money nor love had been lavished. It was a hideous red
brick and belonged, if I remember correctly, to some wealthy
merchant who was adding to his gains by soaking Uncle Sam. It
had three floors. The top or heavenly floor was reserved for the
Consul General, a delightful bachelor. The second floor had been
more or less divided into two sections, the idea being to accommodate two consular families. The ground floor contained the offices,
which were dark and gloomy but the coolest part of the building.
Nevertheless, because of the summer heat and humidity, one
dripped wherever one might be. The saving feature was the location
of the Consulate building on "The Bund," a broad tree-lined avenue

running along the river bank. Fronting the river were great banking and office edifices, the British Consulate and fine residences of wealthy merchants.

In 1927, the Chinese Red revolutionaries had forced the British to give up their concession in Hankow but the Nationalist Government, which had succeeded the Red regime, had set up a good municipal administration under K. C. Wu, now a political refugee in the United States. Although foreign concessions were an especial target for vilification and abuse, they were frequently used by the Chinese as safe havens, and were much admired. In the cool of the evening, when the temperature dropped from 102 to 96, Chinese by the thousands would appear on the Bund to gossip and chew watermelon seeds, to air their pet birds and admire the trilling songs of their friends' birds, to discuss some business deal or plot against the Government.

The importance of Hankow both in a political and economic sense was impressed upon me when I arrived, which was as it should be. To do a successful job, a consular or diplomatic officer must feel that his post and its problems are of vital concern to his Government, and that he is not only making a definite contribution toward strengthening friendly relations between his country and the one in which he is serving, but at the same time that he is furthering his country's legitimate interests.

In the summer of 1932, Hankow was the center of the Nationalist Government's political and military power in west-central China and it represented a point of control over both the Yangtze River, with its heavy volume of trade, and the railway, which ran north to Peiping. Nevertheless, the Government's position in the Hankow area was precariously maintained because of the uncertain allegiance of some of the warlords in the north and the hostility of the Communists to the south. The strength of the latter had increased as a result of several unsuccessful campaigns launched against them by the forces of Generalissimo Chiang Kai-shek, from which they had profited greatly by the capture of large quantities of arms and munitions and the defection of troops. Another massive anti-Communist campaign was in progress but was no more successful than previous expeditions, perhaps because Hankow was alive with Red agents who could be counted upon to keep the Communists well informed.

Hankow was also important to the Nationalists because it contained one of the largest foreign concessions to be turned back to China. I am sure they were aware of the close scrutiny with which the foreign powers were watching the new Chinese municipal administration of the ex-British concession. They realized that the treatment of foreigners at Hankow would have considerable bearing on the course of negotiations in progress at Nanking for the abolition of extraterritorial rights.

The settling-in process of a bachelor is always a nightmare. The question of furniture and furnishings for one's quarters and where to find the necessary funds is likely to bring on the jitters. I took over Government quarters on the second floor, and was lucky because they contained a few sticks of furniture. There are exceptions but, in general, consular furniture is not only old, scarred and shabby but there is invariably a tell-tale sagginess about it—the consular sag. During the course of the many moves a Foreign Service Officer makes from post to post quite a bit of furniture with the consular sag is picked up because one simply has not the cash to buy anything else.

The Hankow consular district included vast areas of western and northwestern China. It ranked second after Kalgan in territorial expanse. American business interests were concentrated in Hankow and consisted of oil and tobacco companies, a branch bank and several import-export firms, with a small but congenial American business community. Up country were to be found hundreds of

American missionaries scattered over a wide area, often living in remote and not easily accessible towns and villages.

It was the duty of the Consulate General to see to the protection of American lives and interests. In this, we were ably assisted at Hankow and along the river by the little flotilla of American gunboats. Up country we had to rely on the local Chinese and the efficacy of our relations and negotiations with the authorities. "Protection work," as we called it at the office, occupied a goodly portion of our time. Sometimes it was humdrum and unexciting, but not always.

"Ekvall murdered near Sian," read a message received at the Consulate from missionaries residing at Sian, the capital city of the province of Shensi.

Our records revealed that he was a duly registered American citizen, the son of Norwegian missionaries who had lived and worked for many years in the far northwestern provinces. Some months previously he had set out for those remote provinces to sell trucks on behalf of the Ford Motor Company.

Telegrams were sent off to the Legation at Peking and to the provincial authorities at Sian, requesting the latter to make an immediate investigation of the reported murder. Communications with distant Sian were so poor that a quick reply could hardly be expected, but time passed and not a word was received from the Chinese authorities of the province, although the Ministry of Foreign Affairs at Nanking notified the Legation that they had sent a prompt inquiry to Sian.

Word came through from the missionaries, however, and what they had to report was not reassuring. From Chinese friends and other reliable sources they had learned that Ekvall had been murdered by men in uniform who were believed to be provincial troops, that the murder had taken place a few miles outside the west gate of the city, and that there was no trace of the body or the car in which he had been riding. The provincial authorities, they added, had taken no steps whatsoever to investigate the crime or to apprehend the murderers.

We pressed the Legation to urge the Government to take immediate action to investigate a crime which apparently had been committed by troops under the command of General Yang Hu-cheng, the warlord Governor of the province, who was a law unto himself. The Consulate repeatedly telegraphed and wrote General Yang, urging him to make a full investigation. Weeks passed. Finally General Yang replied that he had ordered an investigation. Nothing more. We were much disturbed as was the Legation, which decided to send a young Army language officer, Lieutenant Robert Soule, to Sian to look into the case and discover what, if anything, the provincial authorities were doing. He found that nothing was being done.

From Hankow we urged vigorous action to investigate this brutal murder of an American citizen and apprehend the criminals. We proposed that we and the Chinese Ministry of Foreign Affairs send special representatives to Sian. This was agreed to. I was instructed to proceed immediately.

It was in the late fall when I left. The weather was turning bleak and cold. As the train crawled along over a bumpy roadbed, which had often been blown up and twisted as the result of hostilities up and down the Peking-Hankow railway, it was possible to see farmers and their families. They were clad in bulky padded tunics and trousers against the cold and were winnowing the golden grain as they tossed it into the air from flat baskets. Buffaloes, slowly, stolidly, almost majestically, pulled the great stone grinders round and round. Children—there were always children—romped about, scattering a few scrawny chickens. Occasionally a fat sow, belly to the ground and followed by a litter, would add life and confusion to a farmyard.

The scene brought to mind millions of Chinese farmers toiling from dawn to dusk and scratching just enough from the soil to feed themselves and their large families. Superstitious, kindly and hospitable, the farmer has, indeed, a hard lot, for he is plagued by locusts which devour his crops, by famines and floods which destroy his property, and by tax collectors who take what little is left. The daily drudgery is relieved only by a little feasting and gaiety at festivals and on special occasions. Happiness he seldom tastes except from the comforting presence of his wife and children. He is bowed by hardships and adversity and yet he has been the backbone of the country for forty centuries and will continue to keep its life pulsing for centuries to come, no matter who rules over him. China owes much of her greatness to the unceasing toil of her patient farmers.

The going was difficult because when we were about to pass a small station the engineer invariably put on a burst of speed so that his train would momentarily act like the express it was supposed to be. Perhaps he thought of himself as a roaring night dragon who would impress the gaping villagers. I clutched whatever was clutchable as we swayed and clattered over railroad points which I fervently hoped had been well and properly closed. Having thus impressed the station master and villagers, the engineer throttled down his puffing engine and we resumed our crawl.

Next day I changed trains at the town of Chengchow and boarded another "express" on the Lung Hai railway, which carried me directly west to the end of the line and the mud-walled town of Tungkuan on the Yellow River. A few years later the Yellow River was bridged and the railway pushed through to Sian and beyond. At Tungkuan, Lieutenant Soule and a representative of the provincial government met me and we were immediately ushered into the station master's private office where tea, biscuits and fruit were served.

I asked politely after the health of His Excellency, General

Yang Hu-cheng. He was well, replied his representative, and impatiently awaiting my arrival. Such exquisite politeness! We were ferried across the river on a flimsy-looking raft which was covered with passengers, donkeys and baskets of goods. I wondered whether we would make it, so heavily was the ferry loaded and so swift ran the muddy waters of the Yellow River.

We were escorted to a waiting car of really ancient vintage. Bowing, the Governor's representative invited us to take seats in his "poor and humble" car. We bowed and urged him to enter first. After much polite bowing we were finally all seated. The back seat spring groaned as the three of us sat down. Another car was loaded with police and military who were to be our guardians and protectors, while an officer with a large pistol was seated in front, beside the driver.

The latter drove like one possessed along a frightfully dusty road, criss-crossed with ruts and liberally sprinkled with deep holes, some of which he missed by twisting maneuvers executed at top speed. The springs fairly cried aloud in anguish and so did I. It was really an agonizing trip and I paid scant attention to the famous beauty spots in the nearby mountains which our Chinese friend described at length during the trip.

We were driven to quarters provided for us by the Governor. They were clean and adequate although chilly since the only heating was by a couple of little charcoal stoves. I emphasized to the Governor's representative that we must call on him without delay. Meantime I was able to have a long talk with Bob Soule and the missionaries.

Bob Soule, who later in the Second World War rose to fame and to be a general officer because of his leadership in various engagements in the Pacific, had ferreted out additional bits of information concerning the murder. It appeared that the motive had been robbery and that the crime had been committed by ex-bandits who had been taken into General Yang's provincial forces a few months previously. The Chinese authorities contended that the crime had been committed by bandits over whom they had no control.

We went to visit the missionaries, the majority of whom were Scandinavians, and some of whom had been close friends of the Ekvall family and knew young Ekvall very well. They were much upset by the murder of this young man and the attempts of the provincial authorities to conceal the facts. This in turn had led to a certain suspicious hostility on the part of the authorities toward the missionaries who, as they knew, had learned the main details of the crime. The missionaries were relieved to see us and to learn that the United States Government did not intend to allow this crime to be smothered by a polite but meaningless exchange of official letters.

They told us that, in Lanchow, three hundred miles west of Sian, young Ekvall had converted the proceeds of his sales of Ford trucks into gold dust, which he had packed in a candy bottle as a convenient way of carrying his money. This fact had immediately become an interesting bit of gossip in the market place and, as it passed from person to person, the amount became magnified until Ekvall was said to have left Lanchow for Sian with his car filled with gold dust. The missionaries were convinced that General Yang's troops, particularly those nominally guarding the road outside the city, had heard this story and had lain in wait for him.

Several days later, we called on Governor Yang, who was flanked by his Commissioner for Foreign Affairs and by several of his staff. A comment of mine, revealing interest in the past history of the city of Sian, led to an immediate offer to arrange a sightseeing tour. It was obvious that, if possible, our mission was to be sidetracked.

I got it back on the track by reminding him of my purpose in being there and relating the facts we had gathered about Ekvall's murder. General Yang was sulky; he had no wish to discuss the case. To end any hope he might have that the problem would be allowed to drop, I said that we had been instructed to remain in Sian until the matter was settled. At this, he looked more sulky than ever.

"Please tell me, Excellency, exactly what steps you have taken to investigate this crime, in order that my Government may be informed."

He replied perfunctorily that he had ordered an investigation and was awaiting a report. I pointed out that this was what he had told the Consulate General at Hankow three weeks previously. Had there been no information since then? He said rather vaguely that he thought the murder had been committed by bandits.

After a second and equally fruitless interview, I sat down and sent a long telegram to the Legation, which it took me hours to put into code by the dim light of a kerosene lamp. After reporting on the Governor's attitude and the information we had gleaned for ourselves, I urged that further representations be made to the Government at Nanking to despatch its representatives at once, as their presence would impress the Governor with the importance attached to this case by their Government.

Since we had to be our own detectives in the case, we set to work in earnest to see what we could find out by ourselves. We talked to many Chinese, most of whom refused to say anything; those who did spoke guardedly and admitted that they believed the Governor's troops stationed outside the west gate were responsible. But how and where could they have disposed of poor Ekvall's body? And what of the automobile?

We decided to visit some of the little villages near the place where we believed the murder had taken place. Here again we found that the farmers were afraid to talk. As we investigated, we noticed several old wells between the villages and the road. That set us wondering. Might they not have thrown the body down one of those wells?

About a week later a valuable clue came our way. A farmer from one of the villages we had visited came in the dead of night to see one of the missionaries who had befriended him. He said he had been afraid, as were the other men in the village, to talk because the soldiers nearby had threatened to kill anyone revealing anything to the foreign devils. However, after much thought he felt he should tell his friend the missionary that one night he had dimly seen a group of men who looked like soldiers carrying something resembling a body. He had seen them throw the "thing" into an old well nearby and then toss a little earth and brushwood on top. He and the other men of the village who had heard about the robbery and murder of an American believed that his body had been thrown into this well.

Next day we had a chance to talk privately with villager Kao. He repeated his story and gave additional information. He also carefully described the location of the well. "Please, Honorable Consul, do not tell them I told you. They will kill me." We reassured him. We felt convinced that he was telling the truth.

At our next meeting with the Governor we were accompanied by two representatives of the Nationalist Government who had finally arrived. As usual the Governor was polite but noncommittal. I told him we believed Ekvall's body had been thrown into an old well, near the place of the crime and that we even knew the exact well. I asked him to depute a group of officials and military to accompany us the next day to make a search.

This caused consternation. The Governor insisted that he was doing everything possible. I emphasized that we had been in Sian for several weeks during which time nothing had been accomplished. The Governor reluctantly capitulated.

The next day, under a cold blue sky, with the wind whipping

little swirls of dust across the fields, a group of us gathered around an old well. Farmer Kao's directions had been so clear that we had little difficulty in locating it. Farmers who had been rounded up from the nearby village—our informant was not among them—let a rope into the well. A sturdy young man climbed down, hand over hand. Up came brushwood, then several baskets of earth. There was a faint cry. We all looked down. The young man, who was obviously scared, said, "There is a man's body."

Bob Soule and I looked at each other and then at the officials. They looked away. Finally the remains of the poor body came to view. There was no doubt that it was Ekvall, and no doubt that he had been shot. A silent group returned to the city.

After the discovery of Ekvall's body, the Governor felt any further attempts at concealment were futile and that it would be better to make a real effort to unravel the crime and arrest those guilty. He was also probably embarrassed by the presence of the representatives of the Nationalist Government. At any rate, he agreed to issue a proclamation, offering a reward for information leading to the arrest of the criminals. Indeed, he now admitted that these were three or four soldiers from a unit stationed along the road outside the west gate. They had been bandits, he said, who had been taken into his army.

Temporarily, there was little that we could do except wait. Then a summons came from the Governor. He looked more cheerful than I had seen him at any previous meeting. He announced that his troops had tracked down the four men who were believed to have murdered Ekvall and, in a brief encounter, three of them had been killed and the fourth captured. After a long interrogation this man had confessed not only to have taken part in the crime but to have conceived and directed it.

I inquired when the man would be tried. The Governor seemed taken aback at the idea of a trial, and no doubt had intended simply to have the man executed. I pointed out that the Chinese criminal code made express provision for the trial of persons charged with the commission of murder and added I was sure the Governor would want justice done in this legal and orderly way.

After some talk with his advisers, he agreed. I then said that I had an unusual request to make and asked that I be accorded the right to be present at the trial and to put a series of questions to the prisoner through the presiding judge. This request really caused a flurry, but I wanted to make sure, at least to my own satisfaction, that the man being tried had actually been involved in the crime and that he was not some poor felon whom they had decided to sacrifice.

A few days went by, during which I found myself biting my nails. Had I asked too much? But suppose the man actually was innocent and they were making him the scapegoat to settle the case? This last thought haunted me. While waiting for the Governor's answer to my request, I spent much time drawing up a list of questions, the replies to which I felt would show clearly whether the prisoner had really been present and participated in the crime.

To my relief, the Governor's reply was "yes." The trial took place the next night in a great gloomy hall, dimly lit by kerosene lamps. It was icy cold. The judges were seated on a platform behind a long table. I sat below in a chair especially set aside for me. At a signal from the chief judge, there was a clank, clank, clank of heavy chains dragged across the floor. The prisoner appeared, dressed in a dirty gray soldier's uniform, chains around his wrists and ankles. He looked gaunt and ghastly. The certainty of death was written on his face.

The judge read the charges and then the prisoner's confession and asked him if he had stated the truth. In a surprisingly strong voice the prisoner replied that the statements were true and that he and his three companions had killed the American and thrown his body into an old well.

At this point I caught the attention of the chief judge and handed him my list of questions with the request that he put them to the prisoner. He did so. The prisoner seemed surprised but answered all my questions clearly and without hesitation. He described Ekvall's physical appearance, the color of his hair, his eyes, whether or not he was wearing glasses. He described his clothes, the color of the car he was driving, the contents of the car and the candy jar of gold dust. Their motive, he said, was simple robbery and they had not planned to murder the American. However, they knew if they let him go he would immediately raise an alarm in Sian and they would be caught. Therefore, they decided, he must be killed and his body and the car hidden.

He had shot Ekvall in the back of the head and carried his body to a nearby well and thrown it in. By this time it was dark so they had waited until the next morning when, with the aid of some of the villagers, they had pushed the car to a ravine and into a large cave.

At this point, the prisoner broke down, fell on his knees before the judges and begged for mercy. It was a moving sight but the judges passed sentence, ordering his execution for the following morning at dawn.

My first reaction, when I thought of the sudden and savage attack upon young Ekvall, was one of satisfaction. But this faded as I looked at the gaunt and haggard man who at dawn would face the firing squad. And when, in the cold pale morning light I reluctantly attended the grim execution, I thought only of the crumpled body and staring eyes. Justice had been done, the law had been upheld, the right man had been punished. But I was left only with a sensation of profound pity.

In spite of the tragedy and its retribution which were my chief business at Sian, the city in itself proved to be a rewarding experience. The immense walls of the city rose sheer from the flat plain, as massive and impressive as the walls of Peking. Sian and its environs, under such names as Ch'ang An, city of peace, had been the capital of many great rulers. In the time of the famous Tang Emperor, T'ai Tsung of the seventh century A.D., it was not only the center of a great empire stretching into Central Asia and Tibet but the seat of learning and the arts. Vestiges of greatness still remained but when we saw it the place looked seedy and rundown, its trade in the doldrums because of the toll taken by bandits, warlords and Reds.

We visited the tombs of the Tang Emperor in company with our two friends from Nanking, one of whom was well educated in the classics and historical lore. Under the wise and benevolent rule of the Emperor T'ai Tsung, he told us, Sian became a center of learning, poetry, the arts and rare handicrafts. He described tribute bearers and emissaries from Tibet, Annam, India and Persia, marching through the streets in their strange and exotic robes, bearing rare and costly gifts to the Emperor.

I asked if it were true that a Nestorian monk had come from faraway Persia. He said it was so and all had been recorded on a large stone tablet still standing some distance from Sian. But it was not only the Nestorian priest Olo Pen who had been drawn to the ancient city. Many Buddhist priests had come from India, traveling by sea and by land, and had brought with them Buddhist texts, which they translated into Chinese. Emperor T'ai Tsung, who had made this possible, must, I said, have been both wise and tolerant. Our friend agreed and quoted from the edict issued by the Emperor in A.D. 638:

> Truth bears not one name only,
> The sage is not one person only,
> Religions vary with the countries,
> Their influence benefits all beings.

Of course, we also wanted to see the tomb of Emperor Shih Huang Ti of the Chin dynasty who, in 220 B.C., welded together a vast empire by fire and sword and the most ruthless and inhuman methods. The toll of those killed and liquidated ran into the millions, while millions more were uprooted from their homes and moved here and there at the whim of this tyrant. Hundreds of thousands of men, women and children perished in the construction of the Great Wall of China, his principal claim to fame. At his peremptory order, all the classics were burned and reference to the sages or their teachings was forbidden on pain of death.

It flattered his ego and vanity to build immense and elaborate palaces. He was determined that his tomb should be equally impressive. Thousands of skilled workmen and laborers were employed in building a series of huge chambers that were fantastically embellished. In the dome of one of them was suspended a moving replica of the heavenly constellations. The entrances were cunningly constructed to thwart evil spirits as well as tomb robbers. Finally, to make sure that the secret of the entrances should never be disclosed, the Emperor ordered all those employed on the construction of his tomb to be buried alive within its depths.

The Pei Lin, or Forest of Tablets, in a secluded but dilapidated section of the city, was to my mind the greatest wonder in that city of ancient culture. Here were hundreds, literally a forest, of old stone tablets of varying height and size, on which were inscribed Chinese history and literature. No wonder that, for centuries, scholars and artists had come to study these tablets and to make rubbings of them for their libraries. Here in the Pei Lin I felt the strength and beauty of Chinese civilization, which had flowered in spite of blind and savage onslaughts. But to comprehend it one would have to study more than the five cartloads of books prescribed by my Chinese teacher.

9

A Bright Particular Star

I HAD not long been back in Hankow before I was temporarily detailed to Nanking in the spring of 1934 to take over the duties of my colleague, Bob Smyth, who had suffered an injury to his spine. I found him stretched out in the hospital, with great weights attached to his head and feet. It seemed to be a fiendish form of torture.

It had been nearly three years since my last visit to Nanking. Many improvements caught the eye. New government buildings, new residences, new streets, new stores gave the impression of progress and greater stability, which unfortunately was not reflected by conditions throughout the country.

A rebellion in Fukien province involving the famous 19th Route Army, which so gallantly had defended Shanghai in 1932 against the Japanese, had just been bloodily suppressed by Generalissimo Chiang's forces. Many of the warlords of south and southeast China were following an independent policy marked by hostility toward the Nationalist Government at Nanking.

(89)

General Chiang continued his punitive expeditions against the Communists of south-central China and was mobilizing a huge army of over half a million men, supported by a fleet of planes, which later in the year he was to throw against the principal Communist base in the province of Kiangsi in a supreme effort to annihilate Mao Tse-tung's forces. The Communists decided to move from Kiangsi to a new base in northwest China and, like quicksilver, they eluded the Nationalist armies arrayed against them. They commenced a long and incredibly hard trek of nearly three thousand miles to their new base in northern Shensi where they were to establish themselves, strengthen their forces with Moscow's aid, and await their opportunity.

In north China, the Japanese, not content with swallowing Manchuria, had succeeded in forcing the Chinese Government to agree to the establishment of a zone from which Chinese military forces were to be excluded, as a sort of buffer to Manchuria and to Japanese penetrations into Inner Mongolia. Thus they were poised in north China in a most advantageous position from which to make the next move.

Many Chinese with whom one talked were greatly disturbed and disheartened by the inability of the country to unite in the face of Japanese aggression and were critical of Generalissimo Chiang's preoccupation with domestic politics and punitive campaigns. They thought that if he had taken the lead in opposing the Japanese, dissident elements within the country would have rallied around him in united determination to save China. Chiang contended that he must destroy these elements and restore order before tackling the Japanese.

All this and much more was spelled out in the code telegrams and reports pouring into the Nanking Consulate General, which was also the operational branch of the Legation. Our chief there was Willys R. Peck who, as Secretary for Chinese Affairs, had guided our Chinese studies and rigorously examined us ten years before in Peking. His knowledge of the Chinese people, their language and their mentality proved invaluable in the conduct of relations between the United States and China. But there was a whimsical and witty side to his nature which would appear when he was able to put affairs of state out of his mind.

I remember a pleasant picnic on the slopes of Purple Mountain. In inimitable Chinese he mimicked a long conversation between the Legation's number one *t'ing ch'ai,* or general office boy, telephone operator and runner of errands, with the telephone operator of another legation who was his great friend. The private lives and doings of their respective Legation Ministers were discussed in detail and with evident relish. I laughed until the tears ran down my cheeks and my ribs ached.

Back in Hankow for the hot and drippy summer. Consul General Adams left, to the regret of all and, as number two, I was placed in charge, a heavy responsibility but not unpleasant to the ego. As will have been noted, servants and consuls in China were distinguished and differentiated merely by numbers.

Six months later a new Consul General was appointed and I left early in 1935 for home leave, returning to Shanghai a few months later.

There I again found Flavius Josephus Chapman III. Brilliant, erratic, unpredictable, charming and generous, all are needed to describe F. J. His was a temperament that was irked by office hours and regulations, to which he paid little heed. He would turn up at the office at any old time of day but, as one of his chiefs told me, four hours of F. J.'s time was worth ten hours put in by other men.

F. J.'s bubbling humor made him irresistible to his friends, who constantly urged him to correct his wild ways, but without result. Such a temperament, coupled with his impish delight in playing practical jokes on pompous and stuffy members of the staff, led inevitably to a break with the State Department. At the time I arrived, he had joined the Chinese Government Salt Administration and was admired by his superiors for his knowledge of the Chinese language and for his keen mind, nor was he unduly hampered by regulations, so the job suited him.

The Consulate General was located in an ancient pile of red brick buildings, which had been condemned repeatedly as a fire trap. A faint stirring of interest passed through the ranks of the toilers in this old rabbit warren when it was rumored that Washington was considering architects' plans for a new combination office and apartment building to be built on the site of the red-brick monstrosity. The plans, which had been seen only by a privileged few, caused amazement and consternation.

These gentlemen in Washington, who had never seen Shanghai, much less experienced its summer heat and humidity, planned to crowd into the new structure as many tiny little one-and-a-half-room apartments as was humanly possible. "Consular cells" we called them. The moans and groans of the Consul General and his staff were wafted from Shanghai to Washington but without much effect. However, Consul General Gauss, my former boss in Manchuria, fought a good fight and won, insisting when he took charge at Shanghai that the office be moved to decent quarters in a new building in the heart of the International Settlement. But this occurred later.

Meantime, the problem of living quarters was acute. F. J. urged me to share a small house with him. Although fond of him, I accepted his invitation with forebodings, aware that the establishment would be run in haphazard fashion. And so it was. For F. J., out of the generosity of his heart, had taken Chinese off the streets and brought them into the house as servants. The so-called cook served us outlandish concoctions that were quite inedible, leathery and greasy, whether meat or sweet.

"I'm starving; this stuff is impossible," I would groan, pushing back the food. "Can't you fire him?"

"Now, Eddie," F. J. would reply, looking at me reproachfully over his glasses, "you know we can't throw the poor guy out on the street." So we would nibble on crackers and cheese to stave off the pangs of hunger.

The houseboy was just as inadequate, slopping about the house and occasionally languidly flicking a feather duster over the furniture. Clouds of dust would fly into the air to resettle comfortably into place. "Honorable master," he would say, "no use to dust, makes house all dirty." But both domestics were expert accountants, if nothing else, and presented us with fantastic bills for groceries and household items.

Bills piled up endlessly. In spite of our mounting indebtedness, F. J. suddenly decided to buy a car. "Sheer extravagance," I protested. "Now, Eddie"—I was always Eddie at such moments—"calm yourself and listen to me. I'm just doing this to help out that poor Czech automobile salesman, and besides he has such fabulous tales to tell of his experiences."

He bought the car, a tiny two-cylinder affair, of fiery red and so close to the ground it could scarcely hurdle a mud puddle. It was a wholly impractical piece of junk. But F. J. reveled in it and recklessly careened around the crowded streets. He called it the "Red Bug." I tried it once or twice but found my nerves shattered by the experience. After that I preferred the buses back and forth to the Consulate, although they were jammed with humanity and suffocating.

I had my hands full at the office. It used to be a cardinal principle of the Foreign Service that its members should be trained and become versed in the many and varied activities of the Service. A Foreign Service Officer was expected to know the laws governing citizenship, immigration, naturalization, customs and shipping. He must know how to issue passports, visas, invoices and a mass of other documents. He must be familiar with the laws, regulations and customs of the country in which he might be serving. Furthermore, in a country like China, he must know almost by heart the treaties in force between the United States and China and between the latter and all other countries. The troubled times in which we lived made it necessary constantly to invoke the provisions of these treaties and there was much learned argument with the Chinese authorities concerning the meaning and interpretation of these complex agreements.

The Foreign Service Officer also had to be well versed in the system of extraterritoriality, which stemmed from some of the first treaties concluded between China and the foreign powers and which was of particular importance in Shanghai because of the large number of foreign nationals residing there and their extensive business interests. He must be able to promote trade, settle trade disputes or complaints, and to write good reports on the market for silk stockings, locomotives and electric power generators.

Finally, he was expected to make a thorough study of the political situation in China, which was most intricate, and be able to write comprehensive reports, analyzing the situation and suggesting certain courses of action. All in all, a Foreign Service Officer, under the old concept of that species of public servant, was expected to be a jack of all trades and knowledgeable about all of them. It was a good concept. The old-time officer was more flexible and adaptable and could be used by his Government almost anywhere.

Now all is changed, but back in 1935, the old concept still held. I had been doing a good deal of political reporting at previous posts and so welcomed a spell in the economic and commercial section of the Consulate General. It was quite a job keeping the World Trade Directory Reports up to date. This involved interviewing business concerns of all nationalities in Shanghai, cajoling and extracting from them information concerning their line of business, capitalization, annual turnover and many other items of information which we sent to the Department of Commerce in Washington for the use of American business.

The infringement of American trademarks, copyrights and patents was another matter of concern to our office. The more popular a trademark the greater the swarm of Chinese imitators. We were constantly invoking treaty provisions and Chinese laws and regulations regarding the infringement of trademarks. The Chinese always seemed mildly surprised that we made such a pother about imitations which they regarded as being flattering and indicative of the popularity of American goods and trademarks. The proprietor of a Chinese store was mystified when the Consulate complained about the name he had chosen for his store—U.S.A. Inc. He said he thought the U.S.A. Government would be pleased.

Then there were the general and particular economic and trade reports, describing for the benefit of the American businessman at home the import-export trade and its possibilities. The rounding up of statistics was like the pursuit of a will-of-the-wisp. The Chinese Maritime Customs, which for many years had employed a number of foreigners, was about the only ready and reasonably accurate source. For the rest, one set down in one's report the best statistical guesses possible.

I remember calling on a Chinese businessman who was one of the local agents for a well-known make of American trucks. Cups of tea were placed before us as usual. I told him the Consulate was preparing a report on the automobile market, which would go to American manufacturers and result in increased business for him and other agents. How did his business this year compare with the previous year and how many trucks had he sold?

"Honorable Consul," he replied, "the business of this unworthy company in the year of the Dragon [this year] was better than in the year of the Hare [last year] because we sold several tens of trucks more."

All efforts to find out exactly how many "several tens" might be was unavailing. In his own secret account books he no doubt had set down the exact number, but for general publication, he, like most Chinese businessmen, felt that in vagueness lay safety from the inquisitive and from the tax collectors. At any rate, the statistics we included indicated trends and were welcomed, judging by the number of appreciative letters the Consulate General received. And yet it was increasingly borne in upon us that there is too little understanding on the part of American business-men as a whole of the full extent of the assistance which they receive in the promotion and protection of their interests from a group of hard-working public servants whom they are all too inclined to criticize. A clearer knowledge on their part of the constant support and assistance which they are receiving would do much to change their attitude.

While I was absorbed in these activities, life with F. J. continued to be distracting and full of unpredictable events. I would greatly have enjoyed it, for he was a whimsically intelligent companion, but I had personal problems on my mind.

One evening we were sitting in the living room reading and stirring up a little dust left by the houseboy, as we turned the pages or moved in our chairs. Suddenly F. J. slammed his book shut and leaped to his feet.

"What are you mooning about?"

"Josephine," I replied bleakly.

"She is twelve thousand miles away. You must do something. Man, what can you expect?" F. J. strode back and forth excitedly, his black eyes flashing. I did not suspect that he was about to play a role which almost ended in disaster for me.

"How in the world can I ask her to marry me?" I said dismally. "You know how low my finances are and that we are deep in debt; besides I am only a Consul. She has had everything and been accustomed to so much."

"Don't sit there doing nothing," he exploded. "She won't mind the hardships. But you've got to plan a campaign and make it convincing. If you need money, write to Bob Smyth. Meanwhile, I'll write to Josephine, pleading your cause."

Well, we wrote our letters. F. J. plotted so craftily to win Josephine for me that I almost lost her altogether. He fabricated an imaginary lady and described her in glowing terms. She was young, brilliant, beautiful, and charming. She played the piano divinely (an accomplishment for which Josephine had been striving for years), she was a witty conversationalist; this fascinating creature, F. J. continued, had moved next door and both he and I were finding her absolutely delightful.

The first inkling I had of the kind of assistance my friend had given me was a cable from Josephine declaring in effect that all was over. I was dumbfounded and sought out F. J. Subdued, he explained his plan of campaign, defending himself as best he could. I wrote to Josephine, trying to undo the harm. Months went by and not a word.

From that time on ours was a glum household of an evening, marked by long silences broken when I reproached F. J. for his letter to Josephine. More weeks passed.

Then, on a cold, raw Shanghai day early in 1936, came a letter from Josephine. She was planning to visit Japan in March. The day suddenly seemed dazzling and the heavens filled with bright shooting stars. True, the letter did not exactly answer any of my questions. But if she was planning to visit Japan and had written to tell me so, it might mean the disastrous letter was forgiven. It might even mean more.

"Of course it means more," F. J. declared jubilantly. "You see, I was not so stupid after all." He was taking all the credit but I didn't care. I was too happy for that.

"We will be married in Kobe, Japan," I decided. "And I'm going to start looking for a suitable house and buy a car."

"Sheer extravagance." F. J. smiled approvingly. "I'll get my Czech friend to sell you one."

First I approached my chief, Consul General Gauss, and asked for two weeks' leave in March. Then I dashed to a cable office and sent off a message to Josephine, telling her I would meet her in Kobe. The days rushed by like an express train with hardly time to make all the arrangements. I found a house. It was too large and too expensive. When I moved my few sticks of furniture into it, plus some battered oddments loaned me by F. J., it looked stark and empty.

A staff of servants was needed but I went to the wives of my consular colleagues for help on this, and not to F. J., who would doubtless have prevailed upon me to take some of his pathetic waifs.

With money loaned by Bob Smyth I took ship for Kobe and arrived the day before Josephine was due. Praise be for helpful consular colleagues. Through Kenneth Krentz, our Consul at Kobe, reservations had been made at the *Tor* Hotel, a clergyman engaged to perform the marriage ceremony, the necessary Japanese officials invited to issue appropriate documents and finally Ken had invited us to a wedding luncheon. In fact, I was sure of everything but my bride.

All I accomplished in the daze of that day was to go to a small Japanese florist and order all the flowers he had, so many that they filled the room at the *Tor* Hotel; even the fireplace overflowed with roses so that it was impossible to light a fire against the chilly March air.

(98)

I couldn't eat, I couldn't sleep. Several times that night I jumped out of bed at the horrible thought that perhaps Josephine wouldn't consent to marry me. A little gray light seeped into the room, which was cold but fragrant with rose blossoms.

Five long hours before the ship docked. What would I read in those dancing eyes? Breakfast was repulsive. I walked back and forth across the hotel room, adding to the threadbare condition of the carpet.

Hours before the boat could dock I was standing on the pier almost smothered in another huge bouquet of yellow roses. As people stared I could feel myself blushing. Presently Ken Krentz appeared and then the Reverend Myers. The minutes dragged.

"There she is," said Ken.

"Josephine?" I asked huskily.

"Well, no," Ken said patiently. "Just the ship, so far."

At length the ship docked, I went up the gangplank, found Josephine and had my answer without a word being spoken.

"We're to be married at eleven o'clock," I told her.

"I have nothing to wear! Anyhow, it's too soon; give me a little time."

But the wedding took place at the Consulate as scheduled, with Mrs. Gauss and Ken Krentz as witnesses. It was simple and the ring was made of plain silver and enamel, an old wedding ring such as Mongolian brides wear; but it symbolized the four precious virtues, contentment, cheerfulness, tolerance and understanding, which, growing together in harmony, bloom into the Peach of Everlasting Happiness and the Pearl of Harmony.

We spent our honeymoon at Miyanoshita, a heavenly spot high in the mountains, with a sweeping view. The quiet sounds of nature lulled us as we sat looking at the view, at the twisted pines etched sharply against the sky, and the Japanese gardens spread below us, beautiful replicas of nature's wonders.

The first evening at dinner I looked across the almost deserted dining room and started with surprise. There were two Japanese gentlemen sitting at a table near the window. One had the longest mustache I had ever seen. Preparatory to eating his soup, he carefully stretched his mustache to its fullest length and tied the ends together around the back of his neck. After dinner we approached the clerk at the desk and tactfully inquired who the old gentleman was.

"Ah, yes so. He is Mr. Yamaguchi, owner this hotel. Very famous man. I will introduce you."

Thus we met the president of the Mustache Society of Japan, who was exceedingly proud of his eigtheen-inch mustache. For many years we received a New Year's card from him giving a fairly detailed account of the state of his famous appendage.

It was enchantment to be with Josephine. We took long walks in the hills and sat for hours on some craggy rock overlooking the pine-covered valleys that stretched away in dim purple folds. We played the Kreutzer Sonata over and over again on the hotel's old wind-up phonograph until it became fuzzy and scratchy. It was a golden world and Josephine was my bright star.

10

Thunder Before the Storm

I HAD cabled the office the news of our marriage so there was quite a crowd to greet us when we returned to Shanghai from our honeymoon. Josephine looked uneasily at that host of strange faces. Consul General Gauss scared her completely. "Don't change Ed. Let him smoke his pipe," he admonished her, adding, "He used to be such a nice fellow."

"As though I had already ruined you," Josephine wailed afterward.

Home to Amherst Avenue. A high stucco house of pseudo-Moorish architecture with a nice garden behind.

"How nice," Josephine murmured, and I knew she did not like it. Kindly friends had sent flowers, which helped to distract the eye from the shabby furniture with drooping springs, covered in well-worn black Chinese silk. The dining room was not too bad, with a set of borrowed furniture, but there were no rugs, and no pictures. The year before, I had taken my few rugs, pictures and oddments of small furniture home to help my parents furnish the house

(101)

they had bought in which to retire after forty-five years in India.

"Everything is lovely," Josephine assured me. She looked around. "Let's see the upstairs. Where is the linen closet?"

I threw it open with a flourish, revealing three sheets, three pillowcases, three towels. She laughed. All was well.

"Telephone, master, office wantchee you," said our houseboy. I had to go, leaving Josephine to get her own bearings. Perhaps it's better that way, I thought, and easier for her to recover from the shock.

She was not long alone. The door burst open and in bounded F. J., holding a big box in his hand which he dumped into her lap. It contained five hundred engraved calling cards in sizes and styles appropriate for all occasions.

"I expect, my dear Mrs. Stanton, that you will be a proper consular wife and do your duty by Eddie," he said severely, demanding from others that conformity with convention which he absolutely ignored in his own life. "And mind you," he went on, "don't ever let him down or I'll haunt you wherever you may be."

Inauspicious as this welcome was, Josephine shared my affection for him and he was a frequent and welcome visitor until his life ended under tragic circumstances. We felt the loss deeply, as did his many other friends.

The Yankee in Josie was horrified by the extent of our indebtedness. She urged that we immediately embark on a campaign to liquidate the debts, denying ourselves everything but necessities. We couldn't manage without servants, who are essential in Oriental countries where marketing is a nightmare of unintelligible prices, screaming country vendors, thousands of milling shoppers; while the Western housewife is puzzled by the lack of anything familiar in the kitchen and incapable of cooking over the little charcoal stoves which are standard equipment. But after we had paid the servants, the rent and food bills and set aside a little something against our debts, there was really nothing left. Occasionally we attended one of the symphony concerts given by the municipal orchestra, taking seats in the top gallery, although it was not considered the thing to do.

Josie found our cook excellent and a specialist, according to his own claim, in soufflés. But we did not have a single Pyrex dish. Imported articles were so expensive that we couldn't afford to purchase one. Eventually we scraped together enough money, and I can well remember the day we went to a department store and bought our first Pyrex dish. Josie was as happy about it as though I had given her a diamond. The cook also was pleased and gave us a delectable cheese soufflé that evening. The purchase of the Pyrex dish was a notable achievement, but it was years before I could buy her any clothes. Fortunately, her good mother sent her boxes of dresses from time to time, which filled that feminine void about which I could do little.

For more reasons than one it was lucky that we were in love. Josie's Shanghai friends belonged to the smart set, gave grand parties, joined numerous clubs, rode in the hunts, played polo, and amused themselves by buying jewelry or playing bridge of a morning. But if her part in this social life had to be curtailed by our finances, at least all was harmony and peace within our home. Each day life with her was a thrilling experience, fresh and filled with contentment, the period in a man's life when he feels that such attainments and capabilities as he may have, reach their maximum.

So I was pleased when the Consul General assigned me to the political section of the Consulate, from which vantage point one could see the unfolding progression of political developments throughout China and more particularly in Shanghai.

Reports coming in indicated that the Communists, after their long and incredible trek from central China, caused by the massive campaigns directed against them by the forces of Generalissimo Chiang Kai-shek, had reached northern Shensi and established their headquarters at Yenan, a small dusty village located about a hundred and fifty miles north of Sian, where I had spent two months back in 1933 investigating the murder of the young American, Ekvall.

In the year 1936, this province of China assumed particular political importance and not alone from the arrival of Communist forces from various parts of China, who were for the first time united into a powerful force. In Sian and its vicinity, young Marshal Chang Hsueh-liang, son of the Old Tiger of Manchuria, had settled down with a hundred thousand of his men, their families and many thousands of refugees after having been driven from Manchuria by the Japanese. Our reports indicated that he was becoming increasingly disgruntled with the Nationalist Government for its failure to supply him with sufficient funds to pay his troops. Nor was the Young Marshal happy over the Government's unwillingness to resist Japan's encroachments, which had resulted in the loss of Manchuria and parts of Inner Mongolia and mounting pressure upon north China.

General Yang Hu-cheng, a familiar military figure to me, was also in Sian. He, too, claimed to be receiving very little recognition and financial aid from the Government. With the arrival of the Communists in north Shensi, both the Young Marshal and General Yang redoubled their recommendations to Generalissimo Chiang to form a united front against the Japanese. The Communist leaders, Mao Tse-tung, Chu Teh, Chou En-lai and others, expressed similar sentiments, which in part were no doubt sincere and in part related to the need to recuperate their strength and rehabilitate their forces.

It was into this tense and dramatic setting that Generalissimo Chiang flew in December, 1936. He apparently believed that in personal talks with the Young Marshal and General Yang he could convince them that he, too, was a patriot who burned to attack Japan but that it was first necessary to liquidate the Communists. From all accounts of what has come to be known as the "Sian Incident," the Generalissimo talked and argued with the generals at Sian for days.

Suddenly, word was received at Nanking and Shanghai that the Generalissimo had been arrested on the night of December 11, and was being held prisoner. This was electrifying news and caused the capitals of the world to buzz with speculation and activity. The Government of Nanking was, of course, seriously concerned but it was divided as to the best course to pursue. The Minister of War advocated a huge military expedition to liberate the Generalissimo but Madame Chiang and others feared such a move would mean his death. The Soviet Government accused the Japanese while the Japanese Government accused the Soviets and said it was a Communist plot.

There was no evidence to substantiate the latter charge, but it is a fact that Chou En-lai and other Communist leaders arrived in Sian the day after the Generalissimo was arrested and it is certain that they were consulted by the Young Marshal in the formulation of the demands made upon Generalissimo Chiang.

For a week these demands, the most important of which called for the cessation of hostilities against the Communists and the adoption of a policy of armed resistance to Japan, were discussed and argued by the Young Marshal, General Yang, the Communist representatives, and the Generalissimo. Though each participant claimed there was no yielding on his part, a sufficient meeting of minds was achieved so that when W. H. Donald, the Australian adviser to the Generalissimo and a close personal friend of the Young Marshal, arrived, to be followed a little later by Madame Chiang and other representatives from Nanking, it was agreed that the Generalissimo should be released and flown back to Nanking. In fact, it was made to appear that he had never been detained but had merely been the "guest" of the Young Marshal.

Perhaps even more puzzling to the Westerner was the picture of the Young Marshal also flying to Nanking "to receive punishment in order that discipline might be maintained." Here was conduct inscrutable and baffling. Did the Young Marshal expect to be named to an important post in the Government, which he had perhaps been privately promised by the Generalissimo in return for the part he played in effecting his release? Or was it a case of remorse and a sense of guilt which impelled him to submit to disciplinary measures? The drama of the Young Marshal ended with his arrest, trial, punishment and pardon, after he arrived in Nanking, and his subsequent banishment. It would be interesting to talk to him now at his secluded retreat on Formosa.

Relations between the Nationalist Government and the Communists did, in fact, improve to a point where in May, 1937, the latter petitioned to have their forces included in the national armies. Were the Nationalists and the Communists drawing together in face of the impending blow from the jingoists of Japan? The threat hung over both. Its imminence could be gauged by events taking place in Inner Mongolia and North China, but the lessening of tension between these two Chinese political groups and their partisans seems to have been dictated primarily by expediency.

These events were much talked about in our "shop," the political section of the office, but to most residents of Shanghai they seemed remote and far away, and personal affairs much more important. Josie and I were occupied, too, with personal affairs. We had never liked the would-be Moorish stucco house on Amherest Avenue. It was a happy day, therefore, when we were able to move into an attractive wood-paneled apartment with a nice terrace. The rooms were smaller and oddly shaped so that our furniture, with the addition of one or two new pieces, made the apartment look comfortable. We were very proud of our new home, which we occupied with our two dachshunds, Wiener and Schnitzel.

I had sent to Peiping for my former houseboy, tall, elderly Lou, who walked with slow, dignified steps. He had been faithful and was well trained. But his wife, who insisted on accompanying him, was a terror. She had no sooner arrived than there was trouble between her and the cook's wife. Angry voices and screams pierced the air because the servants' quarters were attached to each apartment. We did our best to ignore these verbal battles, which seemed to grow in intensity. Both husbands were henpecked in the extreme but, when we remonstrated with them, they made it clear that either they would all go or the wives would remain.

Josie suddenly developed a terrific rash on her arms and back. The doctor said it was lack of mineral matter in her system and started a series of calcium injections, which were fashionable in those days. The rash persisted. Finally he said, "Could you possibly have any vermin in the apartment?" Josie was indignant and stoutly denied such an unimaginable thing. One night she had an intolerable attack of itch. She got out of bed and switched on the light. There on the white sheet she saw a tiny scuttling black creature and then another.

"Ed," she screamed, "get up, get up." She has never quite forgiven me for sleepily turning over and advising her to forget it and go back to bed. She slept on the sofa the rest of that night.

Next morning she sent for the exterminator, a little Australian who appeared in a snow-white coat with a band of eager helpers and a deal of equipment. Josie told me later that he rubbed his hands together in eager anticipation before tackling the job.

She went out that morning with some friends, glad to be absent from the scene of operations. When the car returned at the end of the morning there, in front of the apartment building, stood the little man in his white coat. As she alighted from the car he called out happily, "We found an army of them in your bed, madam."

I had frequent occasion to meet the local Chinese officials, and we also came to know a number of exceedingly interesting intellectuals, artists, writers, businessmen and politicians. But this upper crust of Chinese society in Shanghai had its inevitable snobs. I recall one evening when Josie received the snub of her life. It was at a dinner given by charming Chinese friends. Some of the guests did not speak English. The ladies were all smartly dressed in the latest Shanghai fashion, a long tight-fitting gown of beautiful flowered silk, slit on both sides almost to the knee. They were immaculately coifed and expensively jeweled, and many of them wore in their sleek hair fresh jasmine flowers woven into brooches.

Josie had been watching a young Chinese lady, whose beautiful face was like a cool, aloof mask. She was sitting all alone and it seemed only polite to engage her in friendly conversation. Josie admired the round clasp of fresh jasmine flowers she was wearing and asked her how they were put together. There was a long silence while the proud but expressionless beauty slowly turned her head in Josie's direction. Then, looking at her coldly, she said in perfect English, "I did not ask my maid."

In sharp contrast to the pleasure-seeking, wealthy Chinese and foreigners living so comfortably in the Foreign Concessions was the abject misery of thousands of tattered, starving Chinese. They lived jammed together, frozen by the penetrating cold of the Shanghai winter, suffocated by the summer heat, eking out the barest existence. They lived squeezed into hovels, crudely patched with oddments of rusted tin or torn matting, scarcely to be called shelters from the elements, or crowded into little boats of all sizes and descriptions along the filthy canals: playing, eating, sleeping, giving birth and dying in these flimsy shelters. Many thousands more huddled together in heaps in doorways or in the streets, with absolutely no protection from the elements. The enormity of their destitution and need made one sick at heart; it was everywhere and on every side.

Over these pitiful humans towered the great turbaned Sikh policemen in the International Settlement who in their smart uniforms regulated traffic. It was not a pleasant sight to see these giants deliver a kick or smart whack on the back of an emaciated ricksha coolie, his breath forcing his distended ribs in and out in painful gasps as he paused for a moment to rest. Most of the well-to-do folk, accustomed to these harrowing sights, passed rapidly in their motor cars without a glance, except one of irritation if delayed by a panting ricksha coolie or half-starved families sprawled in the street. The chauffeur would lean out of the car, hurl a string of curses at them, grind into second gear and drive on with a flourish.

On the evening of July 7, 1937, Japanese troops, forming a part of their Legation guard at Peiping, were engaged in one of the sham battles they so dearly loved to stage, near the little village of Lukouchiao. It is a small shabby village, whose only previous claim to fame arose from the fact that Messer Marco Polo crossed over its stone bridge on his travels to the capital of the Great Khan. Ever since then the bridge has been popularly called the Marco Polo bridge. The Japanese military suddenly announced that their troops had been fired upon by the troops of General Sung Che-yuan, for whom they had no love because he was the only Chinese general in north China who had resisted their efforts to take over Inner Mongolia and to nibble into north China.

From Shanghai we watched these events with much concern because it was obvious that Japan's military leaders had decided the time was ripe for major moves in China. This piecemeal conquest was a deadly technique which they had carefully conceived and

skillfully employed. It called for "incidents," whether real or manu-
factured, and the swift employment of force to protect Japanese
"rights and interests."

The United States and the governments of the other great powers
did, indeed, protest these aggressive moves, but there was lacking
the will and the determination to take collective action. The dismal
failure of the efforts of the League of Nations with respect to
Japan's seizure of Manchuria in 1931 was fresh in the minds of the
world's statesmen. The seizure of Manchuria, the fortification of
islands in the Pacific under Japanese mandate, the denouncing of
the Treaty on Naval Limitation, were acts which indicated that
Japan's leaders were bent on pursuing their grandiose plans for the
conquest of China and the establishment of a mighty empire in
Asia and the Pacific.

The events in north China, together with the bellicose statements coming out of Tokyo, caused a heavy, palpable tension to
fall over Shanghai, where anti-Japanese sentiment had reached
fever pitch. When we heard, during the first week in August, that
the Japanese Government had ordered the evacuation of all their
nationals from Hankow and the Yangtze River it seemed ominously
clear that the next move was to be in Central China and we sur-
mised that operations would commence at Shanghai. The Chinese
populace sensed the tension, and fearing a renewal of the horrible
hostilities of 1932, began to stream out of Hongkew, the Japanese
quarter of Shanghai, and Chapei, the Chinese-administered section
of the city, into the comparative safety of the International
Settlement.

On the evening of August 9, a Japanese naval officer and sailor
were shot and killed by Chinese guards at a military airfield on
the outskirts of Shanghai. No valid explanation was ever given by
the Japanese authorities as to why Japanese naval personnel should
have intruded into a Chinese military aerodrome, but the Japanese

Consul General declared that the incident was of a grave nature. An effort was made by the Chinese Mayor of Shanghai, O. K. Yui, to settle the incident to the satisfaction of the Japanese, but the arrival of Japanese naval and marine reinforcements on August 12 made it clear that they had determined to take action.

On Friday, August 13, sniping broke out between Japanese marines and Chinese troops, while both sides erected barricades and defenses and moved up reinforcements.

Shortly after I arrived at the Consulate that morning, Consul General Gauss called me into his office and expressed his concern for the safety of a number of Americans residing on the outskirts of the city and well within the Chinese lines. With his authorization and approval, I set out by car to find out what had happened to them and to bring them into the Settlement. It was a hot, sticky day. When we came to the border of the Settlement, a patrol of municipal police and volunteers shook their heads when I told them where I was going. It was dangerous, they said, because the Chinese had been laying mines along the roads and under the bridges.

I left the car and started walking. The area seemed deserted and for about a mile there were no signs of military activity. Suddenly, a Chinese sentry leaped from a little foxhole he had dug into the road bank and challenged. He didn't understand my northern dialect very well but after I had repeated a number of times that I was from the American Consulate he nodded and beckoned me to follow him.

At first I could not fathom the reason for taking such a zigzag course or walking so gingerly. Then I remembered what the Settlement police patrol had told me: mines. The temperature seemed to shoot way up and perspiration poured more copiously than ever. It was like walking for miles on red-hot coals. Actually, a few hundred yards farther on we came to a sand-bagged defense post surrounded by barbed wire and manned by twenty-five soldiers under a young officer. He could understand my dialect, was friendly, and volunteered to show me the way.

I was only too pleased to accept his offer since the thought of being blown sky high by a land mine was anything but pleasant and seemed a poor way to leave a lovely wife and a fairly promising career. But first, the inevitable cup of tea. While we sipped it, the young officer talked. His family had been living in Hongkew, the Japanese section of the city. He was bitter in his hatred for the Japanese who had killed his parents in 1932.

"They are like the scorpion, wicked and cruel," he said. "They know no pity. They kill my father and mother for no reason. I hate them." A mild-mannered, pleasant young man he appeared to be, but his eyes blazed with fury. "We must drive the dwarfs into the sea," he declared.

His was the type of determination and spirit that caused thousands of Chinese soldiers to stand fast and die. We started out, threading our way cautiously through the land mines. Judging from the way we zigged and zagged, they had been laid in great profusion. We finally reached the homes of the Americans only to find they had left the previous day for the International Settlement. The return journey was the same flirtation with eternity but we were lucky.

Later that afternoon, both sides opened up. The roar of artillery was to be a familiar sound for many days to come.

11

How Much Bitterness Must We Eat?

THE next day was to be known as "Bloody Saturday." The Settlement was jammed with thousands upon thousands of sad-eyed refugees, sitting on the streets in little family groups and clutching nervously at the small bundles that held their meager possessions. The air began to vibrate with the roar of Chinese planes, attempting to bomb the Japanese cruiser *Idzumo*, lying in the Whangpoo River just off the Japanese Consulate General.

A barrage of anti-aircraft fire met the planes, which turned and flew back over the Settlement. There, to our horror, their bombs suddenly hurtled down upon a huge crowd, with the most ghastly and bloody results. What I saw was unspeakable. A thousand were killed and as many more were injured. Many of those tragic victims were refugees who had fled to the Settlement for safety. An accident—but a horrible one—and an accident that was to be repeated in the days to come, as fighting grew in intensity.

A few days later, Josie and a friend of hers were shopping

in downtown Shanghai—for one clutches at the normal under abnormal stresses—when a frenzied mob of refugees surged down the street in a mad desire to escape from the battle zone. They were driven by wild hysterical fear that transcended all other emotions, all reason. The two girls sat petrified in the midst of this tidal wave of fear-crazed humanity who clawed at the windows and swarmed right over the car, as they might any obstacle in their path.

Eventually, the Settlement police channeled this flow of terror-stricken human beings into various side streets. But it was pitiable, my wife told me, to see little children, stark panic on their faces, rushing back and forth looking for their parents.

These grim adventures, plus the mounting pile of problems at the office, made sleep elusive. Even the electric fan failed to drown out the crackle and boom of gunfire. At the Consulate, feverish plans were made, in consultation with our British and other colleagues, to evacuate as many women and children as possible. Washington arranged for vessels of the Dollar Line to stand by. Josie flatly refused to leave me but I pointed out that, in the Foreign Service, orders are orders, and the wives of the staff had to set an example, especially in view of the unpopularity of the evacuation order. No one could tell how the fighting would develop or whether the International Settlement and French Concession might not be overrun by hostile armies. At any rate, the tragic events of "Bloody Saturday" made it apparent that dangers to the civilian population from bombs and shellfire were very real.

We worked long hours, making the necessary arrangements. Always there was our chief to guide, direct, encourage and consult. Whether at eight in the morning or at midnight his mind was clear and incisive, and his grasp of the many complex problems was phenomenal.

The war gathered momentum as the Chinese made a desperate

effort to cut the Japanese forces in two by penetrating deep into the heart of the Japanese section of the city. Japanese bombers dived and strafed Chinese positions. Shells and fragments of bombs continued to fall in the Settlement, killing and wounding many more civilians. Fragments fell on our terrace grim souvenirs of death.

The arrival of ten Japanese transports loaded with troops indicated that the militarists had in mind more than a local war at Shanghai. The bombing of Nanking and other places along the Yangtze River including an American missionary hospital, and the imposition of a naval blockade along the coast, confirmed our belief that the Japanese action at Shanghai was part of a carefully planned pincer strategy. One arm of the pincer was to close on Shanghai and Nanking while the other was squeezing Chinese resistance out of north China.

The drab day came when Josie was to leave. A flat-bottomed ferry boat was to take the women and children down the Whangpoo River to its mouth, where a Dollar Line ship was standing by to receive them. Just as they were boarding the ferry, an air raid commenced and the sky was torn with screaming shells and whining bombs. We who were supervising the evacuation found ourselves in a terrible quandary. Should the ferry go and run the guantlet or should it stay and chance falling shells or bombs? We decided it was better for the ferry to push off lest the situation worsen. Women and children were ordered to lie flat on the decks. Josie reached out over the deck rail. We held hands until only our fingertips touched as the boat pulled away.

Much later, we heard that the ferry was fired on farther down the river. And after these experiences, the evacuees received a cool reception from the round-the-world tourists who were passengers on the luxury liner and distinctly annoyed at this interruption of their pleasure cruise.

The next day, August 26, we were astounded to hear that

the British Ambassador and his party, while motoring from Nanking to Shanghai in a car clearly marked with the Union Jack, had been fired upon by Japanese planes. The Ambassador was wounded but fortunately recovered. The Japanese formally apologized as demanded by the British Government, but they sought to gloss over the incident as an accident caused by poor visibility. The attitude of the British Government stiffened noticeably as a result of this seemingly deliberate and unprovoked attack.

Both we and they were deeply concerned by Japan's open aggression in China, the severity and barbarity of her military actions, the stoppage of foreign trade, the threat to foreign enterprises, and the danger to the lives of our nationals. Decisions were reached by both governments to despatch forces to Shanghai to protect the International Settlement, and efforts were made through diplomatic channels to persuade the Japanese Government to cease military operations and enter into negotiations with the Chinese Government. China herself appealed to the League of Nations, which after considerable discussion and deliberation condemned Japan's action in bombing open towns and defenseless civilians and recommended that all measures hampering China's defense be avoided. It was hoped that President Roosevelt's historic speech in Chicago denouncing aggression would be heeded. However, neither the action of the League, nor speeches by foreign diplomats, nor aroused public opinion in Great Britain and the United States made any impression upon Japanese leaders, who had committed themselves and their country and who, as a Japanese Foreign Office spokesman declared, were determined "to fight to the bitter end, until China reconsiders her attitude and drastically alters her anti-Japanese policy."

During the first month of the war, the Japanese attempted to dislodge the Chinese forces from their positions, which ran west from Woosung at the mouth of the Yangtze River through a strong point called Tazang, through Yangtzepoo and Hongkew, where Japanese residents were concentrated, and then into Chapei, the Chinese section of the city. There were heavy shelling, bombing and savage hand-to-hand encounters. Japanese progress was slow because the Chinese troops fought with great tenacity and courage from houses and buildings which they had turned into veritable fortresses, and from entrenchments along the canals which criss-crossed the countryside.

Civilian deaths mounted in the battle zones, until the streets were littered with unburied corpses. Men, women and children who had run from death until they could run no farther died at last, trapped, without knowing why. Refugees continued somehow to escape from these horror zones. I saw some of these poor unfortunates stagger, exhausted, to a Settlement barrier. One old man, his eyes wild with the terror of his recent experiences, gasped, "They killed my son with their sharp knives, shot my son's wife and little child, and burned my store. How much bitterness must we eat?" He fell in a huddled heap, while the Chinese Settlement police gave him a little hot tea and a bowl of soup to revive him. Such scenes were a daily occurrence.

Had the Japanese soldiers lost all sense of decency and humanity or was this a calculated policy, designed to intimidate the Chinese civilian population and break their spirit? These continuing acts of brutality, coupled with the repeated statements made by the Japanese military of their determination to "scourge" the Chinese, pointed directly to the use of brutality as a planned instrument of policy.

On September 19, the U.S.S. *Chaumont* arrived at Shanghai and landed the 6th Regiment of United States Marines. It was heartening to see the Leathernecks appear and we were all down on the dock to greet them. The British and French also sent contingents and presently the borders of the International Settlement and French Concession were guarded by regular, well-equipped forces. They took over these duties from the Shanghai Volunteer Corps, who had rendered signal service during the early and trying stage of the hostilities.

For the next few weeks, the Japanese launched savage attacks against Tazang, the capture of which would force the withdrawal of Chinese units from Chapei where they had repeatedly thrown back the Japanese in bloody fighting. Tazang fell on October 26. That night the Chinese defenders of Chapei commenced to withdraw, setting this huge area ablaze as they did so. From my apartment balcony I could see the huge conflagration which shot long fingers of flame into the black sky. It was an awesome sight. Next morning Shanghai was covered with a dense pall of smoke. Great fires were still raging. The destruction was appalling but the determination to leave nothing but smoking ruins to the conquerors was understandable, and Shanghai was thrilled by the heroism of the lone Chinese battalion which fought on doggedly until overwhelmed.

The war shifted to the western outskirts of the city; the nights were made hideous by the roar of Japanese artillery and the rumble of shells as they passed over the apartment building and landed with a crash in the Chinese western defense sector. Tired as I was from long hours in the office, I found sleep out of the question. Night after night I lay rigid, staring up at the bedroom ceiling, waiting tensely for the next barrage of shells to rumble over with a deadly, hollow sound, expecting that sooner or later they would fall short.

I found that tinkering with my old watches relieved nervous strain and was glad I had taken up this hobby in Peiping, where one could find wonderful old English and French timepieces. At first I had been intrigued by their beautiful enameled cases and then by their delicate and finely wrought mechanisms. The Chinese, who had not devised a practical timepiece of their own, were equally fascinated when they saw the clocks and watches which early English and other traders of the eighteenth century brought with them to China. These were much sought after and the more fanciful the clock, with moving figures, singing birds, and chiming mechanisms, the better they liked it. The Empress Dowager Tzu Hsi had a fabulous collection of clocks. I remember seeing one in the Palace Museum in Peiping, which stood five feet high and was shaped like a Chinese pagoda. On the hour, birds appeared from the summit of the pagoda and sang a variety of songs, while the doors of the base opened and a little figure resembling a Chinese scholar wrote the time with a brush pen. Fiddling with my old clocks and watches was wonderfully soothing on those nights when the heavens trembled with passing shells.

In the midst of these trying days and nights, I heard Josie's voice. One morning I picked up the telephone to hear a man say, "Would you like to talk to Mrs. Stanton this evening?" He was an amateur radio ham in frequent radio phone communication with another ham in Manila, he explained, and invited me to go to his apartment at seven that evening when, if atmospherics were not too bad, he would arrange for me to talk to my wife. I was at his apartment on the dot of seven. He was twisting a great array of dials and gadgets and talking a jargon I could not understand. Finally he said, "She's there," and handed me some earphones.

She was there. I was so tongue-tied I could not get out a syllable. She kept asking how I was. I managed to stammer that everything was quite all right. Just at that moment there was a thunderous crash as a bomb fell somewhere nearby. Several times later we were able to talk and on the last occasion I told her the joyous news that the consular wives would soon be allowed to return.

November 12 marked the close of the battle of Shanghai after ninety-two days of uninterrupted fighting. Besides the grim toll of soldiers and marines killed and wounded, thousands of civilians had lost their lives and hundreds of thousands their livelihoods. Shanghai's streets were crowded with refugees who sat huddled together in listless groups, staring into space. They moved only when the Salvation Army's soup trucks came around. That organization did a remarkable job in feeding many thousands of refugees who otherwise would have starved to death or taken to looting and pillaging in desperation. Equally charitable and humanitarian services were rendered by Father Jacquinot, who organized an International Relief Committee for Refugees and, after the most ardous negotiations with both the Japanese and Chinese authorities, obtained their agreement to the establishment of a special refugee zone in a section of Greater Shanghai known as Nantao. In the midst of so much savagery and destruction it was heartening to see men of good will care for the needy and homeless who had been through unimaginable horrors.

Josie returned on the last day of November, after being away for five months. I was prepared for that ecstatic moment with a platinum wedding ring to replace the modest Mongolian ring I had given her when we were married, but it was several years late.

So great was the human misery left as an aftermath of the savage battle for Shanghai that at times we felt almost ashamed of our happiness. Personal happiness seemed hardly permissible in the face of the misery, destitution and hunger which stalked through the city. The refugee problem was a stupendous one. Charitable and relief organizations did their best but it was impossible to feed and give shelter to all. The winter weather was upon us. Many, thinly clad and half starved, died from exposure. Daily the vans of the Public Health Department made the rounds in the early morning, collecting for burial the gaunt bodies of those who had died during the night. The problem was further aggravated by the refusal of the Japanese to reopen the areas in the native city and in their own section where many thousands of the refugees had formerly lived and where some would doubtless have found their houses or stores still standing.

Another tragic group contributed to the multiplicity of problems confronting the city. Jewish refugees from Germany and Austria commenced to arrive by shiploads. At that time, Shanghai was probably the only large city in the world which could be entered without passports and other papers. Tens of thousands of the victims of Nazi persecution flooded into Shanghai. Some were dangerously broken in body as a result of the horrors of concentration camps. Others had not been physically affected. But all were deeply scarred and wounded mentally. It was astonishing, therefore, that so many of them were bursting with optimism and to see how they immediately set about laying the foundations of a new existence. They adapted themselves to what could only be described as the most unfavorable conditions with a determination and cheerfulness that filled all of us with admiration.

Shanghai was picking itself up in rather dazed fashion from the debris and shocks of the recent battle, and the war had rolled on toward Nanking when we received a flash at the Consulate that the little United States gunboat, the U.S.S. *Panay*, had, on December 12, been bombed and sunk by Japanese planes at a point about twenty-eight miles from Nanking on the Yangtze River. An unknown number had been killed and wounded, while the survivers had escaped under fire to a small village on the bank of the river.

We were stunned. Later reports coming in indicated that the U.S.S. *Panay* had been under bombing attack for well over an hour in the middle of the afternoon, that visibility was good, and that it was impossible for the Japanese planes to have mistaken this clearly marked American naval vessel for a Chinese ship. Furthermore,

Japanese surface craft in the vicinity had sent a detachment of sailors aboard and had later strafed her with machine-gun fire as she was sinking.

Shanghai buzzed. The capitals of the world buzzed. There was intense indignation in the United States. Our Government immediately sent an extremely stiff protest to the Japanese Government, demanding formal apologies, compensation and the condign punishment of the pilots and officers responsible. The Japanese authorities, some of whom were alarmed by this open attack upon an American naval vessel, did the correct thing so far as apologies were concerned.

In Shanghai, Japanese Consul General Okamoto immediately called on Consul General Gauss and tendered his apologies and regrets. He looked to me to be genuinely concerned and worried. The Japanese Government agreed to compensation. They were, however, evasive with respect to punishment of the pilots and the senior air officer in command of the unit.

We learned later that the attack on the U.S.S. *Panay* and a similar attack upon H.M.S. *Ladybird*, a British gunboat on patrol on the Yangtze River, had been instigated by a hot-headed young Japanese colonel who was violently anti-British and anti-American and who, with or without the knowledge of his superiors, had encouraged similarly minded junior officers to create incidents.

Looking at this event in the light of the Japanese attack upon our fleet at Pearl Harbor a few years later, it seems probable that the Japanese military and naval leaders, who were even then planning for an eventual attack upon us, regarded the *Panay* Incident as target practice for bigger events to come.

For a few days the *Panay* Incident overshadowed the Japanese assault and capture of Nanking, after bitter and savage hand-to-hand combat. To the further shame of Imperial Japan, her troops were allowed to indulge in days of butchery and looting. The "rape of Nanking" shocked the world and hardened the hearts of the peoples of many countries against Japan. The Chinese Government withdrew to Chungking, where the diplomatic envoys of the United States and other countries eventually established themselves.

To give some semblance of legality to their conquests, the Japanese created puppet regimes at Nanking, Peiping and in Manchuria. On March 28, 1938, the "Reformed Government of the Republic of China" was proclaimed at Nanking. Later it was headed by the well-known Chinese political figure, Wang Ching-wei, who at one time had been a close supporter of Dr. Sun Yat-sen, and had occupied important posts in the Nationalist Government. However, relations between the Japanese and their Chinese collaborators failed to run smoothly, while the resentment of the people in the occupied areas against Japanese rule was a mystifying irritant to the empire builders in Tokyo.

Shanghai, for the next few years, was throttled by heavy-handed Japanese control over the area surrounding the city, while the International Settlement and French Concession, where foreign interests and residents were largely centered, was subjected to continuous pressure.

Japanese insistence on holding a "Victory Parade" through the International Settlement touched off the first incident. It was followed by many incidents, caused sometimes by Chinese terrorists throwing bombs at Japanese, but more often by the intrusion of armed Japanese units into the Settlement and French Concession. We also went through a grisly period when severed heads or hands appeared in front of houses or stores of Chinese accused by their compatriots of collaborating with the "enemy." The fact was that the Japanese were irked by the presence of foreign authorities, foreign troops and foreign naval vessels which sought to preserve the neutrality of the Settlement and French Concession and to protect the lives and properties of their nationals.

Demands were made on the Shanghai Municipal Council to increase the number of senior Japanese police officers on the police force, for greater representation in the Council and voice in its affairs. We were daily involved in negotiations with the Japanese authorities regarding these and other vitally important matters. I spent long hours at the Japanese Consulate General discussing and arguing these problems with my opposite number but it was evident that they were merely messenger boys for Japanese military headquarters.

The most serious of our problems with the Japanese grew out of their flagrant disregard of American rights and interests. Our citizens were not permitted to reoccupy their properties in the Japanese-controlled areas or to carry on their normal activities, whether commercial or religious. Only after endless negotiations could passes be obtained, permitting American citizens even to visit their properties, the majority of which had been badly damaged during the hostilities.

Even more vexatious was the question of claims for damage inflicted on American property. It was a tremendous job getting together the detailed data required by the Japanese. Negotiations were discouraging. After a particularly exasperating and futile all-day session I told Consul General Gauss, "They are just stringing us along and have no intention whatever of paying any of the claims."

To get Japanese military or naval units out of American property was equally difficult. We were successful in a few cases. One was the evacuation of the battle-scarred Shanghai University, a large Baptist Mission educational institution. These once handsome buildings had been a target for Japanese naval guns and then occupied for many months by Japanese units.

After weary weeks of negotiation it was agreed that we might visit and inspect the property in company with Japanese military and consular representatives. The buildings were still partially occupied. They were a shambles. Floors had been ripped up and used for firewood as had all desks and other furniture. All metal fittings had been removed and sent to Japan, which sorely needed scrap to build its battleships and manufacture its weapons of war. There were gaping holes in roofs and walls. Months passed before the military was induced to return the property to the Baptist Mission.

The Japanese had no intention of permitting foreign business to resume, except on their own terms. To an increasing extent all trade was controlled by them. A depressing dead atmosphere descended slowly, like a black cloud, over Shanghai. Its foreign residents were glum and so were we at the Consulate.

We decided to attempt to lift this pall of gloom by an evening of music. One of our friends, Mary Stewart Toussaint, the wife of the Netherlands Consul General at Manila, was visiting us. She had a magnificent contralto voice. Josie planned a musical evening to introduce her to Maestro Paci, conductor of the Shanghai Symphony Orchestra and to other music lovers.

The guests assembled, Mary's lovely voice soared in some Schubert lieder. Tears of appreciation streamed down the maestro's cheeks. The evening was going to be a success.

Then the doorbell began to ring as late comers drifted in, calling, "Good evening." The dogs, Wiener and Schnitzel, barked an enthusiastic welcome. And my clocks—all my clocks—began to chime and strike the hour, not together but in a fitful, wayward fashion and as their fancy dictated. I had fully intended to stop the clocks and had forgotten. The evening was going to be a disaster.

Our singer, a true prima donna, broke off her song and ran angrily from the room. My despairing wife burst into tears and rushed out on the terrace where she seemed to be trying to hide behind a drain pipe. While this melodramatic scene was taking place I attempted to keep our guests happy by what I hoped was bright talk. It wasn't very bright and no one was very happy. Then the two ladies appeared, smiling, arm in arm, and all was well.

I tiptoed quietly from clock to clock and stopped their tick-tock. The dogs were banished. Then I sat down in the back of the room, mopped my brow, and at length heard in peace the lush beauty of Mary's contralto.

12

Sharp Taste of Humiliation

IN FEBRUARY, 1940, orders came from Washington assigning me to Nanking for a period of six weeks to report on the Japanese puppet regime, under Wang Ching-wei, and on Japanese efforts to extend the influence and prestige of this creation of theirs.

We had seen a good deal of Japanese travel and "sanitary" restrictions around Shanghai but we were hardly prepared for the strict procedures imposed around Nanking. When we stepped off the train, where we were met by Consul J. Hall Paxton, one of the victims of the *Panay* Incident, we were astonished to find a formidable array of Japanese soldiers and doctors on the platform, all wearing white gauze masks over their mouths. The doctors, who were standing behind little stands on which were placed huge bowls of disinfectant, flourished hypodermic needles. All passengers, most of whom were Chinese, were herded into long lines by the Japanese sentries, ordered to wash their hands in the dirty bowls of disinfectant, jabbed by the doctors with anti-cholera

(127)

serum, and then sprayed from head to foot with more disinfectant from large atomizers. Every Chinese was also ordered to remove his hat and bow low before the sentries. Those who failed to do so were cuffed and slapped.

This was more than the expression of power. It was an ugly picture of a new pattern in the world, of humiliation as an act of policy, of indignity as a code of ethics in dealing with one's fellow humans. It was denial of every civilized concept man had painfully developed during his long and slow climb out of savagery. For eight long years the hammer blows of the Japanese militarists upon the body of the Chinese people were made the more grievous by the mental humiliation of being forced to bow low, to grovel before the conqueror.

Paxton advised us to remove our hats before being told to do so, in order to avoid any unpleasantness. Our cholera certificates, he thought, would satisfy the doctors, but the dipping of the hands in the disinfectant was a must. There was some argument about inspecting our baggage, in spite of our diplomatic passports, but we were finally let go.

On the way to the Embassy a second test awaited us. When we arrived before one of the main gates into the city proper, we could see that a strong Japanese military patrol was stationed there. They, too, wore gauze masks, which we later discovered were standard equipment for all Japanese in Nanking, who believed firmly in their effectiveness to ward off disease. A long line of cars, rickshas and carts had pulled up waiting to pass. Those in the vehicles were forced to get out and doff their hats, bowing before the sentries. They were sometimes permitted to proceed but, at other times, the sentries rummaged through everything, prodding the scared and unhappy Chinese with their bayonets the while.

Our turn came. We sat in stony silence, looking straight ahead as the driver of our car opened the door for the inevitable inspection. The sentry peered in but did not force us to get out. Paxton remarked we had been lucky. He said he spent a good deal of his time protesting to the Japanese authorities against incidents involving attempts by the sentries to force him to doff his hat, descend from his car or to search both the car and his person. This was the much-heralded "new order."

After attempting for some years to operate an Embassy office on the ancient and cramped premises which housed our Consulate General in Nanking, our Government had rented spacious grounds and buildings, especially built for this purpose by one of the Chinese banks. We lived in the "number two" or counsellors' house, with a lovely rose garden and a magnificent view of Purple Mountain in the distance.

There was a small American and foreign community in Nanking. Catholic nuns maintained a hostel for unwanted baby girls and fed pitiful refugee children and war orphans, who lived like alley cats scavenging for their food. American missionaries were still attempting to carry on at the University of Nanking and the Ginling College for women, though there was a good deal of interference with the curriculum and student activities. With the exception of the oil companies, whose products the Japanese needed themselves, our businessmen found it virtually impossible to do any business. Chinese business was dead except for a little retail trade. By contrast, Japanese business was flourishing, the city being flooded with merchandise from Japan.

In order to report intelligently on what was taking place, it was necessary for me to maintain good relations with the Japanese authorities. The Japanese Government had extended quasi-diplomatic recognition to Wang Ching-wei's Government and had stationed several senior diplomats in Nanking. From them I learned that Wang Ching-wei was not content to remain head of a local government in that area but was insisting that his jurisdiction be extended to include north China, where he wanted the Japanese to disband their puppet creation.

There was a difference of opinion between the Japanese militarists of north and central China on this matter of policy, those in the north being disinclined to see their puppet laid away in a bureau drawer. From the diplomatic representatives of the Nazi Government, which had hastened to recognize both the Government of Manchukuo and also Wang Ching-wei's regime, I learned that Japanese diplomats were unhappy over the dilemma facing them. They had had visions of establishing a single Chinese Government under Japanese auspices that not only would be a formidable rival to the Chinese Nationalist Government but which would win the allegiance of the Chinese people and thus bring about the downfall of the latter Government.

The United States, of course, had no official relations with Wang Ching-wei but the latter was most anxious to convince us that he was not a puppet, that indeed he drew a large measure of support from the Chinese people. A few weeks after our arrival, an emissary from Wang Ching-wei appeared at the Embassy to pay an informal call. This first visit was devoted largely to the amenities and the weather, but on later visits he talked more freely, and sought to explain the reasons for Wang's acceptance of the Japanese "invitation" to form a new government.

He dilated on Wang's great love for his country and his belief that by agreeing to work with the Japanese it would be possible to mitigate the unhappy lot of the Chinese people and to spare them some of the miseries and humiliations caused by Japanese military occupation. He insisted it had been a great personal sacrifice for Wang Ching-wei to decide on the unpalatable step that he felt it his duty to take. Because of his close personal association with Sun Yat-sen in the early days, Wang had been popular with the Chinese people and he estimated that Generalissimo Chiang Kai-shek's own popularity was declining, that some elements in the Nationalist Government thought the latter was making a mistake in resisting the Japanese and should negotiate with them. He hinted that these elements were in touch with Wang and that interesting developments might be expected. Of course, these goings-on were of interest to Washington.

The Fourth of July was approaching. Our position in Nanking was a delicate one, with the city under Japanese military occupation. We did not recognize the "puppet government"; the British and their allies had broken off relations with the Germans because of the outbreak of World War II, so we debated the wisdom of holding an official reception on the Fourth. Josie pointed out the social difficulties created by the fact that German and British diplomats were not speaking, that the Japanese were resented by many, including our own Chinese servants, and that food and drinks were scarce in war-twisted Nanking. But it seemed to me more important than ever to maintain the prestige of the United States. Josie wore a worried frown as she scurried about with paper and pencil, trying to make something out of nothing. We agreed that it was essential to serve champagne in order to give "face" to the occasion.

Since the British and the Germans could not meet officially, we solved this problem by inviting the British for "twelve noon, Tokyo time" and the Germans for "twelve noon, Nanking time," one hour later. The Japanese were insisting on using their Tokyo time in China, as this pointed up where the real authority lay. We instructed our servants to receive the Japanese military courteously and to check their clanking sabers without demur, which was no easy task in itself as they resented the conqueror with a smoldering hatred. We must also have an orchestra to play "The Star-Spangled Banner." A few Filipinos and American Negroes were playing in the night clubs of the city and when we asked for volunteers all of them responded enthusiastically.

High noon, Tokyo time. Our servants sucked in their cheeks as they solemnly received the great swords of the Japanese military, our first arrivals. Most of them spoke little or no English and stood about stiffly. The other guests arrived, businessmen, missionaries and the British. Precious champagne, which had cost us dear in more ways than one, was poured.

I invited my guests to join me in a toast to the President of the United States. We raised our glasses, I gave the nod—the pre-arranged signal for the band leader to strike up. There were a few squeaks. Another nod, this one more emphatic. With an outlandish boom and a discordant crash the players launched into what was supposed to be our national anthem. They played as though each man were a soloist, no two instruments in the same key, no recognizable rhythm, no recognizable tune. Meanwhile the guests stood respectfully at attention, holding their shaking glasses, the champagne slopping over the edges, until the last agonizing chord faded away.

Immediately afterward, the British Consul General, like a conscientious schoolmaster, beckoned to his nationals and they departed in a body. Halfway through the narrow gate of the Embassy they met the car of the German Consul General head on. Both cars pulled up abruptly but finally the German backed up, "because I am younger and junior," he explained to me later. Thus a diplomatic incident was avoided.

The July heat was followed by a scorching August. Water from the tap ran boiling hot. Cholera was raging in Shanghai in the crowded Chinese section, where there were hundreds of deaths every day. Rumor had it that the Japanese were burning the cholera cases before they were actually dead, hoping to avoid an epidemic.

Cremation is abhorrent to the Chinese, who believe that their dead must appear in bodily form to take their place in the hall of their ancestors.

Only a few cases of cholera were reported in Nanking but the Japanese redoubled their "sanitary precautions," in great fear that this disease might reach their densely populated homeland and spread like a forest fire. Little booths were set up in the streets of the city, where white masked figures jabbed at each unwilling passerby and forced them to dip their hands into the dirty bowls of disinfectant. We were disinfected wherever we went. Thoroughly irritated, and repulsively odorous, we would return home and plunge into a tub.

Our cook had come down to us from Shanghai; he was an artist in converting the toughish water buffalo meat into delicious stroganoff and ragouts, and concocting desserts from rich but "powerful" buffalo cream. One day he asked us if he could send for his wife. "She makee baby any minute, first time makee baby," he explained. We agreed heartily but reminded him of the cholera restrictions. She arrived in due course and we asked about her. "Look see no very good," he said. "Too much bumpee ricksha man from station. Too much medicine Japanese give her." We understood. The following morning we inquired again.

"Leetle sick. No too muchee." He looked evasive. Later that same day Amah rushed to Josie. "Please missee, cook wife very sick. Have got *huo luan,* cholera. All look see black." We immediately sent for the American missionary doctor who confirmed the diagnosis and shook his head gravely. "There's little chance to save her," he said, "because the disease is aggravated by advanced pregnancy. However, I'll do what I can and promise not to report the case to the Japanese until we've done our best."

Before leaving the doctor said, "Any prolonged case of severe cramps should be reported to me, and the cook's room must be

(133)

thoroughly scrubbed and cleaned with the strongest disinfectant. Don't leave it to the servants."

I insisted on doing the job myself while Josie stood in the doorway sputtering and scolding because I would not allow her to help. The servants thought us absolutely mad.

A few days later I was overcome by agonizing cramps. The doctor came. He was unable to give a certain diagnosis at that stage, but gave medicine galore and put me to bed. "If the cramps continue, you undoubtedly have cholera," he told me before he left.

That was at 6:00 P.M. and no one was allowed on the streets after that time by order of the military, so we realized there would be no help from the doctor until morning. Soothed by his medicine I fell asleep. At midnight I awoke paralyzed by violent pain.

Desiring to do something helpful Josie administered a handful of sleeping pills. Then she settled down for a long and ghastly vigil. She repeated every prayer she had ever learned, plus many she made up, plus Yoga exercises and deep breathing. Panicky, she went into the library for a copy of *Science and Health,* which a friend had given her years before. This she read right side up, sideways and upside down for the rest of that dreary night. I awoke feeling much better. It was Josie who was battered and shaken. The cook's wife delivered safely and recovered from the disease. There were no further cases within the Embassy, though the cholera spread around us.

Wang Ching-wei's emissary called on me again one day and told me that the "President" wished to see me privately and unofficially. Out of curiosity I agreed to an appointment. In the handsome mansion, heavily guarded, I was ushered into an ornately furnished room. Wang made his appearance immediately, sickly and pale looking but with a fine intelligent face. Without indulging in the usual preliminary niceties he launched at once into a lengthy justification of himself. The term "traitor" applied to him by the Chinese had bitten deep into his consciousness. He seemed to be tortured by the scorn and low esteem of his countrymen. He explained that when he had been "invited" by the Japanese to head a new Government he had insisted that all other governments in Japanese-occupied China be abolished. Furthermore, that his Government be given real independence of action without interference from the Japanese. These conditions, he said, had been agreed to. They had also promised to withdraw their troops from Nanking and the area. These promises had not been kept. He appeared to be seriously upset by the perfidy of the Japanese; certainly he found himself in a serious predicament.

His mind was tortured and condemned by writhing conscience, his remorse made the more bitter by the knowledge of his betrayal by his masters. His motives, as he described them, were not convincing. Certainly, well-informed Chinese believed that he was motivated by nothing but self-interest and anger at being dropped from the Nationalist Government.

The summer evenings were lovely. The heat did not abate but the oppressive atmosphere of the days lifted slightly. Massive Purple Mountain in the distance cast violet shadows upon the city. We were swathed in a mauve mist. The chalky dust, which lay thick upon buildings and upon the earth by day, was transformed into silvery blue evanescence in the glow of sunset.

Josie and I loved to bicycle to a quiet spot up on the old city wall to watch the sun sink. There we sat in the twilight, an attentive audience to the drama of Chinese life enacted below us on the outer side of the wall.

Here among the rice fields was a swarming little settlement of flimsy shacks, constructed of torn straw matting held together with rusty bits of metal. They clustered together, leaning upon one another as if for comfort and support. No one ever looked up to discover us sitting there, watching. They were all too busy, the children with their games, the grownups with gossip and household duties. The children amused themselves with bits of wood or tin as happily as though with expensive toys. They rolled hoops, played a kind of hopscotch, devised mumblety-peg. Their shrill laughter echoed against the wall and up into the quiet of the evening. It was a good sound to hear.

Shriveled old people sat in the doorways gazing idly. Women busied themselves lighting fires and cooking the evening rice in great black iron caldrons, padding back and forth and in and out of their houses. A gaunt middle-aged man fascinated us as we observed him, night after night. The cares of the world seemed to be on his shoulders as he dashed back and forth, picking up this and that, briskly brushing up the earthen floor of the courtyard with jerky, nervous strokes, calling out to the children in a shrill voice, never still, never satisfied. A born worrier.

How human all of this was, a cross-section of humanity at the end of the day, the world over. Without comforts or luxuries, yet with their unremitting toil, frugality and stoical patience, these people were the peer of many placed in more fortunate circumstances. Differences of race, religion, environment and customs do not alter the human qualities they have in common with us.

The six weeks in Nanking had stretched into eight months before orders finally authorized us to return to Shanghai. We slipped back into Shanghai life and tensions almost with pleasure. At least we enlivened one evening when the British Consul and his wife, John and Stella Alexander, invited us to dinner. My wife was seated next to a charming Englishman with whom she engaged in animated conversation. When the dessert was passed, Josie was served first, being on the right of the host. So deeply rapt in conversation was she that she helped herself mechanically without turning her head. Horrified, I saw her take spoonful after spoonful of the dessert. Silence fell. Josie looked up. The servant stood beside her, his face bewildered, his dessert bowl empty. With gay aplomb her host leaned forward, patted Josie's arm and scraped back most of the dessert into the bowl to the vast amusement of the guests.

But there were not to be many more gay dinner parties. The war in Europe and Japanese activities in China and the Pacific were inexorably drawing our country into the maelstrom. Watching Japanese activities from Shanghai we strongly advised our Government to evacuate American women and children from occupied China. Our Government provided the necessary shipping but many American citizens who had settled in Shanghai, who owned property there and called the city their home, refused even to think of leaving for the United States. But I told Josie she must make preparations. She sorrowfully packed her best silver, a few pictures and rugs but decided to leave the rest of our things. She hated to dismantle completely the only real home we had had together. This separation would, we feared, be for an indefinite period.

The parting was painfully distressing and oppressive. Husbands returned to their offices acutely conscious that the future was dark and uncertain.

No one knew what lay ahead.

13

War Becomes Total

SHANGHAI began to fill up with Nazi spies and colorful agents who prospered under the expanding Japanese umbrella. Their propaganda against Britain and her Allies was open and vicious. As President Roosevelt hardened his attitude and ordered protective measures against the unrestricted submarine warfare, this propaganda was trained on the United States. Nazi attacks emboldened the Japanese in their diatribes against us, which made it increasingly plain that their big hour of decision could not be far off. We were all racked by the question—when?

Consul General Lockhart, who had relieved Clarence Gauss some months earlier, fell ill in October, 1941. He was taken to the hospital and I was placed in charge of the Consulate. As the general situation worsened we made preparations to destroy the official and confidential papers upon a moment's notice. A radio receiving and transmitting set was installed, operated by a radioman from the little American gunboat, the U.S.S. *Wake,* which had been left behind for communications purposes after all other naval and marine forces had been withdrawn from Shanghai to the Philippines. The office was placed on a twenty-four-hour duty schedule. An air of suspense, heavy and oppressive, gripped us all.

One day, our Naval Intelligence Officer reported that the Japanese Grand Fleet had left its home waters. Part of the fleet had been sighted off the coast of Indochina heading south, while other units were believed to be steaming toward the Philippines. This ominous intelligence was immediately flashed to Washington. We could only wait. Twenty-four hours later the bombs fell.

A loud explosion awakened me at four-thirty on the morning of December 8, 1941. I could hear the sound of sporadic bursts of machine gunfire from the direction of the Whangpoo River, five miles away. The telephone rang in the quiet apartment. Dave Berger, executive officer on night duty at the Consulate, was on the line.

"Ed," he reported, "the Japs have boarded and seized the *Wake*. When they attempted to take over the *Petrel*, the crew blew her up. The Japs seem to be all over the Bund."

"Get as many of the staff as you can and start burning the codes and confidential stuff."

"Already started."

"Don't destroy the radio. Perhaps we can still get off a couple of messages."

At that time there was no word of the attack on Pearl Harbor, but the seizure of our gunboat U.S.S. *Wake,* the attempted seizure of the British gunboat H.M.S. *Petrel,* could only mean war.

The sky over the river downtown was lighted by the blaze of H.M.S. *Petrel,* first British victim of the war unleashed by Japan. There was a sound of machine-gun fire and the occasional crack of a rifle echoing through the deserted streets as I drew up in front of the Consulate. No Japanese guards were stationed there as yet and I dashed into the building.

A number of the staff had already arrived and were sorting and burning confidential material from desks, safes and file cabinets. The Commander of the U.S.S. *Wake* was waiting for me. He had been living on shore for some time with a skeleton crew left aboard. He confirmed that the Japs had boarded his ship at about half past four, had seized it and made prisoners of the crew but there were no casualities. When a Japanese boarding party headed for H.M.S. *Petrel,* the crew blew up the ship and jumped into the river. Some were machine-gunned in the water and others were captured.

A message was sent off to Washington. It was difficult not to be melodramatic. The telephone jangled without pause. Americans calling to ask what had happened, what to do. Consular colleagues calling to exchange information. We were all in frantic haste, anticipating that the Japanese would take over the telephone company at any minute.

My British colleague, Anthony George, appeared. "This is to be a brutal business, Ed," he said. "Don't you think we'd better blow up the power station and the other utilities?"

He was referring to the American-owned Shanghai power station and the British-owned waterworks, mills, bus and tramway service within the International Settlement.

"Tony, in my opinion, it won't be possible to destroy the power station. The Japs must already be guarding it. And while it would inconvenience them to be without light and power, it would have more serious consequences for the Chinese and foreign residents of the city. In any case, do you think we could persuade our people deliberately to destroy their own property, even if it were the wisest thing to do?"

He agreed, although he felt it the duty of a British subject in time of war to sabotage or destroy anything that might be of value to the enemy. The decision was not an easy one for me to make, as I felt much the same way he did.

Rody Hall, our political officer, an enormous figure of a man, who ably tussled and wrangled with the Jap authorities over a myriad of problems, burst into the office. He had been posted to warn us the moment the Japanese entered the Consulate building. "Boss," he roared, "they've posted marines all around the circle in front of the office and there's a machine gun pointed at the entrance of the building."

My mouth went dry. "Hurry the burning. Tell the radioman to stand by to destroy his set but not until I send off a last message." But the words of this last message shaped up agonizingly slowly, like trying to run in a nightmare. It was finished when Rody returned. "They're coming upstairs, boss. Machine guns have been set up in the corridors."

"Everything burned?"

"Not quite."

"We'll have to keep them occupied somehow until it is done."

Lyda Mae, my faithful secretary, entered the office. "They are here, Mr. Stanton."

In came the Japanese Consul with several members of his staff, supported by a naval officer. I gestured to them to be seated as though this were any ordinary call. "Gentlemen, what can I do for you?"

The Consul, whom I knew, looked embarrassed. "Japan is at war with the United States of America," he proclaimed. "Japanese authorities must take over Consulate and confine the staff."

"Oh. Has there been a formal declaration of war?"

They were taken aback for a moment. After whispering among themselves they replied that they did not know.

Play for time, I told myself. The staff must complete burning the papers and dispatch our last message.

"But you cannot do this," I protested, "when you do not even know whether there has been a formal declaration of war. It would be contrary to international law."

The naval officer got the gist of my protest. He scowled and impatiently fingered his pistol and the sword that was almost as long as he was. The Consul was disturbed. He argued at some length with the naval man and they again insisted that they must take over the Consulate. I objected. Finally he said, "We will go and get official paper and return soon." The naval officer looked like a thundercloud. As they left, I could see sentries posted at intervals the entire length of the corridor.

"I am shaky," said Lyda Mae.

"So am I," I confessed. "The Japs will be back within a half hour to take over. Rush the burning. Tell the radio operator to destroy his set immediately after sending the message and signal me when it is done. I'll play for time as long as I can."

The delegation was back within forty minutes. The Consul handed me a fancy paper signed by the Commander in Chief of the naval forces, stating that the Japanese Government had declared war on the United States.

"But this," I pointed out, "does not contain the official text of your Government's declaration of war."

"We've got to confine the staff," the Consul said doggedly.

"Do you mean we are prisoners of war? This would constitute a violation of international law."

"No," the Consul said, adding ludicrously that the confinement was to be only for our protection.

At this point there was a buzz indicating that the burning of papers and destruction of the radio were complete.

I insisted that there was no point in confining the girls of our clerical staff and after further consultation with the sour-faced naval man the Consul agreed to see what arrangements could be made for the girls. While he went off to telephone, the naval man remained, smoking cigarettes constantly and watching me narrowly. I picked up the phone. "No, no," he screamed, jumping to his feet. I felt we were indeed prisoners of war.

The Consul reported that headquarters had agreed to let the clerical staff live at home, subject to control of the Japanese authorities. All officers were to be confined. I demanded that they be allowed to return to their homes for a few days to settle their affairs. This was refused but, as a special concession, we were to be allowed to go home for a few hours, pack one suitcase of clothes and report at the Metropole Hotel, directly opposite the Consulate building, by four o'clock that afternoon.

Arguing against the seizure of the Consulate, I pointed out that, according to international law, the official property and archives of a belligerent country are inviolable and that the correct procedure is for a protecting neutral government, appointed by the belligerent governments by mutual agreement, to seal the archives and the property. They made no reply. The naval officer strode back and forth, his sword clanking. In actual fact, they had already seized the Consulate and were waiting only for our departure to rummage through the files.

Twelve noon, and four more hours of freedom. I made the rounds of the offices telling the staff of the conditions and praising them for their loyalty and efficiency. I was very proud of their conduct.

Profoundly weary and disheartened, I returned to my apartment to say good-by to the servants and give them what money I had. I packed the one suitcase I was allowed and, at the last moment, tucked in an antique watch to tinker with. I looked around, realizing I was unlikely ever again to see the place in which Josie and I had been so happy, or to look at our possessions.

The Japanese had set up what they called a liaison office at the Metropole. The man at the desk checking the "enemy" into "confinement" was a junior consular official. The place swarmed with Jap gendarmes, a dread breed noted for their brutality and ruthlessness. I was asked to assign rooms. When I had finished I flopped onto the bed in my own room, hoping for the relief of sleep. Instead, the incredible events of the day hammered through my mind with painful intensity. These in turn were brushed aside by endless questions and queries about the future. Toss right, toss left.

Suddenly there were wild shouts of *"Banzai, Banzai."* A drunken Japanese officer burst into my room, yelling like a madman. "Japanese navy bomb, bomb, bomb, American Navy. Pearl Harbor. American ships all go down, down, down. *Banzai!"* He capered about, brandishing his pistol, and then staggered out of the room. All that night I walked back and forth, while in the corridor the heavy boots of the gendarme guarding us kept pace with me and my black thoughts. Was it true? How could it have happened? How had it been possible? If true the extent of the disaster seemed staggering.

The first day of our internment dawned, cold and uninviting outside, a suitable complement to the atmosphere within. That morning I had a conference with the Japanese liaison officer on the subject of getting out for some kind of exercise, as well as on the necessity of my going to see Consul General Lockhart in the hospital, as soon as possible.

"Very difficult," he answered.

"But even prisoners of war are allowed exercise," I protested.

Headquarters was consulted, lengthy conferences followed, and at last a pass system was devised. This proved to be a cumbersome and irritating arrangement, but it meant that twice a week we could apply for a pass and walk for an hour, followed at a distance by a gendarme.

Two weeks later, after constant pestering on my part, a special pass arrived for me to visit Consul General Lockhart. Two gendarmes escorted me to the hospital, sitting on either side of me in the motor car. This was my first outing. There was very little activity along the streets, innumerable barriers everywhere. Near the outskirts of the International Settlement, we came to a formidable barrier, bristling with machine guns. Here we alighted and approached the scowling sentries, who snatched my pass and scrutinized it so long that my heart sank; then they beckoned me on. It was good to see Mr. Lockhart looking cheerful and well in bed. He was concerned about his wife, who had left San Francisco by special permission from the State Department a few days before Pearl Harbor. I had no news but promised to do what I could. I was grateful beyond words that he had not been molested.

My worst ordeal followed. Every day for almost two weeks a Japanese gendarmerie officer from headquarters and a consular officer tried to force me to sign a paper, which, in effect, would turn all the Consulate's archives over to the Japanese authorities. They often came at night. The argument went on interminably in an effort to wear me down. Finally they said, "You know, Mr. Stanton, we can do as we please with you."

"I suppose you can," I admitted, "but I will sign nothing." Eventually they gave it up as a bad job.

One day the Chilean Consul General, a good friend, visited me. I had asked him if he would be willing to act as a neutral representative to protect American citizens and their interests in China and he had applied for authorization from his Government. Meanwhile, he confirmed the disastrous news we had received about the attack on Pearl Harbor, the Japanese landings in the Philippines and Malaya, and the seizure of Hong Kong. News concerning American citizens was not good. While the majority had not been molested, the managers of the oil companies and the National City Bank had been interned, as well as J. B. Powell, the outspoken editor of the *China Weekly Review*. They had all been taken to the Bridge House, headquarters of the gendarmerie, which was to become notorious as the scene of torturings and brutalities.

A month later we were all moved into another building known as the Cathay Mansions. There we found the British officials as well as consular representatives of the other nations which were at war with the Axis-Japanese coalition. The change proved diverting; we were not quite so crowded for space and everyone brightened temporarily. But day followed day with a dull and hopeless monotony. Officials shorn of their halo of official prestige lost much of their personality. Many of them sat, sulked and brooded until boredom and melancholia gripped them. They no longer had to make an effort; there was nothing for them to prove and no one to impress, or so they seemed to think.

For six months we went through the monotony of an unchanging routine which became almost intolerable for some of us, oppressed and frustrated by confinement and the unknown. The mechanics of getting up, shaving, dressing were soon completed. What was there to do all day? Sit and stare out of the window. Nothing much to see except brick walls or a bit of garden. But thoughts, thoughts like javelins darted through the mind, leaping from speculation on the progress of the war, to families, to our own chances of being released from captivity, to the annoying habits and mannerisms of various members of our group. I found that my thoughts would gradually merge in to a whirl of despondency and frustration. Unbearable to sit still another instant. I sought relief in pacing the floor. Around and around the room, eyes fixed on the threadbare pattern of the shabby carpet, hoping that its dull texture and endless twining pattern would tie up my thoughts into a tight inextricable knot. It was no use. The same thoughts, doubts, hopes and irritations kept obtruding themselves in a confused sort of sequence, jabbing, jabbing until I seemed exhausted and drained of all thought and yet was not. Day after day, sitting or pacing through the long hours, the mind unsettled, bored, frustrated. Good books the mind did not seem tranquil enough to absorb. Trashy books quickly bored one, while the lurid propaganda constantly thrust upon us by our captors, describing Japanese victories over us and our allies and the glories of the new order of "co-prosperity" in Asia, stirred the bile.

At first we looked forward to meals. The prospect of food and meeting and conversing with the others was a bright one. But as the days and months dragged on the daily fish and rice dishes became flat and finally so unappetizing that we pushed the food away. And conversation? It was a mirror of our confused, brooding thoughts, infinitely dull.

It would have been better if we, the captives, had organized activities to keep us busy but since those cooped up were senior diplomatic and consular officials, each was left to his own devices and such philosophical reasonableness as he might be capable of bringing to bear upon the uncertainty of his fate and the despondent impulses of his mind. As a result the veneer of polish and manners peeled in many cases. There were increasing flare-ups of irritation and temper, especially between those confined to the same room. Being in charge of our group, I became the repository of numerous complaints made by one roommate against another. Complaints about snoring, monopolizing the one comfortable chair in the room, clearing the throat, whistling, pinching cigarettes and such trivialities. A man confined, bored and frustrated magnifies these trivia into grievances which become obsessions. His reason and morale are affected and the baser traits of character emerge. Or is it simply that moral and social standards are superficial and easily vitiated? This may perhaps explain the reactions of some to internment. But how explain the conduct of the few who, by their unselfishness, devotion and service to their fellow prisoners, become inspiring leaders?

The fall of Hong Kong, Singapore and finally of Corregidor, deepened our despair. The gendarmes would jeer at us after each defeat. It was hard to take, but we clung to the hope of ultimate victory, knowing the strength of our nation and the courage of our

people. Occasionally rumors would circulate to the effect that negotiations for an exchange of prisoners were in progress. Our spirits
would rise but sink again when the rumors proved false.

I took refuge in tinkering with the old watch I had brought with
me. For hours I concentrated upon its intricacies, using a hairpin
or a pocket knife as a tool. One day, it commenced to tick and I was
jubilant. At this moment, with a scraping of heavy boots a gendarme
walked in whom I had never seen. He was an ugly-looking fellow.
He sat down, plunked his pistol on my table, picked up my watch,
listened to it ticking, and then dashed it on the floor, grinding it to
twisted bits under his heavy heel. With a pleased expression he
walked out, slamming the door behind him.

What happened to the Japanese in uniform? How could the
smiling, family-loving farmers and storekeepers we had so often seen
in Japan be transformed into these brutes? I recalled a happy holi-
day Josie and I had spent in Unzen in 1938, where we found
charming warm people, who deplored the war in China as much
as we did. They played happily with their children, interested in
the simple details of everyday life. They missed the father, son
and sweetheart sent into China to fight a war they could not understand.

I recalled the charming gentle folk we had found at Miyanoshita
on our honeymoon, devoted to their families and the beautification
of their gardens, to fashioning exquisite things: pictures, screens,
lacquerware; and the wonderful theater that evidenced centuries devoted to the arts. This was a different kind of people. How could
these folk be changed into the uniformed monsters who were rav-
aging China? Did the cult of Bushido and Emperor worship explain it?

A worrying problem was the plight of the Chinese employees
who had faithfully served the United States Government for a
great many years, and who had been dropped abruptly from the

Government payrolls. The Swiss Government had finally been appointed as a neutral agent to act on behalf of Allied nations. The Swiss Consul General, who was permitted to visit us from time to time, sent off a message for me to Washington pleading the loyalty of these people, pointing out that they had stood by us during the crisis and now could not find other jobs. Washington's answer to the request for financial assistance was in the negative. Meanwhile, petitions were pouring in to me from these former employees, describing their situation, imploring assistance. We could only pass the hat among ourselves, but this was meager help.

Another pressing problem was the condition of those Americans interned in the gruesome Bridge House. The Swiss were not granted permission to see them and their welfare was unknown. One could only imagine the worst. I emphasized again and again in the strongest possible language that these Americans must be placed on the list of those persons to be exchanged.

Suddenly, good news, unbelievable news, concerning negotiations for an exchange and return home. Smiles broke out on sullen faces, irritations and petty grievances were forgotten, and those who had not spoken to each other chatted amiably. We were happy also because Consul General Lockhart had been dismissed from the hospital and was moved in with us. After much prodding of the Japanese I had learned that Mrs. Lockhart was in Manila, where she had arrived just as the Japanese struck at Pearl Harbor. After endless talk, she was sent to join her husband in Shanghai in readiness for repatriation.

At about the same time, occasional visitors were allowed to come and see us. It was not our social friends who remembered me at this time but people whom we had been able to help in some small way and who now wished to reciprocate. They brought me goodies, which were expensive for them and involved sacrifice on their part. One day the gendarme on duty ushered in our houseboy,

Lou, all smiles. He proudly presented me with a bag of popcorn, for which he knew I had an inordinate liking. I was deeply touched that he had risked open identification with me by applying for a permit. He gave me news about the servants and I advised him to return to the north with the others, and made arrangements to transmit money to them all. It was the last I saw of him.

The day of the exchange came at last. It was June 26, 1942. With one piece of luggage we were driven to the docks under strong escort and boarded the old Italian passenger vessel, the *Conte Verde*. Happily, all those from the Bridge House, including J. B. Powell, were on hand. The latter arrived on a stretcher, emaciated, his legs swollen with gangrene. The ship pulled away toward the open sea and freedom.

At Hong Kong, we picked up another group of Americans, full of grim tales of tragic happenings. At Singapore, we took on fuel and water and then headed south and west across the Indian Ocean. The Swiss liaison officer on board regaled us with all the war news: the Japanese had occupied Siam, Malaya, Singapore, most of the Philippines, the Dutch East Indies, and were menacing Australia. He related the successes of Japanese and Nazi submarine warfare, which was exacting a huge toll of shipping and transport service. One good bit of news, however, was that in a titanic battle in the Coral Sea American sea and air power had smashed and destroyed many of Japan's finest naval vessels, a telling blow.

We were steaming for the port of Lourenço Marques in Portuguese East Africa, to meet another group headed by Ambassador Grew, evacuating from Japan. As we neared our destination excitement became so intense it hurt. Japanese submarines were lurking thick in these waters. As we came into port, someone shouted, "Look, an American ship!" There she was, a liberty ship, with the Stars and Stripes fluttering in the breeze. It was hard not to cry. The crew from the ship lined the decks and cheered. Then we went wild, shouting, stamping, whistling.

Officials, State Department and others, boarded our ship. We clasped their hands hard and grinned. But now there was work to be done: instructions from the Department, mail to be distributed, money to be exchanged, paper work and more paper work.

Then came the actual exchange—fifteen hundred Americans, civilians, and Allied diplomats for an equivalent number of Japanese. They came down one gangway and we went up the other. The exhilaration and sense of freedom of stepping upon the deck of the *Gripsholm*, which was to carry us home, was wonderful.

The long voyage around the Cape of Good Hope sped by. We were busy writing reports for the Department, recounting the details of the political and economic developments of the past months; preparing lists of American citizens and losses, largely from memory. There were also innumerable staff problems to be solved. In the midst of this activity I felt shooting pains in my leg. The ankle turned black and began to swell hideously. The pain became so intense that I had to give up hobbling around and crawl into my bunk. The missionary doctor consulted could not diagnose my trouble exactly but thought it was a vitamin deficiency of some kind, aggravated by tension. For a long time I was to walk on crutches.

As we approached Rio de Janeiro, we came upon a burning hulk, a victim of Nazi submarines, which operated in packs, attacking convoys and merchant vessels in those waters. We circled around the wreck but could discover no survivors.

The night before our arrival at New York no one slept. At daylight we were all on deck, pacing up and down, peering into the thick morning haze. The mist thinned and lifted. There stood the Statue of Liberty, dimly outlined in all its majesty, the morning sun breaking through the fog, bathing its serene and benign countenance with a faint golden glow. Coast Guard cutters danced about us; ferries and ships in the harbor tooted.

Before noon we docked. An army of immigration, customs and FBI officials crowded into the ship. We were checked and double-checked, squeezed for information—all in alphabetical order. It took hours until the letter S came up.

Four o'clock. The twentieth floor of the St. Moritz. The bellboy opened the door. Josie was backed up against the wall, staring at me. I stopped in the doorway.

"Hello," she said faintly.

"Hi," I whispered.

We could not move.

14

Our China Policy

My physical condition as a result of internment was not as serious as my mental and emotional turmoil so, at Josie's insistence, we went off for a few weeks to a quiet little camp in the Maine woods. As usual, I turned to tinkering with old watches. To concentrate on a little pivot, to cut a pin the exact length required, file, sandpaper, hour after hour. I know of nothing, except music, as useful as concentration on a mechanical detail to help the mind regain its own balance.

What disturbed me was the bitterness of my own thinking. I was constantly harassed by thoughts of the Japanese and the wanton suffering inflicted by their military leaders. Instances of their sharp and deliberate cruelty obsessed me, distorting my thinking, creating a mental haze through which the simple knowledge that the militarists and not the people were culpable could not penetrate.

Hatred is not a healthy companion, but the long patient concentration on the mechanism of the old watch served its purpose and gradually, pushing aside the unpleasant miasma, came fresh clean thinking. I brushed aside memories of the Japanese at bayonet practice on living bodies. Instead I remembered the Chinese among whom I had lived and worked for twenty years, the farmer laboriously tending the land he loves under weather both harsh and soft, under rulers both good and bad, tremendous in his stolid strength, quiet in his patience.

I remembered the Chinese scholar, wise in his knowledge of the classics and his country's history, wiser yet in his understanding that he must master five cartloads of books before understanding the past and comprehending the present. I remembered the quiet repose and dignity of the great pillared halls built to honor the memory of the sage Confucius. I thought of the lights and candles floating in little paper boats or in huge lotus leaves along the lakes, rivers and canals on festival days. I thought of the children playing in mud puddles, of the sun setting purple over the Western Hills, of the reverberating bong of a great temple bell rising into the cool starlit night.

All this I had deeply loved, all this I could think of without pain or bitterness: the charm and simplicity of the people, the wisdom and learning of the philosophers, the grace and symmetry of a porcelain vase. "All within the four seas are brothers," Confucius had said.

But then, how about the Japanese? To exclude them or any human being would be to nullify this noble concept. There should be no exceptions, no exclusions. I had believed in it in the past; somehow I had to relearn to believe in it now. Slowly bitterness drained from the deep pools of the mind and on the lakes of Maine I found peace again. Before long I was ready to emerge from this moment of inner struggle and eager to find the way in which I could best contribute. That meant returning to the job for which I was trained, and to Washington.

The story of wartime Washington needs no repeating. It was two parts discomfort and irritation to one part sense of humor. To the degree that these proportions could be reversed one's sanity was better preserved and reflected in more intelligent application to one's job. We faced with misgiving the necessity of finding an apartment in Washington, seething with its many dwelling seekers. When a kind friend offered us a temporary roof over our heads, we snatched at it gratefully. Two rooms and a bath in a big old house on Rhode Island Avenue. A combination electric grill and portable oven was set up in the bathroom. To reach our apartment we passed through a dentist's waiting room redolent of the smells associated with such needful places of unhappy memory.

The Chinese section of the Far Eastern Division to which I was assigned was working overtime on the many and acute problems that faced Free China in her efforts to keep the Japanese at bay. The Nationalist Government under Chiang Kai-shek endeavored from Chungking, its much-bombed capital, to buy time in which to build up its strength by yielding territory. Aside from the determination not to capitulate to the Japanese, the only asset the beleaguered Government possessed was the vastness of its territories. Japanese strength was deployed and committed in the Pacific and Southeast Asia to such an extent that the complete conquest of China was never achieved; the great sprawling Chinese dragon seemed merely to coil and recoil.

Millions of words have been written on the story of our relations with Free China during the war in the Pacific. This period in our foreign relations has given rise to innumerable official documents, books, articles and pamphlets, some in defense, some critical and some factual. A historian of the future with access to all relevant material will, no doubt, place these events in their true perspective.

As I saw it from my desk in the Department in the autumn of 1942, our country was still in process of mobilizing and welding its resources, spiritual, human and material, into a tough bulwark, which was first to repel and then to hurl back the invader of the Pacific. Our own strength and resources and those of our British ally were strained to the uttermost limit by these attempts and the desperate effort to survive the fearful blows being struck both by the Germans and the Japanese. Allied grand strategy called first for a supreme effort to meet the Nazi onslaughts in Europe and Africa, and for a concentrated effort to thrust back the Japanese in the Pacific, leaving the China-Burma theater of operations a poor third. Nevertheless, this period was marked by an earnest desire on the part of our Government to give every possible assistance, both in a political and a material sense, to our friend and ally, Free China.

On January 11, 1943, our Government renounced its extraterritorial rights, thus clearly affirming recognition of China's sovereignty and equality. At President Roosevelt's insistence, China was included as one of the original signers of the joint Moscow Declaration of October 30, 1943. At the Cairo Conference in November of that same year, the President was equally insistent that China should be given every opportunity to become a great power. Our Government was no less zealous in behalf of China during the formation of the United Nations, urging that she be seated on the Security Council. Through these and other political and diplomatic measures the United States sought to ensure for China a place in international affairs as one of the great powers of the world.

This was only a part of the picture as I saw it unfold. Our Government was concerned by the need to assist Free China, which had already been fighting the Japanese for four years, to equip and train her forces the better to defend herself and also to help us by pinning down as many Japanese divisions as possible while we struck in the Pacific. In this respect our record was both good and bad. The constant, almost daily, pleas from the Chinese Government for planes, munitions, military supplies and equipment of all kinds, and for consumer goods to combat inflation and the dire shortages that existed, were most sympathetically received. We promised a good deal but were by no means able to implement those promises with the rapidity that the Chinese Government thought justified by their extremity.

Our country was the principal arsenal of all those countries joined together in repelling and defeating the Nazis and Fascists in Europe and the Japanese in the Pacific and in South Asia. The demands upon our human and material resources were gigantic. Furthermore, global strategy, determined in concert with our Allies, called for the major effort to be made in Europe and the Pacific. In consequence, we found ourselves limited in what we could do to aid China.

Nevertheless, in the State Department we felt, particularly those of us in the Far Eastern Division, that there was insufficient recognition of the political importance of not merely giving Free China moral and political support but clothing this support with real substance by assigning a higher priority to China in Allied military strategy and in the logistic support this would imply. The Department's recommendations to the White House on this subject were underscored by reports being received from our Embassy in Chungking, from time to time, to the effect that the lack of tangible and visible support in the form of planes and supplies was giving impetus to a sense of frustration and defeatism that tended to spread like a cancer among some elements of the Government, especially the small group which had, for a long time, advocated coming to terms with the Japanese.

Another serious obstacle was the lack of land communications into isolated Free China. This meant that practically everything we sent had to be flown in over the Hump, a most difficult and dangerous stretch of the Himalayan Mountains. In time, the trickle of a few hundred tons monthly increased to almost twenty thousand tons a month. Nevertheless, even with a trickle of supplies, General Stilwell struggled valiantly to equip and train Chinese divisions for use in his cherished plan to defeat the Japanese in Burma and to open a road into South China, while General Chennault was intent upon building up an air force which he believed could hold the Japanese at bay in China and ultimately destroy their lines of communication back into Japan itself.

These efforts were marked by conflicts in strategy and conflicts of personalities. Our British allies being hard pressed in Europe and Africa, and having suffered disastrous defeats in Malaya, were reluctant to engage in a major campaign in Burma. On the other hand, Generalissimo Chiang was not inclined to commit a substantial portion of his forces in the reconquest of Burma, where his troops had been routed by a Japanese offensive in the summer of 1942, unless the British would agree to do what they did not want to do.

In addition, our own military men did not see eye to eye on the question of strategy in the China-Burma theater of operations. Some were staunch advocates of increased operations by ground troops in Burma; some equally ardent in their support of stepped-up air operations from airfields in China. A Japanese offensive in the summer of 1944, which probed up the Yangtze River toward Chungking and south at airfields in Free China, was not stopped by intensive bombing, nor was General Stilwell, in spite of his enthusiasm and determination, able to make much headway in northern Burma. In September, 1944, Stilwell, whose personal relations with the Generalissimo had steadily deteriorated because of his irascible temper, was withdrawn from China. It was not until early in 1945 that the fruits of his training program and planning ripened into operations which cleared the Japanese from northern Burma and opened a land route into China.

There were, of course, other important factors that affected both the political and military situation in China and our relations with the Nationalist Government. Perhaps the most significant of these arose from the continuing hostility between the Nationalist Government and Kuomintang Party on the one hand and the Communists under Mao Tse-tung on the other. The honeymoon that occurred for about a year in 1937-1938, when these two political groups agreed to some measure of military co-operation in order to meet the Japanese advance, was followed in the next five years by a steady deterioration in relations as the result of suspicions, mistrust and the bitterness of the past. The Communists strove to increase their strength while the Nationalists sought to contain them by establishing a fairly rigid blockade around the areas occupied by the Communists.

The talks that took place between the Kuomintang and the Communists in June, 1943, served only to strain relations still further as the latter refused to abandon the Government they had established in Yenan and to place their armies under Nationalist command. The blockade was intensified and by the summer of 1944, when the Japanese launched a major offensive, there were almost three hundred thousand Nationalist troops and an even greater number of Communist regulars and guerrillas arrayed against each other. They were taking no part in operations to halt the Japanese offensive, let alone to throw back the invader. Furthermore, it had become apparent that the Kuomintang and Nationalist Government's leaders were so preoccupied by their feud with the Communists that the prosecution of the war had become of secondary importance. They felt, and perhaps with some justification from their point of view, that the war would certainly be won by the United States and that it was to their advantage to conserve their strength to cope with the postwar problems which would confront China, including the Communist bid for power.

On the other hand, our Government was deeply concerned and troubled over the enormous sacrifices, especially of our young manhood, which we were being compelled to make in the hard and savage struggle to drive back the Japanese in the Pacific. While there was no lessening of our friendship for and desire to aid Free China, there was keen disappointment over the failure of the Nationalist Government fully to mobilize its resources and prosecute the war with vigor and determination. To hasten the day of victory and to save American lives it was essential, in the thinking of President Roosevelt and his military and other advisers, that all Nationalist troops, including those blockading the Communists, as well as the Communist forces, be thrown into action against the Japanese.

The exigencies of war dictated the effort made by the President and his diplomatic and military representatives in China, which the State and other Departments of the Government supported, to persuade the Nationalist Government to permit full use of all forces in Free China against the Japanese. These efforts were not successful, but I am convinced they were made in the best interests of the United States at a time when we were engaged in a herculean struggle.

In today's type of global warfare, countries are banded together which have the most diverse and opposite political ideologies, the only common denominator being the desire of self-preservation in the face of aggression. It was in such circumstances that we found ourselves allied with Communist Russia. Not because of any love for Communist doctrines or their system of government, but because we were fighting common enemies and needed one another's aid. If we bear in mind the exigent nature of the war in the Pacific and our intense desire to spare the lives of our young men, I think it will be easier to understand this phase of our China policy over which there has been so much controversy and misunderstanding, including the passing of harsh judgments upon some of my colleagues who deserved better of their countrymen.

The fact is that basic policy objectives governing United States relations with China remained unchanged from the outbreak to the conclusion of the war. That policy, conceived in lasting friendship for the Chinese people, aspired to see China become a strong, united and well-governed nation devoted to the welfare of her people, and a leader in world affairs. This is what our Government sought to achieve and my colleagues and I, who had some small part in formulating and implementing this policy, felt not only that the objective represented a continuation of our traditional friendship for China but that the efforts made to implement it were sound and sensible in the light of wartime demands.

That our Government was anticipating the emergence of China from the war as a great nation and equal partner was implicit in the decision taken to draft and negotiate with the Nationalist Government a new treaty of friendship, commerce and navigation. The treaty was to stress friendship, equality of sovereign rights, and full reciprocity. It was designed to spell out the rights of citizens of the two countries freely to trade, travel, reside, acquire property and to carry on legitimate religious and commercial activities in the country of the other party. Matters of taxation, trademarks, navigation, as well as the protection of persons and property, were to be included.

The State Department set up a drafting team that included myself. We met with our counterparts from various other interested agencies of the Government. The job of drafting, a new experience to me, was tackled slowly and systematically with long and protracted sessions. Each point had to be considered, discussed and regurgitated. Searching examination was made of the legal, political, economic and financial implications of every provision to be included in the treaty. Chinese laws and regulations, Federal laws and regulations, and the laws and regulations of all the forty-eight states had to be weighed carefully and our drafts of the various treaty articles adjusted delicately to meet all requirements.

I told Josie one evening, after returning from a particularly long and involved session on the subject of the right to own real property, that to draft a provision on this subject, which would have any substance and at the same time meet Chinese law and the laws of our individual states, was infinitely more difficult than adjusting the mechanism of an old watch.

"Give me the old watch any day," I said as I watched her rolling out in what seemed expert fashion a piece of dough. We were in our new apartment on R Street and Josie, who had graduated from a neophyte in cooking, informed me that she was going to bake some biscuits. Something went wrong, however, because the dough, instead of lying placidly as it should on the pastry board, entwined itself round her fingers, her hands, and finally her arms, in so affectionate an embrace that I was called in to peel it all off. Needless to say, there were no hot biscuits that evening.

The drafting of the treaty progressed slowly but steadily. Each long session gave rise to such a cloud of legal jargon that I despaired at first of ever comprehending what was really meant, and upon requesting enlightenment, couched in plain and simple language that laymen might understand, found that the lawyers themselves were sometimes confused. They would listen when I urged over and over that the legal phraseology be made intelligible to the laymen. I stressed the point that the average person turning to the treaty for guidance in the conduct of his affairs would expect it to give him the information he needed. Furthermore, I never let them forget that the English text had to be translated into Chinese. If we were not sure of the meaning of the former we could not hope for any clarity in the latter. They listened and strove mightily to make the language of the treaty as simple as possible.

We all worked together in harmony but it was not until April, 1945, that the first draft was presented to the Chinese Government. I was particularly pleased with the Preamble to the Treaty, which read:

The United States of America and the Republic of China, desirous of strengthening the bonds of peace and the ties of friendship, which have happily long prevailed between the two countries, by arrangements designed to promote friendly intercourse between their respective territories through provisions responsive to the spiritual, economic and commercial aspirations of the people thereof, have resolved to conclude a Treaty of Friendship, Commerce and Navigation.

As I left Washington for Vancouver, to which I was transferred, I felt that the treaty, upon which we had spent so much time, thought and earnest effort, should be added to the long list of political, military and financial measures taken by the United States to manifest its friendship and high regard for China. The record shows, it seems to me, that the United States has been in the past and continues to be Nationalist China's best friend.

Vancouver is one of the most beautiful cities in the world with its ever-green mountains capped with dazzling snow, looking down protectively over a winding land-locked harbor. V-J Day arrived and the city went wild. We went wild, too. The Canadian authorities decided to mark the day by impressive and solemn ceremonies in which consular representatives were invited to participate. My morning coat and top hat were hastily prepared for the occasion, shaken, pressed and brushed. Just as I was saluting the flag, standing at attention, there was a plop as a low-flying sea gull left its calling card upon the top hat held across my bosom. I was to lay a wreath at the War Memorial and there was nothing to be done but to carry this mortifying badge throughout the rest of the ceremonies with as much sang-froid as possible.

For a few months we settled down, enjoying ourselves tremendously, after having moved in and out of two houses at great expense and labor. Then a telephone call came from Washington. John Carter Vincent was at the other end, informing me that I had been appointed Minister to Thailand.

15

Thai Means Free

Two weeks later, in June, 1946, in the old State Department Building in Washington, came the solemn but thrilling moment when I took the oath of office as Minister to Thailand. The days had passed in a blur of activity known as "consultation." Most clearly remembered was my call on President Truman, who recalled that Thailand was the only sovereign and independent country in Southeast Asia and said he felt we should give that country both political and material support. The President expressed the particular hope that Thailand would rapidly increase her exports of rice, which were desperately needed by the hungry people of neighboring countries.

There had been daily conferences and consultations in the Department, where our policy with respect to Thailand was being hammered out and at which I was briefed on problems concerning rice, tin, British, French and Chinese relations with Thailand, claims of American citizens for damages and many others, including, of course, those dealing with the functioning of the Legation and its staff. There were calls on officials of the Thai Embassy in Washington, whom we found cordial and helpful.

When we finally boarded our plane, Josie, who was wearing slacks on the advice of all the knowledgeable ladies she had consulted, discovered in dismay that the other feminine passengers aboard the plane were clad in trim suits.

"Never mind," I consoled her, "when we bail out you will be glad." But my feeble attempt at humor did nothing to restore her confidence.

On arrival at Calcutta we were met by our air and naval attachés from Bangkok and early one morning set off in our air attaché's DC-3 with two officials of the Thai Government.

Over the Bay of Bengal we ran directly into the heart of a monsoon. Much has been written about the monsoons, those torrential downpours that saturate the parched, baked lands of India and flood the rice fields of Burma and Thailand with sheets of cool water. There is praise and thanksgiving on the earth as this life-giving deluge greets the hot, withered land. But in the air, all is turbulence and violence as great masses of rain-bearing clouds, towering twenty thousand feet, are whipped by lashing winds and pierced and rent by jagged bolts of lightning. Into such skies our air attaché, Colonel Vance, launched his plane.

Our pilot and his navigator tried to go under or around the storm. It was no use. The plane rocked, plunged, up and down, side-slipped or fell like a leaf for a hundred feet or more. Fortunately, we did not realize the tremendous power of that storm as we clutched our seats and tried to appear calm. Nor did we know until it was all over that it was the first flight made by Colonel Vance in this particular plane, of which he had just taken delivery at Calcutta, and that it was the second worst storm through which he had ever flown. Blissful ignorance.

At length we broke through the clouds. Below us spread a great river and patches of farmland. This was Thailand. This Land of the Free, for the word *Thai* means free, is a lush tropical country about the size of the state of Texas. Densely forested mountains fringe its northern and western frontiers where wild orchids and wild animals abound. A broad central plain, watered by the river Chao Phya and its tributaries, is the country's life blood and wealth. From its thousands of green and yellow rice fields come food for its people and a rich revenue from the export of over a million tons of surplus rice each year to rice-hungry lands. In the south, millions of rubber trees grow in the jungles and rich deposits of tin ore lie along its western shores. Fish abound in the rivers, in the lakes and in the canals that crisscross Bangkok and mark the great central plain like the divisions of a checkerboard. Tasty sea fish swarm along the coasts, where the blue of the sea and the green of the waving coconut palms stand out against the chalk white, sandy beaches. These fifteen million Thai and three million Chinese may not each have a radio, an automobile or a refrigerator, but of rice, fish, vegetables and fruits such as the luscious mango, the creamy bananas of twenty and more varieties, the rich coconut and the cheeselike durian, there is an abundance. Blessed by nature and supported by their religious reverence for Buddhism, the Thai are a happy, contented people.

We had a blurred glimpse of a sprawling city and the sparkling glitter of temple roofs, before landing, and then stepped from the plane into a hot wind and burning midday sun. Our chargé, Charlie Yost, and his wife were there to greet us and several members of the Legation staff. Mom Luang Pikthip Malakul, who later became one of our good friends, formally welcomed us on behalf of the Minister of Foreign Affairs and the Thai Government and presented Josie with a large bouquet of orchids.

As we stepped into the official Legation car, a dilapidated Chevrolet, a straight, slight little chauffeur saluted us smartly. He had twinkling eyes and smiled a gay welcome. This was Nai Chin, or Mr. Chin, who was to play an important part in our lives for years to come. Driving toward the city, sixteen miles away, the steaming air seemed to suck one's very breath away. Nevertheless, we hung out of the windows of the car, craning our necks for a first impression of the new land which was to be our home.

What we saw was not too encouraging. The monsoon season had just begun but the rains had not yet filled the canals, which we saw on every side. Those separating the road from the ramshackle huts that faced the highway were almost dry and filled with debris and redolent with refuse. The landscape stretched away, absolutely flat, but was relieved by the light green rice tips that were just appearing and by groves of trees and clumps of swaying bamboo.

A temple sparkled in the bright sunlight, the yellow of its roof tiles looking like burnished gold, its slim spires piercing the blue skies. It reminded us of Chinese architecture, except that there was a sharper upsweep to the roof and a sense of joyousness about this Thai temple. And that, we learned, was a reflection of the country itself. For the Thai are a joyous, smiling people. Everyone smiles, children, farmers, storekeepers and pedestrians.

We were in the city now. The streets were crowded with bicycles; three-wheeled rickshas or samlors; automobiles; little tram cars of ancient vintage; swarms of people walking, shopping, eating, gossiping. Mangy dogs ran in all directions, looking for scraps. Over all one heard a babble of cheerful but unintelligible sound. The women, for the most part, wore blouses with a wrap-around sarong, called a *pasin*. The men wore jackets and Western trousers, while the children were as free of clothing as nature and the hot climate dictated. But the women were all in black and the men wore black armbands. For a moment I wondered why, because I had heard that Thai costumes were exceedingly colorful. Then I remembered. Their young King was dead and the entire nation was in mourning for him.

Meantime, Charlie Yost was briefing me on the political situation. My departure for Thailand had been darkened by the news of the tragic and mysterious murder of His Majesty, King Ananda Mahidol, who on the morning of June 9, 1946, was found lying on his bed in the Grand Palace with a gaping bullet wound in his forehead.

"The death of King Ananda," Yost said, "overshadows everything." Ugly rumors had commenced to circulate, linking the Prime Minister, Pridi Phanomyong, and some of his supporters with the young King's death. These rumors were so persistent, in spite of the official announcement describing the mysterious death as an accident, that the Government had appointed a Special Commission of Inquiry, charged with determining the cause of death.

The Legation compound consisted of three old wooden houses, built in tropical style with deep verandahs, which stood in a garden. They had been repaired and remodeled many times during the last fifty years with the few pennies allotted for the purpose by our Government, but not since the war. Two luxuriant traveler's palm trees on either side of the central house and the brilliant flame of the forest trees in the rear were the only attractive features of the property. Charlie Yost explained that once upon a time the houses on either side had been residences for the staff, while the upstairs of the central building had been the Minister's quarters and the downstairs his office. The central building still played its accustomed role but the other two buildings had been turned into offices.

The first person to meet us as we stepped from the car was Babu, the Indian watchman, a benign and friendly old man, clad in the long shirt and *dhoti* worn by Indians, which were none too clean. He had wrapped a small length of white cloth around his head by way of a turban. After greeting the assembled staff, both American and Thai, the servants and the gardeners, we mounted the narrow, rickety stairs to the "Minister's quarters."

These consisted of a huge barnlike space, separated into two bedroom units. A modicum of privacy was achieved by swinging half doors and lattice work above the partitions. There were no windows, the sides of the house being entirely open, but some protection from sun and rain was afforded by bamboo blinds. The openings were screened, or at least they had been screened. Much of the screening had rusted into large, jagged holes.

I don't know what Josie had expected, but the partitioned rooms, the depressing bits of furniture, and the antiquated bathroom with large earthenware pots to hold water quite stunned her. We knew when the Yosts were ready for lunch because they had the other bedroom and one could hear every word through the lattice.

The rooms were furnished with requisitioned Japanese furniture and consisted of a set of green leather chairs, square and clumsy, arranged in two austere rows facing each other. One corner, more cheerful than the others, was equipped with half a dozen well-worn rattan chairs. No pictures, no curtains. Two faded grass rugs covered a section of the floor but gaping holes stared at us.

The next morning, accompanied by Charlie Yost, I went to pay my respects to the Minister of Foreign Affairs, Nai Direk Jayanama, a slight man in his thirties with a sensitive, intelligent face. He had been one of the group who, under the leadership of Pridi Phanomyong, had rendered valuable service to the Allies during the war by supplying information concerning Japanese military operations through an organization known as the "Free Thai."

Thailand had been occupied by massive Japanese forces, who landed along her southeastern shore on the same day our fleet was attacked at Pearl Harbor. Under Japanese pressure, the Thai Government, which at that time was headed by Field Marshal Phibul Songgram, who today is again the country's Prime Minister, declared war on Great Britain and the United States, and collaborated, at least superficially, with the Japanese. As a Thai statesman explained it to me, "We Thai bend like the bamboo but we do not break." They bent under Japanese pressure but secretly organized an underground resistance movement which spied out Japanese military movements and attempted to sabotage their activities. Taking these various circumstances into consideration, our Government wisely decided not to treat Thailand as an enemy country upon the conclusion of the war. That decision restored the links, broken temporarily, in the chain of friendly relations, dating back to 1833.

After discussing arrangements for the presentation of my credentials to the Prince Regent who was acting on behalf of young King Phumiphon Adulyadej until his coronation, I expressed deep sympathy over the tragic death of the latter's brother, King Ananda. I gained the impression that the Foreign Minister not only mourned his young Monarch's death but that he was greatly troubled by its political implications.

After we left the Ministry we drove past a great walled enclosure, many city blocks in length, which glittered and sparkled in the bright sunshine. The gracefully tapering roofs of the buildings within rose one upon the other to form a pyramid of bright color in yellow and green, the ends of the roof lines melting into slender ornaments that curved up into the blue sky. These were the royal palaces and the royal chapels, the most famous of which was the Temple of the Emerald Buddha. Equally fascinating were the bell-shaped structures covered with gold leaf and dominated by highly ornamentated spires that looked as though they had been sprinkled with every imaginable jewel.

That afternoon the Yosts took us to call on Her Highness, Princess Poon Diskul, one of the daughters of Prince Damrong, who was renowned and respected throughout the country for his intellectual attainments, his statesmanship, his administrative ability and, above all, for his kindly interest in the welfare of the people. He had died during the war, mourned by the nation and especially by his daughters who had lived their lives in him. The diminutive princess, who spoke good English, talked vivaciously, chiefly about her father and the library which she was arranging as a memorial to him and for the use of the public.

During the night the most violent cramps seized me. Josie was awakened by a loud crash and, rushing into the bathroom, found me lying face downward on the floor in a pool of blood with a large gash on my forehead. She called for the Yosts, who helped her drag me onto the bed and sent the car to fetch the doctor. Dr. Waddell of the Seventh Day Adventist Hospital came and stitched up my head and diagnosed my condition as acute bacillary dysentery with possible concussion of the brain.

I felt foolish and frustrated to be laid low at the very outset of my assignment to Thailand. Dr. Cort of the Presbyterian mission, who had come down from the city of Chiengmai at the request of the Thai Government to serve as one of the foreign doctors on the Commission of Inquiry set up to determine the cause of King Ananda's death, was also consulted by Dr. Waddell. There must be an x-ray picture taken they decided. The only portable x-ray machine in town was with the Indian medical unit attached to the contingent of British troops, which had been sent into Thailand on V-J Day. Although the medical unit was leaving the next day, the Indian doctor in charge kindly agreed to bring his machine to the Legation that night. On a teakwood bed, which weighed ten times the ordinary bed, I was carried downstairs by a dozen men and deposited in the middle of one of our offices. The doctor took his pictures and developed them at once. The conclusion, "No concussion," was cheering. I was stuffed with sulfa drugs and carried, less carefully this time, back to my bedroom.

As I lay for a few days while my head mended, my thoughts

kept returning to the death of King Ananda and its significance in the developing political situation, as well as its impact upon the people. Hazily I recalled bits of Thai history which I had been reading.

My thoughts drifted back to the ancient Thai kingdom of Nanchao, which flourished during the early Christian era in the southern provinces of China and was divided into six well-organized principalities. According to Chinese historical records of the seventh to the tenth centuries, these independent people defended themselves fiercely against many expeditions sent against them by the Chinese Emperors in an effort to subjugate their proud, free spirit. Valuing their freedom, they began to move into northern Burma, Thailand and Indochina during the eleventh and twelfth centuries and, when the golden hordes of Kublai Khan swept into southern China in the middle of the thirteenth century, a great exodus of Thai took place from their ancestral homes located in what is known today as the province of Yunnan in south China.

Kingdoms were founded in northern Thailand. The greatest of these was the kingdom of Sukhothai, which in the latter half of the thirteenth century flourished under King Rama Kamheng, who is greatly revered among the Thai people today because of his prowess as a warrior, his wisdom, his benevolence and his solicitude for the people. To him is attributed the invention of an alphabet for the Thai language. His was the inspiration for the casting of many of the finest statues of the Lord Buddha, his the inspiration for the encouragement of artistic handicrafts, and his the inspiration for the maxims and sayings which every schoolboy in Thailand repeats by heart today. He was just to his people, who might summon him at any time, day or night, by striking the great bell he had caused to be hung in front of his palace gate.

In central Thailand an even greater kingdom arose, which in time conquered the northern kingdom. Its capital was built on an island formed by the confluence of two tributaries with the Chao Phya River. It was called Ayuthia and lies forty-five miles north of Bangkok. Early Dutch, Portuguese and French merchants, missionaries and envoys who visited the capital city of Ayuthia in the sixteenth and seventeenth centuries describe its straight streets, great markets and many beautiful gilded temples.

Here at this capital of a great kingdom, which comprised all of modern Thailand and stretched into Cambodia, Laos and Malaya, the arts flourished and Thai culture and civilization reached their zenith. But it was not a period of tranquil, unbroken peace. The expansion and consolidation of the Kingdom meant almost constant warfare. The Khmers or Cambodians were driven from the central regions back to Cambodia and at last vanquished at their capital city, Angor Thom with its world-famous temple of Angkor Wat. With the Burmese to the west battles raged constantly. Many expeditions were sent by the kings and princes of Burma against the Thai. Sometimes they sought merely to seize a white elephant thought to possess miraculous powers and sometimes to destroy rising Thai power and splendor. In 1767, Ayuthia, the beautiful Thai capital, fell after a long siege to powerful Burmese armies. The city was sacked and destroyed, the Thai King captured, the people scattered or made captive.

Nevertheless, the Thai spirit of freedom survived even this mortal blow and within fifteen years the Burmese legions had been driven from the country by King Taksin, and a new dynasty of Chakri kings under King Rama I commenced a long and notable rule from Bangkok. Such illustrious rulers as King Mongkut and his son King Chulalongkorn opened Thailand during the nineteenth century to Western technology and influences. But even more important, they devoted themselves to the welfare of their people. King Mongkut daily received the petitions of his subjects and advised them on innumerable matters from the manipulation of window wedges to the inelegant practice of throwing dead animals into the waterways. His son, King Chulalongkorn, who succeeded to the throne upon his father's death in 1868, is venerated as the Abraham Lincoln of Thailand, because he abolished slavery, remodeled the courts of justice and the whole system of governmental administration along Western lines, improved education and constructed railways and irrigation works.

As I lay on my cot trying to forget the throbbing pain from the cut in my head, I thought of the enlightened and progressive rule the Thai had enjoyed under recent monarchs and of the urge to substitute a Western democratic system of government arising from new ideas absorbed by Thai young men, studying abroad. They had heard much about liberty, equality, fraternity and representative forms of government adopted by Western nations. Their imaginations had been fired and two young men studying in Paris, Pridi Phanomyong and Pibul Songgram, joined a group of likeminded Thai who carried out a bloodless revolution on June 24, 1932, ushering in the present era of constitutional government.

The gash in the head mended rapidly and I was able to present my credentials on the Fourth of July, 1946, as planned, although I looked anything but a distinguished diplomat with a bandage around my head. The Brahman astrologers attached to the Royal Court, who always determine auspicious dates and times at which to receive foreign envoys, had selected this date. It seemed a happy augury for future relations between the United States and Thailand.

Since full dress was prescribed for this formal ceremony, which was to take place in the throne room of the Grand Palace, my staff and I attired ourselves in white tie, stiff shirts and collars and full evening regalia. We all looked a trifle ridiculous, dressed in this headwaiter's garb in the middle of a hot morning.

We were ready and mustered at the Legation at the appointed time. The royal cars, which were to convey us to the Palace, drew up; two cars out of a storybook. They were Daimlers of bygone days, painted a bright royal red, with chauffeurs and footmen in white and blue uniforms. I climbed in, taking care not to mar the well-brushed look of my top hat.

Our cavalcade entered the courtyard of the royal palace, a handsome towering building with yellow tiled roofs but westernized marble façade. The palace was surrounded by buildings of lesser size but striking in the grace and brilliancy of their Thai design and ornamentation. Tamarind trees and a variety of shrubs, meticulously trimmed and cut into fantastic shapes, adorned the paved courtyard. In front of the marble stairway leading up to the palace stood a guard of honor in bright red uniforms and white helmets, which one of the Thai kings had had copied from the dress uniform of a famous British regiment.

The chief of protocol met me and escorted us into a handsome marble reception room where hung portraits of the kings and queens of the Chakri dynasty. I was introduced to the Grand Marshal of the Royal Court, a dignified old gentleman, covered with the most magnificent array of decorations and sashes I had ever seen. He spoke good English and explained in detail exactly where Prince Jainad, the Regent, acting on behalf of young King Phumiphon, who was not of age, would be standing in the Throne Room, where I was to stand, where the staff was to stand, how many paces we should take before each bow, and many other details, for these matters of protocol were of the utmost importance to the Thai.

Before the immense and richly decorated doors of the Throne Room, my staff and I took up our positions. The Grand Marshal gave three taps on the floor with his long jeweled baton. The great doors slowly opened and we found ourselves looking into a magnificent room, richly gilded and decorated. At the far end was the King's throne on a dais with the seven-tiered umbrellas behind, the number of umbrellas signifying his royal rank. In front of the throne stood the Regent, bedecked with medals. On his right was a line of court officials, on his left the Minister of Foreign Affairs and officials of the government.

Dressed in our somber black, we advanced the prescribed number of paces into the room. I stepped forward, while the Regent looked at me in friendly fashion, and made a short speech, recalling the close and friendly ties that had existed for over a hundred years between the United States and Thailand and conveying the President's personal greetings and good wishes to King Phumiphon, as well as his deep sympathy over the death of King Ananda.

The Regent accepted the Letter of Credence from the President and placed it on a golden tray shaped like a lotus leaf, which was held by a court official standing near him. In reply the Regent stated that Thailand would never forget the understanding with which the United States treated her during the war and recalled how much Americans, missionaries and others, had done for his country.

At the conclusion of the Regent's speech, I was introduced to him and we conversed in English. I found him wise and friendly, an estimate confirmed by our close association during the years that followed. When I had presented my staff, we retired, walking backward and bowing to the Regent and the throne, in accordance with the procedure laid down by the Grand Marshal. A memorable occasion and a colorful and impressive ceremony. I felt the Thai were right to retain the trappings of royalty and a meticulous protocol because these tended to preserve respect for the King and established authority.

That afternoon we held a reception for the American community by way of celebrating the Fourth, although we were ill equipped to serve some seventy persons who were expected. The community was not large, consisting of members of the Presbyterian and Seventh Day Adventist missions, members of the YMCA and a handful of businessmen. There was a mighty scurrying on all sides and the belongings of others were borrowed right and left. The Ursuline nuns provided four china teapots. Two ladies poured while the servants continually filled and refilled the small china pots. It looked like a chain gang.

Josie was preoccupied with problems of the household and of the domestic staff. The Yosts had done the best they could to gather together household supplies of linen, glass, crockery and cutlery. A few coarse bed sheets had come from confiscated Japanese supplies, stiff khaki bath towels had been donated by British troops, while the cutlery and most of the china were unmistakably United States Navy issue. However, Josie was proud of the dozen or so gold banded plates with the Department of State seal in gold, which had been buried in the garden by Babu, the Legation's loyal Indian watchman during the war. Until our own boxes arrived, a year later, these gold-banded plates helped Josie to keep her head high.

Ah Ngee, a tall lanky Swatow Chinese of middle age, was the Legation's major domo, housekeeper, butler or number one boy. I had noticed with amusement that he and Josie had eyed each other with speculative curiosity upon their first meeting, aware that they were to be partners in much activity, and perhaps a bit apprehensive of one another. The Yosts had told us that Ah Ngee was a superlative servant who had worked at the Legation for some twenty years. My wife preferred to reserve judgment for she had observed that Ah Ngee ran the household with a heavy hand, submitted gigantic food bills for meals indifferently cooked and ordered authoritatively from the stores without consulting her.

She had a talk with him. "Cook must go," she told him. "He make bad food and take plentee money. Find me good new cook."

Ah Ngee had replied, "Madam likes I can go too?" "No, I need you very much help me run the house." This established her as the commander in chief of household affairs.

All of Bangkok was closely following events connected with the death of King Ananda. I was told privately that the Special Commission of Inquiry, on the basis of investigations made up to that time, was inclined to believe that the King's death was not the result of an accident. This left only two possibilities: either that it was a case of suicide or that he had been murdered. Later, the majority of the members of the commission came to the conclusion that the King had not committed suicide. The ugly suspicion of regicide gained new adherents and hung like a heavy shadow over the city, while whispers that the Government was doing nothing because some of its members were implicated spread in the market places.

The young King and his mother were leaving Bangkok to return to Switzerland, where he would continue his studies. I requested a private audience with His Majesty so that my wife and I might informally pay our respects to him and his mother. This was granted. We were met at the Grand Palace by several officials of the King's household, walked through large reception rooms ornately furnished with Louis XV furniture, and then into a smaller sitting room. Making conversation with the King's aide while we waited was difficult because we were both oppressed by the deathly stillness, which drew one's thoughts to the picture of a young King stretched on his bed in one of the rooms of the Palace, with a bullet wound in his head.

"His Majesty will receive you," said the aide. We mounted a long marble stairway and were ushered into a gloomy sitting room. His Majesty, a slight boyish figure with dark, intelligent eyes, stood in the center of the room. Behind him was his mother. Josie made a curtsy and I bowed. The aide introduced us and then withdrew. The four of us sat stiffly. We said nothing because court etiquette prescribes that one may not speak until spoken to by a King or Queen.

The young King's face was drawn. There was a sad droop around the corners of his mouth. His mother looked at us with tragic eyes. Her fine features were lined with fatigue and harrowing memories.

The silence grew so oppressive that at last I ventured to say a few words of sympathy. His Majesty merely replied in a low voice, "Thank you." His mother began to talk with Josie, speaking with evident pleasure of her life in the United States where, as a young student nurse, she had met and later married Prince Mahidol. Looking fondly at her son, she said, "The King was born in your country." I commenced talking about photography, which I had been told was one of the King's hobbies. He replied to my questions with animation and his face lighted up. But one could not escape the feeling that both he and his mother had a dread and fear of those ornate palace rooms. They have never lived in them since.

16

Protocol and Politics

NAI PRIDI PHANOMYONG, the Prime Minister of Thailand in 1946, was one of a small group of Thai leaders who, as students, had gone to France. In the course of his studies he sampled a number of isms, including socialism. Being an idealistic young man, he was eager to bring the blessings and benefits of these new Western doctrines to the people of his country and to introduce various reforms. He felt that the absolute monarchy, which had been a feature of Thai rule for many centuries, must be replaced by a more representative type of government. Upon returning to his country he joined the revolutionaries who carried out a bloodless *coup d'état* in Bangkok and proclaimed the establishment of a constitutional monarchy. Nai Pridi, Colonel Phibul Songgram and many other members of the revolutionary group, were included in the government.

His advanced socialistic ideas alarmed many of his colleagues, who feared they verged on Communism. The matter reached a point where a special commission was appointed, headed by a well-known British jurist, to examine the writings and theories of Nai Pridi. He denied that either were in any way communistic and in this contention was upheld by the commission. Nevertheless, he left the country and remained away for a year. Upon his return he was accepted back into the fold and from then on until the outbreak of World War II he held numerous cabinet posts.

During the war, he was appointed Regent to the Government, headed by the present Prime Minister, Phibul Songgram. At the same time, under the pseudonym of "Ruth," he became head of an underground resistance movement, known as the "Free Thai," which greatly assisted the United States and our British allies. At the end of the war, Nai Pridi emerged as Thailand's leading statesman and a powerful political figure backed by the Free Thai, which by then was not only a fairly well-equipped paramilitary force but also a political group devoted to their leader. Phibul was ousted as head of the Government and went into temporary political retirement.

Prime Minister Pridi received me at his combined office and residence, which was pleasantly located on the banks of the Chao Phya River. A stocky man with a crew haircut appeared after a few minutes' wait. As we shook hands he smiled faintly and gave me a searching look. After expressing our Government's appreciation for the assistance rendered by the Free Thai during the war, I touched on the credit of $10,000,000 which the United States Government had extended to assist in the rehabilitation of Thailand. At this point Pridi opened up with great animation about his plans not only to expand the country's economy but to improve the welfare and livelihood of the people. As I came to know him better I found these were subjects on which he liked to dwell.

To my surprise he himself brought up the death of King Ananda, perhaps to impress upon me the fact that his Government was doing everything possible to determine the cause of the King's death. He also recalled that he had been responsible, as leader of the Government at the time of this tragic event, for inviting the late King's brother to ascend the throne, in accordance with the Constitution. Perhaps he deliberately recalled this information as proof that he had nothing against the Royal Family, in spite of the ugly rumors circulating to the contrary. I wondered.

Nai Direk, the Foreign Minister with whom I had already established friendly relations, made it plain to me, in polite diplomatic language, that the Thai were not happy over the prospect of returning to the French a slice of territory in Cambodia which Thailand, in 1895, had been forced to cede to the French, and which during the war Thailand had reoccupied with Japan's blessing. "We regard these as our lost territories," he said.

It was a delicate matter we were discussing, involving Thai prestige and nationalism and I could well understand their sentiments. Nevertheless, in the interest of peace and harmony in Southeast Asia, it seemed politic that Thailand's frontiers should revert to their prewar status, the more so since she had allied herself with Japan and had been induced by them to declare war upon the British and ourselves. The Thai Government had already returned such small enclaves of Burmese territory as they had occupied during the war and had agreed in principle to return to the French the territory in Indochina which they had seized. Furthermore, if someday Cambodia became sovereign and independent, as is now the case, it was certain that the Cambodians would clamor for the return of this territory, which, up to the fifteenth century when the Thai conquered it, had been Cambodian and the majority of whose inhabitants are Cambodian. Nai Direk was also aware that, since this issue had been raised in the United Nations, failure to reach agreement with the French would probably result in France opposing Thailand's entry into that organization.

"And what about exports of rice, Excellency?" I said. Because of our Government's deep concern over the serious food shortages which existed in the countries of South and Southeast Asia, the Philippines and China, we had become signatory to a tripartite rice agreement with the Governments of Thailand and Great Britain. In pursuance of this agreement, a Rice Commission had been established at Bangkok whose duty it was to arrange shipping schedules in accordance with the allocations established by the International Emergency Food Commission set up by the Allied Powers at the end of the war to cope with world food shortages.

"Exports have been very disappointing. Cannot your Government make more rice available?" I pressed. He skillfully countered by emphasizing the difficulties experienced by the Government due to lack of rolling stock, much of which had been destroyed during the war by Allied bombing. "We are making every effort," he said with a smile as he exhaled a cloud of cigarette smoke. He was an inveterate smoker in those days.

I left him feeling we knew one another a good deal better and I had had my first experience of the skill and tact of Thai diplomats. I must say, I became increasingly impressed by their never-failing politeness and rare tact, even when the disagreeable subjects came up for discussion or negotiation. They have perfected the art of polite verbal acquiescence, but this is not necessarily followed by action if the matter is deemed not to be in their national interest.

On my way to lunch I stopped in at the office to see if any telegrams had come in. There were several, including one announcing the arrival the next day of a considerable delegation of bigwigs. We had scarcely recovered from the financial strain of providing for the Fourth of July reception out of our own pockets. However, in view of the instructions from Washington concerning the special treatment to be accorded the delegation, it was obvious that parties would have to be arranged to introduce these notables to the Thai officials.

Josie began to figure. Imported foodstuffs, such as butter, sugar, coffee, flour and canned goods were not only ten times as expensive as at home, but they were hard to find. Plans to entertain the visitors were mapped out but not before my wife had explained her worries and woes to M. L. Pikthip, the friendly protocol official who had first met us at the airport. He suggested that if we would give one party, the Foreign Office would entertain the following evening and furthermore that we could borrow all necessary crockery and utensils from them. This was surely extending the hand of friendship in a practical way.

We managed to lay on a buffet supper for about a hundred persons, including many Thai officials and important personages whom we had not met and whose names, ranks and positions kept eluding us at crucial moments when a member of the visiting American group wished to be introduced to one of our Thai guests. Our first effort at entertaining Thai and Americans—there were to be hundreds of them in a steady procession in the years to come—went off fairly well, but we were woefully out of pocket, since the entertaining allowance we received was not nearly sufficient for even one large party. By contrast, the dinner which the Foreign Minister gave the next day was a most lavish affair with both Western and Thai food, good music and an interesting exhibition of Thai classical dancing. It might just be noted that the United States Government's representative was never able to match the entertainment offered by the Thai Government or the British or Chinese Legations. In a rather forlorn way Josie begged some of our distinguished visitors to arrange to send her some canned goods and other much-needed supplies. As I remember, promises were given but I do not recollect that we ever received as much as a can of baked beans.

The Chinese Minister, Li Teh-chen, a huge man, and the first envoy to have been appointed from China in over five hundred years, was telling me in Chinese about the involved state of Chinese-

Thai relations. He explained, at times rather disconsolately, the ups and downs of his negotiations with the Thai Government concerning the burning issue of immigration from mainland China to Thailand. As conditions deteriorated in China, the number of Chinese immigrants rose to a flood tide of a hundred thousand a year. In 1946 Chinese residents numbered nearly three million and controlled much of Thailand's wealth.

The Thai had been following a policy designed to assimilate the Chinese and, to a considerable degree, had succeeded through intermarriage, nationality laws and in other ways. However, recent Chinese immigrants had displayed a disinclination to become naturalized and assimilated. They wished to remain Chinese and wanted their own schools and curriculums. The Thai were becoming alarmed over the influx of the Chinese, their opposition to assimilation and most of all over the Chinese grip on Thailand's trade and commerce, which in times past they had been only too happy to leave in their hands. There is no doubt that the country has benefited by the settlement during the past two hundred years of Chinese immigrants who by their industry and flair for business have contributed to Thailand's prosperity. But serious problems have arisen between this powerful minority group and the Thai. They still exist and have been made more acute by present Thai realization that the small, hard core of the Communist organization in their country is Chinese, the remainder being "fence sitters" with a sprinkling of loyal supporters of Generalissimo Chiang Kai-shek. Many Thai wonder what the majority of Chinese residents will do when that awful day comes and the Communists attempt to seize control of the country.

During my many comings and goings in and out of the Legation I could not help noticing that Babu, our Indian watchman, was not a happy man. I asked Chin, the driver, what the trouble could be. He translated, with Babu interjecting remarks in his broken

Thai. No proper watchman, it was explained, could be expected to officiate without a proper turban. In fact, even with such a turban an Indian watchman is only half a watchman unless he has a full and complete uniform. Babu went on to describe the splendid uniforms supplied him by other Ministers: the broad red sash across his chest and round the waist, a white drill coat with brass buttons, elegant white shoes. It was not for himself that he asked for a turban and uniform but only because of his official position.

When Josie looked into the matter she discovered that two white turbans would cost thirty dollars. This did not include the uniform, as well as uniforms for messengers and servants, all of whom were clamoring for them. Washington was completely indifferent to this problem. However, in Oriental countries the question of suitable uniforms for the staff is important because local people judge a country by just such externals. There was nothing for it but to find the money ourselves and order several bolts of material from India.

No man in the city of Bangkok could have looked more proud than dear old Babu in his turban and new uniform. And he deserved them, for at about this time we heard the story of Babu's heroism at the beginning of the war.

When the Japanese occupied the city early in December, 1941, all Americans were locked up in the Legation compound until their repatriation was arranged on the S.S. *Gripsholm* eight months later. From one of our missionaries on the spot at the time, we heard the story of the Japanese breaking into the Legation grounds and ordering Babu to haul down the American flag, which was flying from the tall white pole near the gates. In spite of menacing bayonets and rough words, Babu shook his head and stoutly refused. The soldiers converged on the flagpole and hauled down the flag. Just before it touched the earth, Babu stepped forward, gathered it into his arms, untied it from the halyard, much to the astonishment of the soldiers, turned right about face with the flag clasped to his chest and marched back to the Legation building. After the Americans were repatriated, Babu remained on the premises tending a herd of water buffalo to keep himself alive and the grass clipped, and watched over the flag and the gold-banded dinner plates buried in the garden. It was this same flag which was first flown when the Legation's gates were flung open onto a free Thailand.

This account of simple devotion and bravery so impressed me that I reported it to Washington with the request that Babu be granted a suitable decoration for his loyal act. After many months, a Medal of Freedom arrived, complete with citation, ribbon and button. Babu, who was completely overcome by the importance of the occasion, invited many of his friends to be present at the ceremony. They were for the most part Indian watchmen, their wives and children. All were dressed in their best, especially the little girls in starched and frilly dresses.

As I read the citation to Babu and it was translated to him, he stood stiffly at attention, his face solemn, every muscle rigid, but a few tears dripped down his weatherbeaten, kindly face and splashed onto his beard.

An indispensable part of diplomatic life is formal calls which make possible those personal contacts necessary to the successful conduct of a government's foreign relations.

Together, we paid our respects to the Prince Regent and his Princess, a motherly German lady whom his Royal Highness in his student days had met, so the story goes, at a ball in Germany where he was attending a military academy. It was love at first sight. The Prince was informal, very friendly and took evident pleasure in showing us around his residence, a veritable museum of fine gold lacquer cabinets, rare religious and historic Thai paintings and other works of Thai art. Later, we discovered it was most difficult to purchase such treasures because the Thai do not like to sell their belongings. We became well acquainted with the Prince and his family and formed a high regard for his intellectual attainments and the devotion with which he served the young King.

The wives of the cabinet ministers on whom Josie called were all so genuinely friendly that she felt the pall of gloom, which invariably settled over her every time she returned to the dreary Legation quarters, slowly lifting. She was captivated by the quiet grace and winsome charm of the ladies. The attractive, smiling expression of the people, their politeness and good manners and their joyousness are irresistible characteristics which extend even to the poor. By contrast, poverty and economic distress oppress the great mass of the Indian people to a point where they seldom seem to smile but look upon life as a sour, burdensome fate. The millions of Chinese too are so bowed down by the grinding effort to survive they have little time for fun. For the Thai, *sanuk* or fun is an essential ingredient of living. It is a joyousness in life and the art of living that I have rarely seen equaled. Both my wife and I were much impressed by their innate good manners. Even among the country people, one remarked it. They were curious, but not to the point of closing in on one, gaping and fingering as would a Chinese group. Their poise and lack of self-consciousness astounded us. At so many functions children would appear before an audience of notables and act, sing or dance without the slightest trace of self-consciousness. "Wish I was as easy in public," I would whisper to my wife. At many a dinner party I had partners to right and left to whom I could not speak since few of the officials' wives spoke English. Nevertheless, they were not in the least embarrassed and resorted to the nod, the smile or the giggle to convey their friendly sentiments.

We decided that we simply must take up the study of Thai. To obtain a smattering of the language is easy, but we found that more time than we could give would be required to acquire a really good knowledge of the language. Like Chinese it is a tonal language, but the faint resemblance to Chinese tones, over which we had labored many years, was just enough to make spoken Thai confusing. However, the smattering which we did pick up was most valuable to us. The Thai are particularly appreciative of any effort made by the foreigner to speak even a few words of their language and were greatly pleased when we stammered out a few sentences from time to time.

Calling on Thai officials in order to get to know them I found thoroughly enjoyable. Nevertheless, it was time consuming and work at the Legation piled up and we were woefully shorthanded. I found myself lending a hand at everything: coding and decoding telegrams, going over accounts and administrative matters, trying desperately to get the office organized and functioning smoothly. The staff was very willing and constantly overworked but we were frustrated over our inability to prepare the more detailed political and economic reports which the rapidly developing situation warranted.

Shortage of staff was not the only office problem that beset me. The local Thai staff of the Legation complained, with justification, of their acute difficulties in meeting the high cost of living owing to an adverse rate of exchange for the dollar. I did my best for them, laying the problem before Washington. However, I marveled, as I have many times in the past, at the loyalty and devotion of locally employed help of the United States Government, who work faithfully for pittances.

We thought all our troubles would be solved when a State Department inspector arrived. Expectations were high but unfortunately not realized.

One unhappy result was the inspector's decision that Ah Ngee, our indispensable household factotum, who also acted as office messenger, could no longer be carried on the Government's payroll because of some obscure technicality. Ah Ngee was inconsolable when he heard the bad news. He felt he had been fired and could not understand why his long and faithful service was so ill appreciated, although we endeavored to explain the inspector's ruling and assured him he would be better off financially paid by us. However, he always felt he had been shabbily treated by the United States Government. Unfortunately, his was not the only case and office morale sank to a new low since all of us were affected by double trouble in the form of an adverse exchange rate and the rising cost of living. Such troubles seem to beset a Foreign Service Officer continually.

Before she knew it Josie found herself committed to serve on various committees, all of them worthy, organized to launch and carry on charitable works. Her first American caller was Miss Genevieve Caulfield, a blind American who had taught English in Japanese schools for many years. In 1938, this valiant soul arrived in Bangkok from Japan at the request of officials of the Thai Government to organize work for the blind in their country. However, upon her arrival she found little interest and no facilities. The greatest difficulty arose from the attitude of the Thai toward the handicapped in general.

Like the Hindus, the Thai believe that blindness or other handicaps are the result of a person's Karma, the reaping of one's own acts, whether good or bad, in a previous incarnation. Therefore, many of them felt that the blind had better be left alone, kindly treated but ignored as far as education is concerned. It is not that they are unkind; merely that fate having decreed blindness, it is better not to meddle. Under these disadvantages and without money or backing, Miss Caulfield set about her work; undismayed and refusing to be discouraged. She gathered together a small group of Thai and foreigners who worked to better the lives of the blind in

Thailand. The war interfered, but because of her blindness and her knowledge of the Japanese language, the Japanese military allowed her to remain behind when the other Americans evacuated the country, and to remove her small group of blind students to the seaside to escape the terrifying bombings.

"I expect you, Mrs. Stanton, to give us your full support," she said. "Come to the next meeting of the committee and I will explain what you are to do." The challenge appealed to Josie, who plunged into the work and eventually became vice-president of the board. Today the school for the blind is flourishing.

"We want to organize a YWCA here," Mrs. Eaking of the Presbyterian Mission announced. "Will you help us?" Another challenge. The establishment of a women's group, which would enable Thai women, especially that group of Eurasians who found it difficult to enter the usual social levels, to meet, mingle, learn languages, handicrafts, cooking and other useful activities, was urgently needed. The problem was how to present a plan, essentially Christian, to a devoutly Buddhist group, with no interest in the religious objectives of the Young Women's Christian Association. After much discussion a compromise was worked out and the Thai ladies whom Josie invited to tea were immediately interested. The work developed and expanded, growing into an influential force for good in the community.

For Josie it was a pleasure to work with the Thai in these activities because it gave her an opportunity to become intimately acquainted with them and to form close, personal friendships.

17

A Python in the Garden

No COMFORT, no privacy," my wife moaned, referring to our living quarters. She was right. Not a single door shut off our own rooms from the offices below, with the result that people were constantly bursting in upon us without warning. Nor could we enjoy the evening's coolness in the garden, where we had all the seclusion of an aquarium. Even at night there was no guarantee of privacy as diplomatic couriers locked their precious diplomatic pouches in the office safe downstairs and then got me out of bed long before dawn to unlock the safe for them before they flew out of town. Only a well-worn, thoroughly indoctrinated, persistently patient career diplomat could have tolerated such conditions.

After a lengthy exchange with the Department we received authorization to rent a "suitable residence," and turn our own quarters into badly needed office space. Josie went happily on the prowl in search of an adequate house. The possibilities were not numerous as most of the larger residences were in a state of utter dilapidation; none of them had been painted since before the

war, gardens had returned to jungle, gates and fences sagged
drearily. It was evident that the occupation forces, both during and
after the war, had had little regard for the property of others.

My wife found an attractive house set in a large garden but
it was snatched from under her eyes by a businessman who offered
a higher rent. She found another, a handsome stone mansion,
but at the last moment the Chinese Military Attaché offered a
higher rent. Landlords simply would not believe that the great
American Government was not willing to pay any fancy rental they
might choose to ask.

One day we were driven to the residence of the Prince Regent
along a bumpy dirt side street. The road was called Witayu, or
Wireless Road, because of the location of a naval wireless station
at one end of it. During the rainy season the road became a muddy
mess and was almost impassable. But there, set far back, with an
avenue of magnificent dark spreading rain trees leading to it,
we saw a sprawling sagging house, painted chocolate brown,
shutters hanging precariously; indeed, the whole house listed
to one side. The extensive garden surrounding the house was
crammed with rusted war junk, remnants of jeeps, trucks, gun
carriages and tanks left there by Japanese troops. The property was
encircled by a wide canal containing more rusted junk, which
jutted out of the water at grotesque angles.

Nevertheless, the possibilities of the place kindled Josie's imagina-
tion. She found it in shocking disrepair. The Japanese troops had
burned spots on the teakwood floors with their charcoal braziers,
the plumbing had been wantonly smashed and ripped out; not
one inch of electric wiring remained. The fine tile floor of the
enormous porch or patio was indelibly stained by motor oil
drippings.

Chin, who always knew everything, told her that the property
belonged to the Ministry of Foreign Affairs. He told me privately

that it was utterly unsuitable for us. After looking it over, I agreed with our driver. "Besides," I pointed out to my wife, "who do you think is going to pay for the thousand and one renovations? Washington most certainly will not."

But I did not reckon with the ingenuity of a woman who has made up her mind. "Leave it to me," she said.

She telephoned Nai Direk and asked if the Foreign Office would undertake the necessary repairs if the United States Government were to rent the place. Taken aback, he agreed. An army of workmen was set to the task of cleaning and renovating, a stupendous job that took months, complicated by the lack of materials in postwar Bangkok. Paints, plumbing fixtures, wiring of all kinds, fans, hardware, almost everything needed had to be located after lengthy search in secondhand shops or in the "Thieves Market," and all of it was of inferior quality.

In a store in the famous Thieves Market, we met, in the course of seeking for equipment, a family of Thai brothers born of Chinese parents. Over the years they became helpful friends and from them I learned much about the political sentiments of the Chinese in Bangkok. Their shop was a tiny dark hole in the wall cluttered with a weird assortment of junk. A pink advertising card in Thai and English read:

> Dealing Hardware, Mechanical Tools, Timberjacks, Funnel irons. Ships and Boats Appliances. Agent for famous instruments Samson, Hercules and Stock. Barbells, Dumbells, Swing bells and Cattle hells, etc. etc.

Innumerable times we sat in the little shop, sipping iced coffee that was nauseatingly sweet, and discussing many things, greeting the babies who arrived annually. The eldest son with a robust mother, a frail wife and seven skinny children lived in two tiny, dark, damp rooms, without ventilation or sanitation. At times the "boys" visited us, usually at New Year's, and always uncomfortably dressed up. Before we left Thailand they took a highly colored photograph of us all together, enlarged it to gigantic size, and hung it conspicuously in their shop.

With dramatic suddenness it was announced early in August that Prime Minister Pridi was resigning and would make a good-will trip around the world in the capacity of Thailand's senior statesman. I was not entirely surprised, because ten days previously when I had seen Prime Minister Pridi he had appeared obviously troubled. Public suspicions regarding the cause of the King's death had mushroomed into the most sensational rumors and had grown into the settled belief that King Ananda had been assassinated. My mind focused on what Pridi had said to me when I saw him last: "It is terrible to have people always whispering against me. I am very tired." He looked tired and now he was leaving the country. Would his dramatic action still the rumors I wondered? Why had it not been possible for the Government to get to the bottom of the affair? Six months later three members of the Royal Household were brought to court charged with complicity in the King's death. The case dragged on for years, finally ending in a verdict of "guilty" against the accused. The fact that the whole country followed the trial with solemn intensity and that the circumstantial evidence presented tended to link Pridi and one of his aides with the regicide has caused serious political repercussions in Thailand.

One hot afternoon when I went to see the Foreign Minister he appeared visibly upset. After discussing some of the problems which were on my mind, he spoke of Thailand's desire to be admitted into the United Nations and of his Government's efforts to ensure that there would be no obstacle to admission. Now a cloud had appeared. The attitude of the Soviet Government was not friendly because of an anti-Communist law which had been in effect in Thailand since 1933. He was afraid the Soviets would veto Thailand's application for admission unless this law was rescinded. This, he told me, was the price they would have to pay but he was not sure whether their Parliament would agree. It was a genuine dilemma, but later Parliament agreed to rescind the law and Thailand was admitted to the United Nations. This was the country's first taste of Communist pressure and has not been forgotten.

When I left the Foreign Office I bumped along Wireless Road and into the driveway of our home-to-be. There I found my wife sitting cross-legged on the tiled patio, surrounded by Chinese painters. All were intent upon a bucket of paint into which various colors were being poured and stirred. I dragged her away as we had several engagements. While dressing for dinner and struggling with my tie in a heat that turned everything limp, my mind kept reverting to office problems, but I knew Josie's thoughts still centered around the house and the paint pot. I was not surprised when she said, "But didn't Nai Direk say anything to you about plumbing fixtures for the house?" "No, I don't think so" was my reply, which she regarded as highly unsatisfactory. But I was as keen as she was to get out of the uncomfortable quarters in which we were living and which were badly needed as offices. "When can we move?" "Oh, as soon as I get that Williamsburg blue just right," she replied.

The Diplomatic Corps was invited to attend the "Hundred Day Rites" of the Lying in State of the late King Ananda to be held in the magnificent Royal Chapel. The Protocol Division decreed "full dress mourning" must be worn, the ladies to be attired in long black gowns, the men in uniforms or white tie and tails with black armbands. We carried handsome floral wreaths which were laid, immediately upon entering the chapel, before the altar, with its many gilded tiers, high upon which rested the great golden and diamond-encrusted urn containing the remains of the late King. The chapel is a lovely hall, the lofty ceilings being decorated with fine gold and red designs. Colorful frescoes adorn its walls. With bow and curtsy we laid the flowers. The Thai knelt low, heads bowed, the palms of their hands joined together in respectful obeisance. This deep genuflection is executed with the utmost grace.

Seated strictly according to rank and protocol, we rose when the Prince Regent entered. He commenced the rites by lighting candles surrounding the golden urn until it was suffused with a soft golden glow. Our thoughts fixed upon the young King stricken down so mysteriously.

Although the atmosphere remained solemn through the several hours of ceremony, there was an easiness in the midst of the formality. One could whisper, smoke or sip tea from a table within reach.

The priests sitting cross-legged on a platform along the wall of one wing of the chapel intoned the Buddhist scriptures, their eyes closed, their hands clasped, lost to the world it seemed. At suitable moments the Thai congregation responded to the prayers. The soporific melodious chanting, beautiful, impressive in its hidden meaning, carried one away. One found oneself mesmerized, swaying to the sound, at peace. It was dreadfully hot, one became soaking wet and yet the beauty of the moment made one forget the heat.

The frail and aged Prince Patriarch, Chief Priest of the Buddhists, now slowly ascended to a gilded and railed platform high above us. Sitting cross-legged, holding long thin sheets of palmleaf parchment, he read a eulogy to King Ananda. Though Chief Priest, he too was dressed in simple yellow robe, barefooted, one shoulder bare.

The Prince Regent laid folded packets of yellow cloth before each priest. While a broad brocade ribbon was laid under these gifts and attached to the urn, the monks recited verses calling down blessings upon the deceased Monarch. Buddhists believe that blessings are transmitted to the dead through the consecrated ribbon.

The rites were concluded with more bows before the urn. We left the chapel feeling as we always did during the many ceremonies we were to attend in the years ahead of us, both stirred and much impressed by the Thai, who conduct their services with such poise and perfection.

Subsequently we often visited the chapel with visitors from the United States. Candles were usually burning, priests chanting. It was fascinating to watch the people who quietly came and went. Government officials or noblemen dressed formally with decorations, people from the city, farmers from the country. Here came an old woman, the style of her hair and dress bespeaking customs of the past still followed in the little country villages. She fell to her knees when she perceived the magnificent urn. Prostrating herself, the palms of her hands joined, she bowed her head to the floor three times. Slowly and gracefully she moved her body forward across the floor on an elbow, and laid her tribute of flowers before "her" King.

Our first Thanksgiving Day in this faraway land simply had to be celebrated in accordance with some of the time-honored traditions. There was a baseball game and sports for the children while the entire American community enjoyed at least a taste of turkey, trimmings and other goodies. In the cool of the evening, they sat in the Legation garden and sang with nostalgia.

The paint dried on the walls of the renovated residence in Wireless Road and we prepared to move in February of the year 1947. When she discovered, however, that our garden held a python, in fact several of them, Josie displayed a decided reluctance to enter the new premises until the giant snakes had been removed. A snake charmer, an ancient fellow, was called in, sniffed the air knowingly and admitted the presence of a reptilian monster, but could not locate its lair.

In our time of need a young Filipino named Johnny Royola appeared at the office. He was a big-game hunter, a procurer of mammals and reptiles for American zoos and museums. He offered eagerly to rid us of the pythons. Anyhow, he was itching to use a shiny new, all-steel, lasso-like gadget which the inventor claimed had merely to be slipped over the head of the serpent. With the help of the gardeners he searched the gardens for some time before he found the entrance to one python's hole on the far bank of the canal. The snake appeared to be sleeping off its last meal and was not therefore inclined to emerge.

Johnny lit a smudge and the snake slowly began to uncoil and move toward the mouth of the hole. Johnny waited, his steel lasso ready. He slipped it over the head of the huge python as it appeared. He held the head tightly enough but the coils started to whip sinuously around his body. The gardeners fled in terror. Johnny yelled for help as the coils wrapped more tightly, offering increasingly large sums of money to anyone who would come to his assistance. One old man turned back, seized the snake by the tail and by prodigious effort was able slowly to unwind it. When the pressure was released Johnny managed to force the head of his prize into a large gunny sack. The remaining yards of snake were then stuffed into the bag, the mouth tied, and it was taken to his camp on the edge of town. Later we visited the camp and were shown the "Stanton python," its mouth taped with adhesive.

"I'm punishing him," Johnny explained. "He bit me this morning but now he'll never bite me again."

That visit to his camp was exciting. An ugly female chimpanzee, high in a tree, suddenly swooped down and, hanging by one long powerful arm from the branch, grabbed Josie's hair. Johnny immediately leaped at the monkey and extricated my wife before any serious damage was done. The female chimp, Johnny explained, does not like other females of any species.

With one python removed, we were ready to move into our new house. The great sprawling structure was a delight. The garden was enchantment itself. We did not mind the erratic wheezy plumbing or the electric wiring which kept breaking, or the secondhand locks and catches which broke at once and left us open to thieves and prowlers who were numerous at that time. It was the typical hundred-year-old house that constantly needed repair, but it had great charm and atmosphere and we loved it. Almost overnight the garden began to bloom. The flowers and shrubs we planted were sent us by our Thai friends: cannas, hibiscus, gardenias, orchids and sweet-smelling jasmine.

When Prime Minister Pridi resigned he turned over the reins of government to one of his staunch supporters, an ex-naval man, Rear Admiral Thamrong Navaswasdi. Some changes were made in the cabinet but Nai Direk remained as Foreign Minister. I found the new Prime Minister a jaunty, likable person with a good sense of humor. He was also an astute politician and gifted with a "golden tongue" as the Thai described his forensic talents.

The new Government promised a good deal. It declared it would take active measures to solve the mystery surrounding the death of the late King and to bring down the rising cost of living. Both were matters of great public concern. A more thorough investigation of the circumstances surrounding King Ananda's death was indeed undertaken and charges preferred in the courts against several suspects, but the case was not concluded until five years later. To combat spiraling prices, various drastic measures were taken, but were of no avail.

As I pointed out to the new Prime Minister on more than one occasion, artificial restrictions on exchange and trade resulted in an increase rather than a decrease in living costs and directly affected all government employees, who became more susceptible to the lure of corruption. The plight of Government servants was serious, inasmuch as their salaries, based on prewar wage scales, were totally inadequate to meet living costs fourteen or fifteen times as great as those prevailing before the war. Prime Minister Thamrong, a sensible and intelligent man, saw in time that restrictions were no remedy and threw them all out of the window, saying, "They were no good as medicine and will kill the patient."

The growing importance of Thailand in international affairs and our increasingly friendly relations with that country led our Government to propose that the diplomatic missions in our respective countries be raised from the status of Legation to that of Embassy. This being in accord with the wishes of the Thai Government, announcement to this effect was made simultaneously in March, 1947, in Bangkok and in Washington. Similar action was taken by the Thai and British governments at the same time. In May, I had the honor of presenting my credentials to the Regent as the first United States Ambassador to the Kingdom of Thailand. His Royal Highness, Prince Wan Waithayakon, was named by his Government first Thai Ambassador to the United States and served with distinction in that capacity for a number of years.

During my first ten months in Thailand it had given me great satisfaction to see and to feel the good will that princes, Government officials, students, merchants and country people felt for the United States. This was based on the friendly relations which had existed for over a century. The selfless labors of American missionaries had also won many friends for the United States. Medical missionaries had introduced anti-cholera and smallpox serums and had helped to bring these diseases under control, while in the educational field they had contributed greatly toward the establishment of a sound system. The respect and affection of the Thai people for our missionaries was constantly emphasized by people of all ranks. When Dr. Edwin Cort of the Presbyterian Mission Hospital at Chiengmai, retired in 1947 after forty-seven years service in Thailand, hundreds of poor people traveled for many miles to say good-by.

"Paw," they called him in Thai. These good people sat on his porch and in his garden for days to catch a glimpse of him or his wife, a nurse and dietician also well beloved. They wanted to say farewell and to offer a small gift of a few eggs or fruit or a bouquet of flowers. In the postwar years he had not only continued his labors at the hospital and at one of the finest leper colonies in the East, but had also directed the distribution of medicines, which churches in the United States had donated for the care of the sick in Thailand. A grateful Thai Government decorated him and joined the people in bidding him Godspeed.

A year after we had left behind us the green hills of Vancouver our goods and chattels arrived, having moved by a circuitous route and rested for weeks on docks in strange ports of call. The arrival of our belongings was opportune for we were able to use them at the largest reception we had undertaken so far. For some time I had been negotiating a reciprocal treaty with the Thai Government to establish round-the-world air services through Bangkok. These negotiations had progressed satisfactorily and Pan American Airways was to bring into Bangkok one of its giant Constellations, which was making a good-will survey flight round the world, packed with celebrities. Since the inauguration of regular air service through Bangkok was an important event, we invited a staggering number of Government officials, royalty, prominent Thai and others. Our newly arrived china and glassware came in very handy. A few months later a regular Pan American service was inaugurated, which has proved to be of real benefit to Thailand and the company.

Early morning is an enchanting part of the day in Bangkok, with a particular coolness and freshness in contrast to the heat and humidity which rush from the earth as the hot sun burns into it. We were awakened early by the shrill shrieks of the priest birds which, the Thai say, summon the priests to matins promptly at daylight. These big black birds pierce the still morning air with a long-drawn-out "Whooo-Whooo," a cry which begins about middle C and ascends the scale, increasing sharply in volume until, with an ear-splitting scream, it fades away, only to be taken up by its mate from another end of the garden.

One stuffs the pillow over the head but simply cannot shut out the sound. And so it is best to get up. By seven o'clock we were eating our breakfast on the wide upper verandah overlooking a long sweep of the garden. This was the most enjoyable part of the day. Here we had privacy, although early-morning visitors were not unknown. Here we could drink in the fresh dewy beauty of the garden.

There were always blossoms and bloom and during the hottest season of the hot year many of the trees burst into pink and yellow flowers whose heady fragrance hung over the garden and filled the air with humming bees. The gardeners carried buckets of water slung across their shoulders from the canal for the morning water-ing ritual, trotting rhythmically across the garden in their bare feet, the water sloshing gently back and forth in their pails. The enchant-ment of the morning gave us strength for the day ahead. It was also the only time in which we could discuss quietly the hundred and one problems, big and little, which made up each day. Josie sat at breakfast with a paper and pencil beside her, an abject surrender to efficiency, I told her. My head would be buried in yesterday's local papers, trying to fathom from the conflicting news reports what was actually going on.

At five minutes to eight, promptly, the car crunched its way slowly round the driveway and my day began, its tightly packed schedule commencing with the reading of all important incoming telegrams, dictating replies as fast as possible, then conferring with Government officials, colleagues of the diplomatic corps, businessmen, the staff or visitors passing through town.

When I returned to the house at night there were always guests in the garden. Iced tea helped to revive flagging energies and made it possible to climb upstairs and, in the stifling heat of our sunbaked bedroom, dress for the round of evening cocktail parties and dinners. These were useful; sometimes I could transact more official business at a party than in the office. After a while one became adroit at maneuvering one's way through the crowds at a reception and cornering the person with whom one wanted to talk about official matters. Within an hour the views or replies extracted might be on the air to Washington, or later dispatched by one of the Embassy's faithful code clerks. These parties were not "pink teas" but really hard work.

To escape temporarily from the discomfort of the "hot season," which bakes out one's energies as effectively as it does the moisture from the earth, we spent a week end at the seaside. The journey took several hours as we negotiated an endless series of mudholes, deep ruts and corrugated stretches of road which caused our teeth to chatter like the ague. Chin drew our mud-covered car to a halt at a broad, swiftly flowing river across which we were to be ferried. A barge, already loaded to capacity, lay waiting, crammed with rickety busses, jammed with passengers, and piled high with enormous baskets containing squawking chickens, vegetables, fruits, odoriferous fish, and a miscellaneous collection of goods going to market. At length Chin skillfully engineered the car onto the barge along two slimy planks which skidded crazily as the barge slid to one side in the current.

Up steamed a busy little launch, wheezing and sputtering alarmingly. The ferryman cast off with a push of his big pole. The current caught our barge broadside, and both barge and launch swung rapidly into the current and drifted at horrifying speed downstream. The members of the crew leaped up from their siestas, the helmsman shouted a stream of orders. Half a dozen men crowded in fascination around the gasoline engine, tapping levers, tightening and loosening screws, pouring oil into various parts of the engine, tying things up with bits of wire, bailing out water.

Then the chief engineer opened the throttle wide. The poor engine, already shuddering at the tortures inflicted upon it, shrieked in protest and set up such a shaking I was sure it would fall apart. We inched our way across the river in the teeth of a mighty current seeking to pull us downstream but landed on the other side, shaken and dazed. Our Thai fellow travelers merely laughed and joked. That's the wonderful thing about the Thai. They never seem to worry, although we learned later they actually do.

18

The Water-Jar Constitution

For some time Thai friends had been telling me that groups in opposition to the Government of Prime Minister Thamrong were becoming unusually active; that a military group headed by Field Marshal Phibul Songgram was likely to attempt to seize control; and, to clinch the matter, that a famous astrologer had predicted there would be a *coup d'état* on the night of November 8, 1947.

I went directly to see the Prime Minister to inquire about these rumors. He laughed them off and said that he heard them daily, hourly. "But, Excellency," he said, "the Commander in Chief of the Army is with me, the Police are with me, and I have the Navy in my pocket." He patted his pocket jauntily and seemed to be in high good humor.

But there was a *coup d'état* on November 8, just as the astrologers had predicted.

That night, in the ramshackle theater of the fine arts, His Highness Prince Dhani Niwat was delivering a lecture on the origins of the shadow play. He described how, in ancient times, the projection of shadows onto a white wall or from behind a white cloth attached to branches of trees had developed a dramatic art at an early date in Thai history. The figures, which were often taken from the famous Hindu epic, the *Ramayana,* were cut out of leather and maneuvered across the screen much as marionettes are animated in puppet shows.

Suddenly a Thai friend, sitting directly behind us, leaned forward and whispered in my ear, "There's trouble. The tanks are out."

It was midnight when we stepped into the cool star-studded night. "Yes," said Chin in a matter-of-fact way, "many soldiers with guns and tanks." As we drove home we saw soldiers at street intersections and a few whippet tanks stationed at intervals.

As soon as I reached home I called our military and naval attachés and asked them to scout the town, reporting to me from time to time. There was no sleep for us that night. Early next morning they handed me a printed proclamation issued by a military group, which declared that the Army, in accordance with the will of the people, had decided to overthrow the Government of Prime Minister Luang Thamrong, charging it with gross corruption, with failure to clear up the mystery of King Ananda's death, and with inability to lower the cost of living. The proclamation further declared that Field Marshal Phibul Songgram had consented to assume the post of Supreme Commander of the armed forces.

My British colleague telephoned, asking me to come to him at once to meet an "important personage." On the large cool verandah of the Embassy residence I found Ambassador Thompson and Prime Minister Thamrong himself, the latter drawn and tired but, as always, self-possessed and jocular.

"Excellency," he said, flicking his hand graphically, "they have kick me out. General Adul of the Army promise me everything is O.K. but he have not tell me true."

He described dramatically how, at a benefit ball the night before, an aide had sidled up and tipped him off that the military were on the way to seize him, how he had skipped out the back way as they entered at the front, and had hidden himself all night in a car. He was, he said, leaving immediately for the naval base some eighty miles away where his Government—and he emphasized that it would remain the only legal Government, as he had no intention of resigning—would carry on under naval protection.

I remembered with some irony his confident statement that he had the "Navy in his pocket." He left, waving airily, saying that he would see us soon.

Sustained by strong coffee, Thompson and I compared notes. I told him that a Thai military officer had appeared in the middle of the night at my residence with the news that Pridi had slipped into a small boat on the river and disappeared into the mist just as troops were battering down his front gate.

Neither Thompson nor I liked this overthrow of the Thamrong Government by force; the flouting of the constitutional processes simply set back the hands of the clock. We agreed that the Thamrong Government, like its predecessor, was corrupt, perhaps even more so; that the other charges against it were equally true. Nevertheless, we deplored the rule of force, the possibility of civil war as well as numerous diplomatic complications which might arise.

Later that morning the Bangkok radio blared forth the proclamation. Followers of Pridi and Thamrong, who had not already skipped town, were rounded up. The Prince Regent, acting on behalf of the absent King, was approached to approve what had transpired and to promulgate a new constitution drawn up by the military group. It came to be known as the "water-jar" constitution, because Colonel Luang Kach, the most active figure in these events, had kept it hidden in a large red earthenware water jar.

Later the Prince Regent told me it seemed to be in the best

interest of the country to acquiesce in what had been done in order to avoid bloodshed. "As you know," he told me, "bloodshed is abhorrent to us as Buddhists."

In answer to my question as to whether there might not be danger of civil war if Luang Thamrong were to hold out, he replied that he felt Thamrong would not wish to plunge the country into war and would probably leave quietly, to reappear on the scene at a more propitious moment. The Prince Regent proved to be correct.

Meanwhile, Pridi silently fled to Singapore, where the British gave him political asylum, before he went to China. Fortune was not kind to this statesman who had planned and worked to give his country democratic rule, to raise the standards of living and promote the welfare of the people. Instead, he was forced to flee the country with the dark stigma of implication in King Ananda's death attached to him, and is now apparently a puppet in the toils of the Chinese Communists and likely to be used when they so decide.

Nai Khuang Aphaiwong, another former Prime Minister, a delightfully animated and witty man, was established in office as Prime Minister. As cabinet colleagues he selected some of the most intelligent, capable and honest men to be found in the Kingdom. They represented solid talent and integrity and yet—like that shadow play we had witnessed the night of the *coup d'état*—we were seeing but shadows. The reality lay with the military group behind the scenes, which had come into office through unconstitutional means. We knew many of the members of the new cabinet personally and had the highest regard for them. If they had had real authority they could have given the country the clean, intelligent government it needed. Most knowledgeable observers felt that the new Government could not last; that, once having served the purposes of the military group, it would be pushed aside, the curtain lifted, and the real power, Field Marshal Phibul, would emerge.

The Water-Jar Constitution

In the weeks to follow, my secretary frequently announced, "Colonel Suranarong is waiting to see you." The colonel and other emissaries from the military group and the new Government called often, seeking to explain what had happened, dilating on their good intentions. The purpose of all this persuasive effort was to obtain diplomatic recognition for the new Government from the United States, Great Britain and other foreign powers.

I explained to them some of the complexities involved in diplomatic recognition of a Government that had not come into power by constitutional means. I pointed out, too, that the new "water-jar" constitution called for elections in February, and that it would be wise to wait and see what happened at that time.

In periods of stress and strain our house always became a busy center as politicians, their wives and friends tried to talk to us privately rather than appear at the Embassy. On more than one occasion there were opposition groups in the residence at the same time, one upstairs, one down.

A few weeks after the overthrow of the Government, Poonsuk, Pridi's wife, appeared quietly with her charming sixteen-year-old son. She was almost unrecognizable, weary, untidy, her face squeezed by anxiety. She begged my wife to take her four children into safekeeping. "You are my only hope," she urged pitifully.

Josie was fond of the children but she rightly felt that she could not assume this responsibility. With a heavy heart she pointed out the reasons and Poonsuk departed, discouraged and disappointed. The official visits of politicians were easier to cope with, but where pity and sentiment were involved, decisions were not easy to make.

One morning in late November we were at breakfast when I asked, "Where is that singing coming from?"

Boyish voices, not quite on pitch, were pouring forth a familiar Christmas carol. The Silesian Fathers, Josie explained, had turned the dilapidated old place next door into a hostel for boys and were teaching them useful trades. She had gone over to see for herself, riding on her bicycle, taking candies for the boys in the bike basket. They had put on an impromptu football game for her benefit and cheered her as she left.

"I nearly fell off into the ditch trying to maintain my dignity," she said.

As Christmas drew nearer, the carols were rehearsed regularly. "Let's give a Christmas carol party," Josie suggested. "We'll have the boys next door and the kids from the Blind School, who are also practicing carols. We will invite Embassy children, too, for the fun. It will be our Christmas present to each other."

It was a wonderful idea and the party was planned for Christmas Eve for over a hundred children. The Blind School children were fetched in a truck, while the boys from next door marched over, with broad grins, wearing brand-new uniforms and caps which they had tailored themselves. The first year our Christmas tree was a poor affair, decorated with what we could find. But the children loved it. Even the blind children, who were taken singly to "see" it, ran their hands lightly over it with evident delight.

The Embassy small fry acted as ushers and felt very important, handing out programs with the carols printed on them. We sang with enthusiasm for an hour and though there was a little dabbing of eyes it was a happy affair. The great moment was refreshments. Here the little Embassy helpers were really heroic, helping their Thai friends first, visibly restraining themselves from pitching into the ice cream and cookies, peanuts and popcorn. Pandemonium and confusion reigned as politeness gave way to complete relaxation and the children let themselves go.

While the servants, who had enjoyed the fun as much as the children, cleaned up cheerfully, Josie prepared for dinner for our junior staff members who were alone on Christmas Eve. It was a grand affair with all the best china and silver on parade, for Josie had finally succeeded in making Ah Ngee understand that anyone who came into our house as a guest was just as important as a Royal Highness and was to be treated as such.

All through dinner a procession of carolers appeared, holding lighted candles, their voices soaring into the soft night. Christmas Eves in Bangkok became memorable ones for us.

An urgent telegram from the Secretary of State interrupted my concentration on Thai political affairs. The President had appointed me special envoy and personal representative to the Independence Ceremonies of the Union of Burma to be held on January 4, 1948. On that day the Burmese people were to achieve full independence from the British who had ruled over them for more than a century. The struggle for freedom had been intensified after the war and with great wisdom the British had worked out a series of agreements granting the Burmese the sovereign rights and liberty so dearly coveted. To mark this special event the Burmese Government had invited friendly nations to send their representatives to attend the ceremonies and celebrations.

As our plane circled over Rangoon we could see the city spread out below us, with the might Irrawaddy River, a broad band of silver, encircling a part of it. Thailand and her neighbor, Burma, are both blessed with majestic rivers flowing through their land, great pulsing arteries of life and transportation. The silver glint of the Irrawaddy River, as we prepared to land, was dimmed by the sun rays which flashed from the huge dome of the Shwe Dagon, Burma's greatest temple and shrine to the Lord Buddha.

We landed to find ourselves in what seemed to be an armed camp. This was a period of turbulence for the new Government, political feelings and tensions were running high, with a left-wing Communist group causing as much confusion and dissension as it could. Indeed, the first ceremony symbolized this somber mood rather than one of victory. It began with the laying of a wreath on the coffin of Aung San, Burma's foremost revolutionary in the fight for independence who, a few months before, had been shot to death by gunmen. His body was lying in state in an immense public hall, covered by wreaths, banners and other tributes to his popularity.

Here, as in Thailand, ancient Hindu rituals and the conjunction of the stars were a potent influence. Burmese astrologers had painstakingly calculated the auspicious date and time for one of the greatest events in Burmese history, fixing four o'clock in the morning of January 4. An elaborate ceremony had been planned for the actual turning over by the British of the reins of government to the Burmese. It was dark and chilly but the sky was full of stars that seemed to reach down and hover over the city in benign blessing. The special diplomatic representatives and their staffs were assigned places on either side of the Burmese and British officials, facing freshly painted flagpoles, which were startlingly white in the darkness and spectacularly illumined by giant floodlights. The colorful costumes of the Burmese were a striking contrast to the white uniforms of the British and the somber black of our own dress attire.

The dramatic moment arrived. The Union Jack, which had flown over Burma for more than a hundred years, was slowly and solemnly lowered, as Sir Hubert Rance, the British Governor, and his staff stood rigidly while "God Save the King" marked the end of British rule.

A brief pause. In the rays of the floodlights the five-starred flag of the Union of Burma was raised to the top of the flagpole. There was a spontaneous cheer from the Burmese. Their national anthem was played and, mingling with its strains, were the piercing wails of conch shells blown in conformity with ancient custom.

A few hours later, the Governor gave a farewell reception on the luxuriant lawns of Government House, situated on an elevation overlooking the city. For the last time he reviewed the troops and for the last time held court in his splendid residence before turning it over to the Burmese Government and setting sail on the cruiser awaiting him.

For the next few days there were formal and informal entertainments of all descriptions, interspersed with quiet talks with Burma's young Prime Minister Nu. His intelligence, his zeal to make Burma a country of good government dedicated to the welfare of the people, and his idealism all made me feel he was destined to become a great leader of the new Burma. His deep religious faith shone through his thoughts and his words. He spoke frequently of his desire to enter a Buddhist monastery as soon as it might be possible to do so. Not only I but all his friends and associates urged him to put the needs of his country, particularly at that critical juncture, above his personal inclinations. This he has done and has continued to lead Burma through troubled times, and pressing economic problems.

Back in Bangkok, we found the uncertainties of the political situation crowding in for attention. Elections were held to determine whether the provisional government of Khuang Aphaiwong would be confirmed. The percentage of voters who chose to exercise their electoral rights and cast their ballots was disappointingly small, but the elections were conducted fairly. The Thai are democratic in thought and custom but the majority still have only a vague notion of the meaning of constitutional government and the procedures involved in the election of representatives. This is not surprising, however, since the concept of government by the people was imported from the West only twenty-three years ago. Prime Minister Khuang was returned to office and his Government received a vote of confidence from the assembly. Diplomatic recognition by the United States and other foreign governments followed in the month of March.

The Government had high hopes and set to work to institute many needed reforms. It pushed more vigorously the investigation of King Ananda's death, sought to clean up corruption, and tackled the perennial problem of the high cost of living. It also established a constituent assembly to work on the "water-jar" constitution and endeavored to give it greater democratic substance and safeguard more adequately the rights and liberties of the people. Nonetheless, I had an uneasy premonition that these high hopes would not be realized, because there were indications from behind the scenes that the military group was becoming restive.

It was burning hot in Bangkok. The garden had been scorched brown by the relentless rays of the sun, the city's small canals and ponds were dry and smelly from refuse, the trees were bare of leaves. As if to distract man's attention from the heat, nature provided a luscious feast of color. Brilliant orange red splashed the leafless trees. The Flame of the Forest was in bloom and lighted up the city and countryside. From my office window I looked out onto a red carpet of blossoms which startled one with its colorful beauty. Climbing bougainvillea of purple, crimson and a delicate salmon pink trailed over houses, gateways and fences, adding to the feast of color; hibiscus hedges, deep rose and red, lined the roadways.

We decided to escape from heat and turmoil for a long week end at Siricha on the sea where we had found a small bungalow to rent. It was set among mango and banana trees, with thickly forested green hills and jungle behind. Below, in a little rocky cove, were the skeletons of two wooden ships, said to have been built by the Japanese during the war, which gave to it the atmosphere of a pirate's lair.

We stretched in long canvas chairs, official duties and responsibilities blanketed by the peace of the simple things and nature's prodigal display of beauty. There was no telephone, no electricity, no running water, but there were freedom, harmony and simplicity. In the cool darkness a little moon sailed daintily among feathery clouds. Searching for music to match the enchanted night I turned on the portable radio beside me.

"You are listening to Radio Moscow." Before I could turn the knob, it went on, "Ambassador Stanton, representative of Imperialist America, thinks he controls Thailand. He is planning to make Thailand the base of aggressive attacks against the peace-loving people of China who are fiercely resisting the attacks of Chiang Kai-shek's bandits."

From time to time the Communist press in Bangkok had depicted me as a vampire sucking the blood of little children, or driving a jeep with a diabolical leer as I careened along, flattening out the bodies of babies. But the Moscow attack was something new. Perhaps it was connected with the recent arrival of Mr. S. Niemchina, the first diplomatic envoy to be appointed from Soviet Russia to Thailand. Was this an indication that the Soviets would be taking more interest in Thailand? The peace and quiet were rudely snatched away.

I switched off the radio. "What a horrible beast you are," yawned Josie.

19

The Revolution That Failed

Rumors that the military group was planning further action were freely circulating in the markets and coffeeshops, a sure barometer of events to come, but they were stoutly denied by members of Prime Minister Khuang's Government. Nevertheless, the rumors were correct. After a few months in power, Prime Minister Khuang was told to resign by a military delegation headed by Colonel Luang Kach, who had executed the *coup d'état* in November, 1947.

Nai Khuang took the blow gracefully and resigned with a shrug of the shoulders. "The Prime Minister's seat is too hot for me," he told me.

There was no surprise when Field Marshal Phibul Songgram was invited to step from behind the shadow curtain and assume the duties of Prime Minister. The Parliament gave him a vote of confidence and thus, by a turn of the political wheel of fortune, he was back in office. He has remained in control of the country's affairs ever since. A most attractive-looking man, slim, erect, with graying hair and a disarming smile, his modest manner makes it difficult to credit stories of his past dictatorial ambitions. Speaking partly in French, partly in Thai, he explained at our first meeting his part in the political events of the past six months. He had, he said, emerged from retirement only because of the pleadings of the younger military officers, many of whom had served under him, and had acted from motives of patriotism.

He spoke of his Government's plans for the future, which had a familiar ring, being concerned with solving the mystery of the King's death, dealing with corruption and the high cost of living. In the field of international relations, he stressed his determination to support the United Nations and to strengthen friendly relations with the United States. His subsequent unswerving support of the United Nations and the United States have been notable features of his foreign policy. My first meeting with Field Marshal Phibul left the impression of a man of magnetic charm and pleasant friendliness.

Diplomatic life is a mixed casserole of official duties and official functions. Both grew steadily and especially the burden of official entertaining. Josephine attempted to keep up-to-date lists of princes, princesses, changing Government officials and cabinet ministers, members of the diplomatic corps, residents of all nationalities and the business community. Official receptions, dinners and lunches had to be carefully thought out, while the physical labor of writing and addressing thousands of invitations became tremendous. We were so shorthanded at the office that I could spare her none of the secretaries. At a reception my wife voiced her need and a distinguished Thai official of the Department of Commerce immediately offered to "give" her his daughter.

So it was that Koblab Sombatsiri came into our family. Chubby, bespectacled, good natured, she arrived three mornings a week. She was shy, giggly and inexperienced at first but she could type a little, she had a correct knowledge of Thai etiquette and she was willing.

Furthermore she could telephone in Thai to the Protocol Division of the Ministry of Foreign Affairs, which was consulted many times a day on questions of procedure, seating arrangements, arrivals and plans for VIP's who were flooding the Embassy.

Koblab became practically a member of the family. And then she fell in love. Romance had blossomed in Japan, where she had been educated in a convent and had met a young Thai student. As he came from an impecunious family her parents did not regard him as a suitable match and produced a number of suitors of greater substance. From then on the piles of invitations were scattered by her heaving sighs. After leaving our house she would meet her Thom at the tennis club. Josie encouraged her to thrash the matter out at home but Thai family traditions with respect to marriage and the deference shown to parents were not lightly cast aside in spite of the impact of twentieth-century notions fostered by wildly romantic Hollywood scenes, which were watched nightly in the movie theaters.

For three years she stolidly refused the suitors proposed by her parents, which made home life disagreeable. But her father eventually capitulated, the heavy sighs evaporated, and though the negotiations were complicated, she finally married her Thom. With the birth of her first child Koblab asked Josie to become its "foreign mother," a role which Josie loved.

It seemed more than mere coincidence that Serge Niemchina, first Soviet Minister to be appointed to Thailand, should have arrived just a few weeks after an important Communist party meeting held in Calcutta during February, 1948, at which orders were issued to lanch armed attacks in Burma, Malaya and Indonesia in a bid to seize power. In Indochina, the Moscow-trained Communist leader, Ho Chi Minh, was already engaged in savage guerrilla warfare against the French. The emphasis in Thailand was along organizational and propaganda lines. When I first arrived in Bangkok, in the summer of 1946, only two out of a dozen Chinese-language papers were following a pro-communistic line, extolling all that Moscow did, exulting in the victories of the Chinese Communists over Generalissimo Chiang's armies, and bitterly attacking the United States. With the arrival of Minister Niemchina, the volume of Communist propaganda noticeably increased and so did its virulence. In the weeks following the Minister's arrival, I was perturbed to see, as I scanned the Chinese Communist press, that diatribes and vilifications put out in China during "Hate America" week, were being printed in Bangkok the next morning.

Fragmentary information was also coming into the Embassy about the more intense efforts of the Chinese Communist party in Thailand, the hard core of which had existed since 1926 or 1927, to infiltrate and organize Chinese laborers, trade guilds, schools and such societies as the Chinese Chamber of Commerce. This information was confirmed by the Chinese Ambassador, but he was quite as worried by the intention of Field Marshal Phibul's Government to reduce drastically the annual Chinese immigration quota from ten thousand persons to two hundred.

This continued to be one of the most serious issues in Chinese-Thai relations and was of equal concern to Chinese Nationalists and Communists. In these circumstances, Ambassador Li did not feel the time opportune to make representations to the Thai Government concerning Communist propaganda and other activities.

Although the Prime Minister knew of the guerrilla campaigns being carried out in the countries surrounding Thailand and something of the Communist activities within his own country, he did not at that time take the matter seriously. He knew little about Communism, he told me when I discussed the matter with him. He was thinking more of the threat posed by a large Chinese minority population in Thailand to the economy of his country and the livelihood of the people. It would be best, he thought, to prohibit further Chinese immigration into the country.

I agreed the problem was a real one, but pointed out that Thailand had greatly prospered as the result of Chinese business acumen and that the high degree of intermarriage between the two peoples had produced many close bonds.

With a smile the Prime Minister replied that this was true, but that the new Chinese were different and did not want to become Thai.

I suggested that harsh restrictive measures might harden the Chinese community against his Government and turn them toward the Communists.

"Maybe so," he replied. "My Government will study the matter."

So the Chinese immigration quota was reduced to two hundred a year amid the lamentations and the criticisms of the Chinese residents. For the Communists it was a sharp local issue which fell into their propaganda basket, in spite of the Government's warnings and the occasional detention of some minor editorial writer. The Chinese Nationalist Government, suffering defeats at the hands of Communist armies, was no less concerned because they did not wish to see Thailand, a prosperous land of refuge, prohibited to them. All this must have been pleasing to the Soviet Legation, which by all accounts was very busy.

The American University Alumni Association, composed of over two hundred Thai graduates of American colleges and universities, included among its members cabinet ministers, officials, businessmen, bankers and writers, all drawn together by common interests stemming from having lived and studied in the United States. We looked forward to their lunches and meetings where hospitality and informality fostered friendships and enabled us to understand our Thai friends better. Its annual show was always a gala event and in 1949 was held on February 26.

We were laughing at a hilarious skit, in which the American Ambassador had gone off with the prettiest girl in the cast, when my military attaché leaned over the back of my seat and whispered, "Mr. Ambassador, the Bangkok radio has just announced the formation of a new government headed by Nai Direk. Trouble is expected."

Nai Direk had been Minister of Foreign Affairs under Pridi Phanomyong. If the report were true, it meant that Pridi had staged a comeback and was attempting to overthrow Field Marshal Phibul's government.

We continued to sit through the performance and later moved on to an enormous outdoor dance floor lit by strings of gaily colored lights. Among the guests were both followers of Phibul and men loyal to Pridi. They talked only of the show they had just seen but their thoughts, like mine, were on what was going on outside the gate.

One of my military aides appeared. "Troops and marines are out in force. The Royal Palace seems to be in the hands of the Navy. Naval vessels in the Chao Phya River have been readied for action. Navy marines are moving out from the Navy wireless station on Wireless Road (where we lived) and fanning out, setting up barricades and machine-gun posts. It looks as though the Army and Navy are set for a clash, with the Army supporting Field Marshal Phibul and the Navy backing Pridi."

"Is there any news of Pridi?"

There was a rumor, he told me, that Pridi had been seen in the Grand Palace, wearing a naval officer's uniform.

The party went on. We danced a few duty dances but the gaiety had vanished, people were quietly slipping away. There was a stir. The dashing figure of Deputy Chief of Police, Colonel Phao, appeared with a contingent of police, and looked around suspiciously. At last we could escape.

The drive home was eerie. There was bustle and commotion. Tanks, troops and police dashed around. Road blocks, barricades and machine-gun posts were being set up. Some of the Army's guns pointed toward the Royal Palace, others toward Wireless Road. Our driver had thoughtfully mounted a small American flag on the fender of the car, which helped us to pass through the road blocks. At the entrance to Wireless Road we ran into a formidable fortification, which bristled with guns of all descriptions and swarmed with naval marines.

I asked the young naval lieutenant who allowed us to pass, "What's the trouble?"

"Revolution," he answered succinctly.

As we entered the house the telephone was ringing with more information from the staff in regard to the deployment of forces on all sides. There had, I was told, been sporadic firing around the Grand Palace. I sent off a short message to Washington. Half an hour after our return, the house shook violently with the rattle of machine-gun fire and the boom of artillery. From the balcony we watched the sky lighted with tracer bullets and mortar fire. The booms and bangs continued all through the night, coming closer and spreading around Wireless Road, which proved to be the center from which the marines were conducting operations against the Army. At daylight, our assistant naval attaché, Lieutenant Curts, an intrepid young man of unusual ability, appeared after having experienced a number of thrills and dodged bullets to reach us.

Curts had managed somehow to get into the Navy wireless station at the end of our road to talk to a senior marine officer. The latter told him the Navy was demanding that Field Marshal Phibul include in his cabinet a number of naval officers and institute certain reforms. Naval vessels in the river had their guns trained on Wireless Road and on important Army positions. At a given signal they would open fire.

At this point, we heard a prolonged rumble and saw a long line of Navy trucks, heavily armored, moving past our house, accompanied by truckloads of marine reinforcements.

Heretofore, the Thai had taken considerable pride in the fact that they had carried on their revolutions and politics without the shedding of blood, but bitter feeling between Navy and Army had resulted in casualties on both sides. Pridi undoubtedly felt resentment against the military group, which had ousted him and his party and issued a warrant for his arrest as an accomplice in the alleged assassination of King Ananda. On the other hand, his friends had repeatedly told us that the idea of Thai killing Thai was abhorrent to him.

Concerned about the safety of American citizens, my staff got word through to them by phone and messenger to remain quietly at home or gather at the Embassy, where we had a small store of supplies. Fortunately, no one was hurt though some of the staff who lived within the area where the fighting was most severe had narrow escapes with shells exploding in their gardens and bullets plowing into the walls of their houses. Because our house was set far back from the street, we received only stray bullets and bits of shrapnel.

Twelve hours after the revolt was launched, the fighting died down. As soon as possible I got in touch with Field Marshal Phibul and learned that Pridi had personally directed the revolt, at least in its early stages, and that he had been seen at the Grand Palace. The plot had miscarried because the Commander in Chief of the Navy and many other senior naval officers changed their minds and failed to support Pridi, nor did the support he had expected from certain Army units materialize. His only solid support, in fact, had come from the naval marines. Phibul added that he was in touch both with the Commander in Chief of the Navy and senior marine officers and hoped that differences would be ironed out speedily and all "misunderstandings" cleared up.

For public consumption, the explanation given was that Pridi had plotted to overthrow the Government and stirred up misunderstanding between Army and Navy. Harsh measures were taken against the Navy, which was gradually purged of pro-Pridi elements, particularly in the marine corps; furthermore, for a time, the entire Navy was allowed to wither and droop for lack of funds. Even more severe measures were taken against Pridi's civilian supporters, fifty or sixty of whom were arrested for alleged complicity in the revolt. Four of Pridi's staunchest supporters were shot, an unheard-of reprisal, which shocked the Thai people. The failure of the revolt left Field Marshal Phibul and his supporters more firmly in power than ever, but it also left a residue of bitterness among the scattered and disorganized followers of Pridi, which the Communists are seeking to exploit and which later was to be the cause of fresh attempts instigated by them to overthrow the Government.

With the monsoon rains the thirsty earth trembled with the energy of new life. The buffaloes slogged stolidly through the mud in the paddy fields, preparing the ground for the tender rice seedlings, which the laughing farmers' wives planted. The whole country seemed to come alive.

And during this time we began to know the enrichment of delightful Thai friendships. Captain Pluang, in charge of the district police station at the end of our avenue, was a frequent visitor at our house. He was a graduate of the Bangkok Christian College, a Presbyterian school for boys. He liked to drop in on us, unannounced, "to see if everything is all right at the Embassy." He was tall, excessively thin, gentle and sincere, and very sad. He wept unashamedly when he told us of the wasting illness of his tubercular wife and her eventual death. She left him with two small children who sometimes accompanied him, handsome youngsters and very spoiled.

"You are father and mother to me," he said one day. "Americans are so kind."

Josie's special delight was the afternoons she spent with her tiny friend, Princess Poon, at the modest bungalow which she had built after her father's death. Here the two women sat, shoes off, feet tucked under, talking of a dozen things, tasting new dishes, laughing. Priests came there to discuss philosophy, friends from the Fine Arts Theater to talk of the new play, people came for advice. And often there were ceremonies to mark the dates of the birth or death of her famous father, Prince Damrong. At the first such ceremony, Josie was startled when the little princess took her by the hand and said, "Please come to meet my father," and led her to a large portrait beside an improvised altar, where the princess knelt with her head touching the floor.

Another friend, Prince Dhani, a notable figure in intellectual circles, delighted in talking to me of the history, art and archaeology of Thailand. Through him I learned much about the legends and ceremonies of this colorful land and saw many of the latter in his company. He told me about the ceremony of the *thot kothina* and how it originated centuries ago from the practice of Buddhist monks visiting the graveyards of the poor and lowly whose relatives could not afford to have them cremated. The monks gathered the tattered scraps of cloth in which the bodies had been wrapped and put them on. By so doing, they ensured future bliss for these poor ones. From this had come the custom of presenting robes to the priests. The King himself and those he designated joined in this rite, thus perpetuating an ancient custom of merit.

With Prince Dhani we made a fascinating excursion to the old capital city of Ayuthia. We spent a night at the Summer Palace, where the buildings are an unusual mixture of East and West, both in architecture and furnishings. The most striking building is the Chinese palace built by grateful Chinese residents and presented to King Chulalongkorn at the time of his coronation.

Beside a little artificial lake rose one of the most beautiful Chinese pavilions I have ever seen. The royal audience hall, which we next visited, transported us from ancient China to ancient Thailand. The gilded throne, the royal umbrellas, swords, golden bowls and other regalia were reminiscent of the great Thai Kings of the past. Prince Dhani led us into a room whose walls were covered with fascinating pictures of battle scenes and important episodes in Thai history during the period when Ayuthia was the capital of the kingdom. These pictures are painted on glass in vivid colors.

That evening we were introduced to some delicious Thai dishes whose preparation had been superintended by Prince Dhani's wife and his sister, Princess Siphan, a recognized authority on Thai recipes. A steamed fish curry wrapped in banana leaves was served us. The princesses explained that the curry paste is made from dried chilies, shredded lemon grass, chopped garlic, grated rind and peppercorns to which is added fish, coconut milk, eggs, green onions and fish sauce. Steamed for half an hour in its banana-leaf wrapping it has a rich full-bodied flavor which whets the appetite. This was followed by a coconut custard made from thick coconut milk mixed with scented water, palm sugar, eggs and young coconut meat. The custard is strained, placed in the coconut and steamed. Cooled and chilled, it is a dish fit for a king. One cannot resist being a complete glutton and eating every morsel of this ambrosial concoction.

Replete and content, we sat on the broad verandah in the still evening coolness with the river murmuring by below us, and watched Prince Dhani giving audience to the many officials and country people who came to pay their respects. By flickering candle-light these visitors knelt before him, palms joined together in salutation, and then settled themselves comfortably on the polished teak floor to make their reports and discuss their difficulties.

The custom of prostration before the King and the nobles was abolished by decree by King Mongkut, a hundred years ago, but the habit is so deeply ingrained that many Thai of the present generation follow this old custom. Watching the Prince advising the country people about their problems I thought of earlier days and the old Thai Kings who had bells hung outside their palace gates in order that their subjects might summon them forth in time of need to give advice or dispense justice. The continuation of this paternal relationship appeared to be both a comfort and a benefit to the people.

The next morning we attended a *kathin* ceremony at the royal chapel of the Summer Palace. Crowds of villagers and youngsters dressed in their best were lined up to see and greet Prince Dhani. As he passed them he stopped, smiled and chatted for a bit. It was a quaint chapel, for the exterior had been copied almost entirely from European Gothic architecture, but the interior contained all the paraphernalia of a Buddhist temple. It seemed to typify the complete liberalism of religious thought which is a striking characteristic of the Thai people.

From the Summer Palace we motored to Ayuthia. Today, this ancient capital city where the Thai Kings reigned for over four hundred years is a thriving town of rice and lumber mills but for many years, following its destruction by the Burmese in 1767, nothing remained but ruins of once splendid palaces and temples almost obliterated by the jungle. In one of these sites a towering figure of a Buddha image is framed within a jagged opening. In sublime repose he meditates, perfectly preserved, in striking contrast to the ruins around him.

We returned to Bangkok on a river launch by way of the winding Chao Phya River. There was talk about *phi*, or spirits. We had been in Thailand long enough to realize how universal is the belief among the Thai in spirits. The peoples of all countries seem to believe, in varying degree, in ghosts and spirits, but the Thai of today, just as did their ancestors, believe implicitly that there are spirits lurking everywhere. Some are good, but most of them are bad. There are the *phi* of dead persons, particularly those who have died a violent death, who haunt localities or houses. There is the big *phi* whose mouth is as small as the eye of a needle so that it can never satisfy its hunger. It sits on a person's chest and utters sinister whistling noises. Another *phi* looks like a man but for feathers and the tail of a bird.

Good spirits, such as the guardian angel of a house, are invisible. Nearly every home, whether in town or jungle, has a little spirit house in the garden, like a bird house, to accommodate this guardian angel. There incense is burned and gifts of food are offered daily. The jungles abound with many varieties of *phi*, benevolent, malign or down-right wicked. One of the most romantic and deadly is the tiger spirit, which assumes the form of a beautiful young maiden to lure the hunter to his destruction.

Spirit worship or animism, it was explained to us, is not an original part of Buddhism but it does represent deeply ingrained superstitious beliefs and customs as old as the jungles in which the Thai people first lived a primitive existence. No Thai, whether of high or low estate, whether educated or illiterate, would dream of doing anything of importance without first consulting one of the many persons in the country who are believed to have supernatural powers with respect to these spirits, or who have occult knowledge and the power of divination. At this point I thought of one of our Thai friends, a prominent lawyer, former cabinet minister and graduate of a British university, thoroughly westernized in most ways, who told me how a group of his friends observed a priest renowned for his supernatural powers throw silver coins into the sea one stormy night. To their amazement, he went on, they saw many fishes raise their heads out of the waves, catch the coins in their mouths and swim back to shore to lay them at the feet of the meditating priest. Our friend is a member of a greatly respected association of astrologers in Bangkok which is constantly being consulted by politicians and the public alike. In fact, political events in

Thailand are so closely linked to astrological divinations that I used to think how useful it would be to have a first-class astrologer on the staff of the Embassy.

It seems to me, we tend—not just Americans but men and women in general—to oversimplify the factors involved in understanding the motives of others and particularly the factors that shape their thinking. The motivating force is often so submerged that one can easily fail to detect the fact that prejudice and superstition are potent elements in shaping both thoughts and actions. My wife and I began to realize that a comprehension of these beliefs of the Thai was essential to understanding them more fully.

Our launch swung around a bend in the river and I was distracted by the pleasing river view. Green rice fields stretched away on either side, a tiny hamlet of thatched huts was set high above the water on bamboo stilts. A pretty young mother with flashing black eyes and irresistible smile was swinging her babe in a cloth hammock; her husband's strong wet body, glistening in the sunlight, emerged from the river holding a few squirming fish. The water buffalo stood nearby stolidly munching rice stalks. A naked brown little body, perched gaily on the buffalo's back, clapped his hand and shouted, "*Chaiyo*" as our launch went by.

On the other bank shining among the treetops, we saw the yellow and green tiled roof of a small temple. The temple landing was decorated with long strings of colored paper flags. An armada of slim kayak-like canoes was tied up at the rickety landing, crowded with colorfully dressed people bearing gifts of flowers or food set upon elaborate silver or gilded trays. Our launch was hailed and the prince was invited to attend the *kathin* ceremonies. We made our precarious way across the narrow teetering wooden planks and seated ourselves on the floor among the country people, who nodded and smiled shyly, making us feel at ease and welcome. The smiling Thai—who can resist them?

These experiences, far from the tangle of politics and social life in Bangkok, gave us a rich, easy feeling of closeness with the heart of the country and the country people, the backbone of the Kingdom. We had previously flown to the south and down the long neck of land which joins Thailand to Malaya. The boom in rubber and tin had brought prosperity to some. But we were fascinated by the white sandy beaches edging the coast in sharp contrast to the pale blue water, the deeper blue sky, the palm trees and jungle vegetation fringing the dazzling beaches. Off shore, fishermen, their wet bodies shining, moved easily with the rocking of their little boats. They stood poised with their fish nets and then with a deft movement cast them in a wide circular silver splatter over the blue water.

These people work, but not too hard, just enough to eat, to gamble at the cockfights, to buy some lengths of bright cloth and an occasional bit of jewelry both as an investment and to adorn their wives. Why work more? Better far to stretch out lazily on the sand or in the cool shade. This is a happy uninhibited philosophy which extracts the maximum of *sanuk* or joyousness out of existence. It is a philosophy which does not perhaps produce works of great genius, yet it is not lacking in the creation of beautiful things. Best of all, it does not yet feel the pressure of modern life nor the exigent demands of imitative conformity.

20

The New Asian Spirit

Because of the rapidly worsening situation in the Far East the Secretary of State suggested the holding of a regional conference of American Ambassadors sometime in February, 1950, if agreeable to the Thai Government. Such pressing problems were to be studied as the recent events in China where the Communists had succeeded in driving out Generalissimo Chiang's forces, the propaganda pouring out of Peiping concerning the "liberation" of overseas Chinese in Southeast Asia, and the successes of Communist guerrillas in Indochina, Burma and in Malaya.

Prime Minister Phibul was obviously pleased when I approached him about the conference and inquired hopefully whether we would not consider at the same time Point Four aid to his country. I assured him the Embassy had been urging such a program be developed as quickly as possible, because it was our policy to support and encourage the rehabilitation of Thailand's economy in every possible way. Only a few months earlier President Truman had issued special orders to return to Thailand forty million dollars' worth of gold found in Japan after the war because he knew how greatly it was needed to strengthen the financial position of the country. The Prime Minister expressed his gratitude for this help and promised that the gold would be used to stabilize the currency. He also thought that his country's credit would in consequence be sufficiently good to secure a loan from the World Bank in order to improve communications, dredge the river for the use of big ships and buy new equipment for the railways.

Preparations for the conference involved not only securing suitable accommodations, not an easy task in those days, for our representatives from countries extending from Pakistan to Korea, but careful arrangements had to be made for the actual meetings. The only room large enough was a dark, gloomy and exposed reception room adjoining my office. The security officers who came to check on security precautions and to see that no listening or recording devices had been hidden in the walls or ceilings were appalled by the half doors and the thin office walls. Lack of security concerned me, too, particularly since a recent blast from the Communist press had made it evident that they were much interested in the meeting. I was worried, also, lest the worn and worm-eaten beams supporting the room where the conference was to be held should suddenly disintegrate and precipitate my distinguished colleagues into the offices below.

The conference opened on February 13. Ambassador Philip Jessup and Walton Butterworth, Assistant Secretary of State for Far Eastern Affairs, had come from Washington and for a few days every plane brought our representatives from far and near. Exhaustive reports were made on the problems facing each of the countries of this area and precisely how they affected our relations with them. The appearance of the new Chinese Communist regime to the north and its impact upon the countries of the Far East and South Asia were thoroughly discussed, as well as what the United

States could and should do to help her friends of this region to help themselves meet the threat. The rising tide of nationalism in revolt against colonial rule was, we felt, an issue of paramount importance. Independence for the countries of Southeast Asia was recognized as the cornerstone of our foreign policy with respect to that area, but we were troubled by the specter of Communist domination of the nationalist movements in many countries.

Technical assistance to strengthen the economies of these countries, to combat disease and to raise standards of living was long debated, as well as the desirability of giving or increasing military aid in particular instances. But of special concern was the problem of holding the friendship of the peoples and the governments of the area. We agreed much could be done to strengthen good will through information, library and student exchange programs, provided they were conceived to meet the particular conditions in each country and were carried out with due regard for the cultural heritage and sensibilities of the people concerned.

Any conference dealing with international political problems, especially those relating to sensitive areas, engender great expectations. The official communiqués issued seldom satisfy these expectations and often give the impression that nothing of consequence was accomplished, that the United States has no policy and is making a bungling mess of things. The fact is, however, that diplomacy, in some of its phases, needs to be conducted quietly if it is to succeed. This is particularly true where the situation is involved and the problems are complex. In such cases, the implementation of basic policy objectives calls for a degree of flexibility often mistakenly dubbed vacillation or worse.

It is my feeling that our long-range policy objectives with respect to Southeast Asia are sound. We seek to maintain the friendliest relations with the countries of this region. We seek their progressive development and well-being. We seek for them the attainment of full independence and sovereignty, an objective born of our own ideals and sacrifices to achieve independence. The granting of independence to the Philippines demonstrated the sincerity of an ideal which has long inspired us and has not been forgotten by the Asian people. This objective our country has been quietly and persistently pursuing with respect to the countries of this region, recognizing that the spirit of nationalism sweeping through Southeast Asia cannot be denied and that colonialism must give way to it.

However, the record of our efforts to implement our policy objectives is spotty. Historians will note that our patient and persistent efforts to persuade the Government of the Netherlands to expedite the granting of independence to Indonesia were largely responsible for that country attaining her independence as soon as she did. In Indochina, our efforts have not been so successful. Our ally, France, has moved with such slow deliberation to meet the wishes of the states of Vietnam, Laos and Cambodia for independence that the recent granting of that coveted right comes at the eleventh hour. I fear it comes too late to enable these newly constituted states to consolidate themselves and establish sound governments capable of standing against the Communist Vietminh. It is unfortunate that France did not follow the path of wise statesmanship in those early days when Ho Chi Minh and his followers were relatively weak and without outside allies.

We have made our blunders in Southeast Asia, as we recognized at the Bangkok conference, but those blunders were made in pursuance of long-range objectives which envisage independence for the countries of the area, sound stable governments and economic prosperity.

It is now more important than ever, I believe, to study and take into account the Asian spirit of modern times. As I see it, it is a blend of the mysticism, religious beliefs and culture of thousands of years with the burning, driving desire of awakened nationalism to attain independence and freedom. This spirit was born of the bitterness and resentment of nearly two hundred years of colonial rule. It explains, in part, their doubts and suspicions of the West and their disinclination to join what appears to them to be Western power blocs, even though they may realize that such collective security arrangements as the Manila Pact are defensive in nature and designed to protect the very liberties which they have so newly won. This attitude seems anomalous to us but I feel it is important that we should try to understand it because it explains in large measure the present foreign-policy motivations of such nations as India, Burma and Indonesia.

There is urgent need on our part to seek to understand the free peoples of Asia in the fullest sense of the word. Understanding between peoples is not built suddenly, once and for all. It is a slow and painstaking process in which genuine interest in other peoples, their thinking, their way of life, creates the mutual trust and confidence needed to cement the structure together. It cannot be built by governments alone but is woven piece by piece, strand by strand, from the mutual respect and friendship of the peoples themselves. In my estimation this is really the key to the intelligent implementation of our policy, one in which the aspirations and needs of our Asian friends, which differ from country to country, are given the special consideration they merit. This is a challenge we can and must meet. We will be wasting time and money and losing precious friends if we draw up programs and plans without this catalytic element which transforms merely correct and self-interested diplomacy into the warm and intimate partnership of friends and equals, dedicated to the promotion of human welfare and human liberty. The new Asian spirit of nationalism, forged by its people and leaders to achieve their own independence, is basically the same spirit that has made our nation great. We would be wise if we, with tact, patience and understanding, fostered its growth so that they too, may enjoy the fruits of freedom.

During the Jessup conference, Prime Minister Phibul's cabinet was in the throes of another crisis, which arose over the question of whether Thailand should recognize the government of ex-Emperor Bao Dai of Vietnam. The British and ourselves had just given Bao Dai diplomatic recognition in the hope, which I felt sure was not well founded, that such support would give his Government prestige and enable him to win the allegiance of his countrymen. However, the fact that Bao Dai was essentially a creation of the French authorities, without real independence, militated sharply against his becoming a dynamic leader of the Vietnamese people.

Prime Minister Phibul was in favor of according prompt recognition, probably to please the United States. He was supported by the military men in his cabinet, but opposed by his Foreign Minister, Nai Bhochana Sarasin. The latter counseled against hasty action and urged the cabinet to await further developments. The issue was debated for days and finally the decision was left to the discretion of the Prime Minister. On February 28 the Government announced recognition of Bao Dai's Government, as well as the governments of Laos and Cambodia.

Next day the Minister of Foreign Affairs resigned because, as he explained to me, he had taken a definite stand on the question and did not wish to embarrass the Prime Minister. However, his relations with the latter remained friendly and he was later made Ambassador to the United States, a post which he holds now with distinction. But there was a good deal of debate both pro and con in the National Assembly and in the press, while Communist publications shouted that Phibul had been forced by the United States to recognize these "French puppets." As in the past, abuse was heaped on me by the Communists who described me as the arch villain in the piece.

21

The King Is Coming

THE sun does not wait," the Thai say, and these events were quickly forgotten as the country was seized with intense excitement over the prospect that the King was returning home from Switzerland and that the Royal Cremation, Coronation and marriage would soon take place. As his fiancée the young King had chosen the bright, pretty, sixteen-year-old daughter of Prince Nakat, Thai Ambassador to the court of St. James.

An army of workmen constructed a pavilion for the cremation of the late King Ananda on the Phra Mehru, the broad, parklike space lined with feathery tamarind trees before the entrance to the Royal Palace. Crowds gathered to watch, napping in the shade or nibbling whenever they wished. The ubiquitous Chinese food vendors, ever alert for trade, set up food stalls under the trees where one could buy a variety of Thai and Chinese dishes prepared in miraculous fashion on small charcoal braziers, served in bowls with spoons or chopsticks hastily dipped in a pail of water into which many other bowls and chopsticks had already been dipped.

It was fun. It was *sanuk*. The King was really coming back and the King had chosen a beautiful young lady to be his bride. They will have children and, the people said, "We will be happy again. Never mind about the Communists. Who are they anyhow? Just more Chinese."

The approach of three great ceremonies was disrupting for an ultra-ceremonial nation. The diplomatic corps was in a dither, the Royal Household was in a dither, the protocol section of the Foreign Office was in a particular dither. Even the Court Brahmans, those mysterious white-robed priests with long knotted hair, who were used only for ceremonial purposes, were said to be in a dither as they feverishly gazed at their astronomical charts and calculated exact dates and times for the events to come.

The American Embassy and the Stanton household were both in a dither. There was the delicate question of a gift for the King from the President of the United States upon his Coronation. Telegrams darted back and forth between Washington and me. I reported on the gifts which the other governments proposed to make. Washington indicated that the United States Government had no funds available for such gifts. I pointed out that we could not be the only country conspicuously failing to make a coronation gift.

Thanks to fast talking by Ken Landon in the Department a fine radio-phonograph with all possible gadgets was purchased because of the King's interest in music.

"The King is coming tomorrow." The refrain flowed through houses, markets, coffeeshops and out into the countryside. The delicate finishing touches were put to the golden cremation pyre, red carpets laid where the King would walk from his special pavilion up the many steps to the jeweled urn where his brother King Ananda rested. At the Royal Landing splendid preparations were made to receive His Majesty when he came sailing up the broad Chao Phya River on the Royal Navy's finest gunboat. Busy protocol officials informed members of the diplomatic corps about the minutest details of what to do, where to sit, what formal attire to wear.

On March 24, the sun rose red and hot as usual, "Although," as Josie remarked ungrammatically, "you can feel the specialness in the air." Damp and overheated, but arrayed in the correct formal attire, we set off in our cavalcade of cars, with Ken Landon, who had come for the occasion from Washington and was staying with us; our counselor, John Stone, and his wife; and all our attachés.

At the Royal Landing, where we were to greet the King, a long red carpet had been laid from the dock to the gilded throne chair in the center of the pavilion, a little gem of Thai architecture with its gay upturned roof eaves. To the right of the throne chair were the royal princes and princesses in full dress, covered with jewels and glittering with decorations. Facing the throne were Government officials and the chiefs of the diplomatic and consular corps. Between the pavilion and the river lesser Government officials and the diplomatic staffs waited on the green lawn.

For some time we heard the reverberating shouts of *"Chaiyo,"* from the people lining the banks of the river and crowded into thousands of small river craft, to welcome their King's return. Suddenly the gunboat glided around a bend in the river and docked. Silence fell over the waiting crowd, and then whistles sounded, music played, the gangplank was set in place and the King of Thailand stepped upon the shores of his homeland. He wore full-dress naval uniform and looked very young and serious as he walked up the red carpet, with retainers holding the royal umbrella over him.

"There she is!" And behind the young King we saw his fiancée, slim and beautiful and tall for a Thai. She was dressed quietly in dove gray, trimmed with white, with high-heeled white shoes. Her first high heels, we learned later. Her head was bent modestly but she glanced up and smiled radiantly, captivating all hearts.

"Watch her," Josie whispered to me, "she is going to be terrific."

A prophecy which proved to be correct, for the girl bride learned quickly to fill a difficult role in a singularly austere court with grace and intelligence.

The King stepped briskly into the pavilion and bowed to each group. As we bowed, Josie nearly upset a little table in front of us loaded with cool drinks. It wobbled, but a diplomatic catastrophe was avoided. The King listened to the address of welcome made by the Prince Regent, and read with composure and poise his own reply, which he took from a golden tray held out by a kneeling court attendant.

When the national anthem had been played and he was about to take his departure, the news photographers, who had come from far and wide for the colorful ceremonies, broke through the lines of guards, closed in on the King and one flashbulb exploded near his face. As a result of this incident, a ban was imposed on further close-ups, which annoyed the press and prevented the taking of many pictures, which would have completed the pictorial record of these historic events.

The King refused to go to the Chakri Palace where his brother had died so mysteriously and was driven to a special palace that had been prepared for him, while the air rang with shouts of greeting and welcome. The people were wild to have a glimpse of their King and they gave voice to spontaneous and excited jubilation. We realized as never before how important a role the monarch plays in the land of the Thai.

At the office we were drawing up plans, in conjunction with the Government's National Economic Council, for economic and technical assistance to Thailand. In discussing the matter with the Minister of Foreign Affairs, I had stressed that the whole program would be joint and co-operative. The Thai Government, he assured me, was in full agreement on this point and wished to concentrate on agriculture, public health, communications and the training of technicians in all these fields. These proposals were in general agreement with our own thinking in regard to Thailand's most urgent needs.

Some jinx seemed to pursue me when it came to making public appearances. In Vancouver it had been the bad timing of the sea gull. Upon arrival in Bangkok, it had been the bandage strapped around my head. With much to do and a host of ceremonies to be attended, I had a new catastrophe.

I came home one afternoon to find Josie entertaining callers with tea and sprightly conversation. When I had recuperated enough from the heat to listen, I discovered that she was holding their shocked attention by relating some of her experiences with the peculiar fauna that inhabited her lovely garden. She told them of the monitor lizards, the *hea*, iguana-type prehistoric-looking creatures which abounded in our canal, and how one had raced around and around our dining-room table until caught by the servants and strung up by its neck to a tree in the garden. There it swung back and forth until it was given to Johnny Royola to add to his collection.

Warming to her task, Josie told of the large apelike monkey with a hideous red-blue behind, which had lived in one of the great trees in the garden for two years, and how it attacked her once when she was rowing the little boy from the Netherlands Legation next door along our garden canal. Then she launched into the story of the green snake which swallowed the *tokay* one day after lunch.

Just at this moment we heard shrill yelps from our dog Judy and saw a great mangy black dog sinking his fangs into the back of Judy's neck. I yanked the dog loose but he turned and bit deep into my left hand. The guests leaped on chairs, Josie called for the servants, who came running, brandishing brooms, while the Thai police guard appeared, guns cocked, and ran in the wrong direction in search of the dog.

At the Pasteur Institute to which we rushed there were no doctors available, but we were finally able to get a young Danish doctor. The anti-rabies treatment, he said, called for daily injections of serum in the stomach for twenty-one days and would result in swelling, welts, high fever and persistent headache.

And he was quite right. I didn't miss one of the ceremonies that followed but the reaction was worse than had been expected and the headache persisted for months. Meanwhile, Josie attended me at the ceremonies, watching like a hawk, and fanning me madly for fear I would faint from the heat, fever and pain. Movies taken of the events that followed the mad-dog episode always showed someone standing or sitting in the front row, hand waving back and forth frantically. It was Josie fanning me, much to my embarrassment.

The ceremonies for the cremation of King Ananda began on March 29 with the most spectacular procession that one could conceive, to escort the King's golden urn from the Chapel Royal to the cremation pyre. The procession was headed by the venerable Prince Patriarch of the Buddhist Church, who was borne aloft high over the heads of the King and the rest in a gilded palanquin carried by men wearing the costumes of former days. His swaying palanquin was followed by the King, royal princes and the chiefs of the diplomatic missions, all on foot. In the center of the procession came the golden urn drawn by members of the armed forces on a magnificent gun carriage. At each of the four corners of the urn Brahman priests knelt, their hands clasped in supplication, dressed in white robes and wearing high white conical hats.

Everyone was in full dress, the princes and officials with their jeweled decorations and swords, the diplomats in formal attire. Even at eight-thirty in the morning the sun was already high and hot, drawing bright sharp gleams from the urn, the royal regalia, the medals, the jewels and the gilded swords. The colored sashes, bright

red and blue ancient uniforms, the saffron-yellow robes of the priests
were brilliant splashes of color in vivid contrast to the mourning
black of the people who lined either side of the broad avenue along
which the procession moved slowly to the lugubrious strains of
funeral music.

All morning long we marched in the blazing, scorching heat. My
stiff white collar wilted and rivulets ran from under my top hat.
The anti-rabies injections smarted as though an army of vicious
red ants were crawling and feasting about my waist. My Norwegian colleague who walked beside me was attired in a heavy white
serge uniform with a three-inch collar heavily encrusted with thick
braid. His face was white and drawn. Evidently he was in a more
parlous state than I.

Three hours passed before we reached the foot of the towering
cremation pavilion and marched solemnly around it three times in
accordance with Hindu custom. The urn was then raised from the
gun carriage onto a tall pyramidal platform built in the exact center
of the pavilion. The fragrance of jasmine flowers floated in the air
from garlands made by the Thai princesses who replaced them
each day.

After a cool lunch at home and a change into another set of
formal black garments, we set off for the final ceremony, which
stirred us deeply. No one could have shared that moment without
emotion. We sat silently as the Prince Patriarch read a eulogy to
the late King. Although withered and feeble, his fine face glowed
with an inner peace. It was strange, amidst these centuries-old ceremonies, to think his voice was being heard clearly by the immense
throng outside through a modern loud speaker. He climbed
down from his high rostrum, slowly and painfully but with great
dignity, to take his place at the head of the yellow-robed priests,
who sat in a long line on a raised platform at one side of the building. The Cord of Blessing was joined to the urn. The King

presented his gifts to the priests and then ascended the steep red-carpeted stairway, sank to his knees before the urn in homage to his brother, lit sprays of sandalwood from the lamp containing the sacred fire and placed them under the urn.

The sun bathed the pavilion and the urn in a flush of reddish hues, suffusing everything with an unearthly glow. To the high clear notes of the Bugler's "Last Post," the slow boom of cannon and the shrill tones of the Brahmans' conch shells, the King knelt in a final farewell, and then slowly descended the long steps back to his monarch's chair where he sat rigidly upright, staring fixedly at the urn. The princes and princesses, carefully avoiding the red carpet upon which their King had trod, ascended the steps, lighted candles and sticks of sandalwood and knelt in homage to their late liege lord. When Government officials and diplomats followed, Josie and I stood on the high platform on which the urn rested, pausing for a moment to look out over the Phra Mehru grounds. Thousands upon thousands of people were standing, gazing in sorrowful silence at the urn, which they could all clearly see, illuminated by shafts of light from the evening sun.

22

What Can We Do for Thailand?

WHAT should the United States do for Thailand? These friendly likable people, who for centuries had cherished their liberty and freedom, now found themselves menaced by the Chinese colossus to the north, the bitter struggle of Vietminh Communists against the French in Indochina, Communist groups striving to overthrow the newly formed Government in Burma, and guerrilla bands in Malaya who were making increasing use of jungle border areas between Thailand and Malaya as they sought to infiltrate the Kingdom's southern provinces. Equally dangerous was the Communist threat from within the country itself.

What would be best for the Thai people? This thought had scarcely been absent from my mind since I had first arrived in the country four and a half years earlier. To try to know and to understand the Thai and to give them in turn a better comprehension of the United States and its people was basic and fundamental. Without a bridge of comprehension all efforts to help might easily be misunderstood.

We were trying to build such a bridge through the dissemination of clear-cut, sensible information, free from propaganda bombast. Through daily bulletins, magazines, movies and special pamphlets, both in English and in Thai, we strove to tell the Thai of our desire to help them remain free; of those same concepts of liberty which we in the United States cherish; and something of our culture, history and development.

Libraries were opened, which became popular with students, teachers, children, Buddhist priests and the general public. Furthermore, with the signing of an educational exchange agreement on July 1, 1950, a program directed by a joint American-Thai Foundation was inaugurated, which brought many Thai students to the United States and many American teachers and professors to Thailand. I know of nothing we have done for Thailand that has generated greater response and good will. It was the best possible counter to Communist propaganda, which charged that the United States was interested only in turning Thailand into a base for aggressive military operations against peaceful Communist China. It will be a tragedy if this and similar programs in other countries are allowed to die, as seems likely, for lack of sufficient Congressional interest to appropriate funds.

That the co-operative educational program we had worked out would be welcomed by the Thai, I knew. But how did they really feel about economic and military aid from us? The official attitude of the Government and its leaders was well known. The Prime Minister, a military man, and his military colleagues in the cabinet were keen to receive it in order to equip and train the armed forces along modern lines. But how did intelligent, thinking Thai with some knowledge of world affairs feel? Were they fearful that economic aid would mean economic penetration and domination? Did they believe that military aid would so definitely align the country with the United States as to bring down upon the Thai the wrath and the might of Communist China? Their politeness is so deeply ingrained they seldom say what they actually feel and rarely say no to one's face. My staff and I sought from our many friends to find the answers to these vitally important questions. For what would it profit Thailand or the United States if we embarked on these programs only to find that they were not really wanted, that they raised doubts, suspicions and resentments and were being hindered in a thousand subtle ways?

As a result of informal talks, we learned there were no special misgivings with respect to economic aid designed to improve and strengthen the agricultural economy of the country, combat epidemics and disease, and improve communications. However, there were fears concerning military aid, because of the possibility that it might stimulate a powerful Communist reaction. It was not until the Communists struck in Korea in June, 1950, an open act of aggression which the Thai hardly believed possible, that these misgivings regarding the rearming and training of their armed forces were largely dispelled.

Our Government decided to send a special economic mission to the countries of Southeast Asia in order to determine the most pressing needs of each country and how we could best help. It was headed by Allen Griffin, a well-known West Coast publisher, with a sincere interest in the people of Asia. The mission, having first spent some time in Indochina, arrived in Bangkok immediately after the Royal Cremation. Joint Thai-American committees were set up and went to work, using the preliminary data and outlines which the Embassy had already tentatively prepared in co-operation with the Government's National Economic Council. Unanimous agreement was speedily reached that agriculture, public health, communications and the training of Thai experts and technicians were the areas of greatest need. The conferences were long and at times tortuous because the Thai Government lacked the statistical data that would have given an immediate and more accurate picture of needs, finances and planning.

At the end of two weeks Allen Griffin was able to announce that he had sent off specific recommendations to Washington and that the mission's work had been completed. All members of the mission were impressed by the co-operative attitude of the Government, which augured well for the future success of whatever program might be approved in Washington. I was happy in the thought that soon American and Thai technicians would be working side by side in the selected fields, representing another step forward in confidence and understanding. But the Congress moved slowly, politics raising its ubiquitous head to retard the implementation of the President's Point Four concept, which had been hailed by the peoples of Free Asia with enthusiasm and acclaimed by them as the answer to many of the problems with which they were struggling.

While we in the Embassy were busy fashioning this economic aid program, the public was intent on the preparations for the King's marriage and Coronation. The auspicious day for the Coronation had been determined by the Brahman astrologers to be May 5. Before this historic event, the Protocol Division informed us it would be fit and proper for diplomatic representatives to present the gifts of their respective governments to His Majesty.

First to be received by the King in private audience was the British Ambassador, as senior ambassador, who presented him with a fine set of the best English china. A few minutes later I was ushered into the King's presence. I found him comfortably dressed in white linen and looking well in spite of his arduous duties. At first, our conversation ran in stilted and formal sentences, the King thanking President Truman for the fine radio-phonograph presented him on behalf of the American Government.

Then the boy won over the King and he asked eagerly, with one of his rare smiles, "Please show me how it works." The machine had been set up in a corner. It had a formidable array of knobs and gadgets, but I had been instructed by the Embassy's radio technician how to manipulate them and demonstrated for His Majesty. Although other ambassadors were waiting to present their gifts, the King became completely absorbed, all his formality and restraint left him, and he talked like any radio fan, making it obvious that he knew a great deal more about it than I did.

The ceremonies crowded fast on one another, the next being the King's marriage to the princess whom he had chosen to be his Queen. It was a love match and very popular with the people. We did not attend the ceremony itself, at which the ancient Queen Grandmother, in her ninetieth year, poured lustral water of blessing over the heads of the royal couple. That afternoon, however, the diplomats were invited to a ceremony marking the first formal appearance of the King with Queen Sirikit.

The following day His Majesty received formal congratulatory addresses from the Government. The audience was held in the ancient Amarindra Hall, or Hall of the Fairies. It is a strikingly beautiful room elaborately decorated with gilded designs. Enormous black lacquer pillars support a magnificent ceiling studded with gold medallions and gilded fairies flying in a scarlet sky. At the far end of the hall we could see through a heavily carved and gilded window into another room where, on a higher level, royalty sat sparkling with jewels and decorations.

It was early afternoon, the hottest time of the day and, with so many persons standing crowded together, the heat was suffocating. Josie fanned me violently while we waited. There was a hush and in walked the King and Queen, looking young but very dignified. The King listened gravely to the congratulatory messages, replied gravely and left the hall, but the Queen smiled captivatingly.

Three days before the Coronation the Royal Scribes began to

write down the King's name and titles on a golden plate, starting at exactly 9:26 in the morning. At 10:38 the court astrologers recorded His Majesty's horoscope on a golden plate. That same day the court Brahmans performed purificatory rites.

Then came the morning of May 5. We were up early because we had to be at the Palace at 8:30. Josie had long before bought an elegant tulle dress in New York for this occasion. When she started to put it on she discovered in dismay that lizards had eaten away great sections of the skirt, but it was so voluminous that the damage did not show.

The diplomats were seated in a superb inner hall, more magnificent than any we had seen. From here, in olden days, the King gave audience to his courtiers and envoys who were grouped before him on a lower level. Writers of the period tell us that from this elevation, framed in a golden window, the King looked remote, the illusion being heightened by a thin gauze curtain suspended in front of him. We were arranged in three groups, as usual, royalty, Government officials and diplomats. For this occasion the ladies had gone all out in lavish clothes and jewelry.

Seated in front of us on three golden chairs sat the pretty young Queen and beside her ex-Queen Ram Bai and the King's sister. The ceremony, or series of ceremonies, lasting for three and a half hours, were such a fabulous blending of exotic colors and ancient Hindu ritual, that they left a dreamlike impression. There was much coming and going by the King to and from mysterious chambers, which still further heightened our sense of witnessing a picturesque but unreal pageant. Brahman priests officiated, dressed in snowy white baggy pants and shirts, covered with embroidered white net jackets. Strange in a country that is entirely Buddhist to find how strong is the Hindu cultural and ceremonial legacy.

During an intricate ritual of purification, the King disappeared through one of the doorways and reappeared clothed in white flowing priestlike robes, embroidered with gold, one shoulder bare. To the boom of guns, the chanting of priests, the beating upon lacquer and ivory drums, the blowing of ivory conch shells, the King was anointed with lustral water. Again he disappeared and reappeared clothed in ancient costume. He seated himself on a figwood throne while eight members of the National Assembly knelt before him to signify the fealty of the people from the eight points of the compass.

Preceded by the priests, the King, dressed in ancient royal costume stiff with gold brocade, marched toward the great throne. The priests flattened themselves to the floor while he seated himself under the nine-tiered umbrella. The Chief Priest intoned old Sanskrit verses in a nasal high-pitched voice, punctuated by violent beating on small drums. A long line of attendants appeared, each bearing one of the twenty-eight symbols of kingship, among which flashed the Crown of Victory, made of tiers of gold sparkling with enormous diamonds and weighing twenty-five pounds. This the King placed upon his own head, the cannon roared out a salute, one hundred and one times, many bands played the national anthem, drums and conch shells added to the joyful din. The King was crowned. God save the King.

Two hours later, after giving audience to dignitaries from the Golden Hibiscus Throne, he was borne aloft on a golden palanquin in a grand procession which included Palace Guards in plumed helmets and scarlet coats, officers of the Royal Household in blue and white uniforms with long swords, bedecked elephants and an immense throng of retainers and Government officials in handsome attire.

And the end was not yet. Twenty-two times more during that hot season I changed into white tie and tails to attend royal functions. But they were so fascinating and historic, so far from anything we had imagined, that the discomfort of my silly "uniform" was as nothing.

At length we returned to the workaday world, where I found new duties piling up. The British Ambassador had been transferred to a new post, which meant that the deanship of the diplomatic corps fell upon my shoulders. At the same time authority arrived from Washington to negotiate an economic and technical assistance agreement with the Thai Government. The next few months were occupied with long and intensive discussions, complicated by the fact that the original provisions drafted in Washington had been patterned after the agreements concluded with European countries, which were not suitable for Thailand.

In vain we pointed out that Europe and Southeast Asia were totally different; Washington eventually yielded, but only partially. Although it gave me great pleasure to enter into these negotiations, I was embarrassed by them. Naturally, the Thai Government assumed we would embark upon the program immediately after the agreement was signed, in September, 1950. The awful truth was that all was uncertain in Washington, and entirely dependent upon Congressional action in appropriating funds. This is the sort of situation that turns the graying hairs of an Ambassador's head silvery white in short order. I felt as though I were walking the plank. At its end I saw all too clearly the bottomless sea of discredited diplomacy. Funds were finally appropriated.

By January of the next year, thirty American experts had arrived. They worked together with the Thai to improve rice culture, irrigation, public health, railways and harbors and to stamp out the dreaded malaria. So far so good, but I kept importuning Washington not to build up a colossal economic mission in Thailand, which would constitute a heavy financial drain on the country, as the Thai were paying administrative, housing, and many other costs. I emphasized that we could ruin a good program by flooding the country with second-rate men who would tear down and not build up good will between the two countries.

At the same time tentative talks were going on with respect to the delicate problem of extending military aid. In view of the Communist threat both from inside and outside the country, I had long felt that a small, well-equipped and trained Army, Navy and Air Force were desirable to meet any border guerrilla action and to help the police combat internal subversion. However, the majority of Thai had little knowledge of Communism and that little did not sound unattractive from the propaganda put out by the Communist press in Bangkok. Indeed, many felt that Ho Chi Minh was a patriot fighting the French to achieve independence for his country. There was considerable admiration for this slight, wispy figure struggling to throw off colonialism. These sentiments made the question of military aid a touchy one.

An additional complicating factor was the degree to which the country's armed forces had become enmeshed in domestic politics and had resorted to arms in the power scramble, as happened in the abortive *coup d'état* of February, 1949. On balance, however, it seemed to me that Communist efforts to engulf all of Southeast Asia were of such gravity that the extension of military aid, which the Government had requested, was a step we must take in the hope that it would unite the armed forces and create the will and determination to defend King, country and Buddhist faith, as the Thai people had done in the past.

The open and unprovoked attack upon South Korea by the Communist forces of North Korea profoundly shocked the Thai. "So this is what the Communists do" was the comment of the man in the street. The promptness with which the United States and the United Nations came to the assistance of the victim created an equally deep impression. A small country like Thailand must have strong friends like the United States and the United Nations, people began to say. The Prime Minister announced dramatically that Thailand had offered to send twenty thousand tons of rice and four thousand men to fight under the flag of the United Nations. He had asked me what response the Government should make to the appeal of the United Nations for assistance. I had suggested rice but was not sure about the advisability of sending troops, since the country might need every fighting man she had to defend herself. But fifteen thousand men volunteered, including Buddhist priests! Thai units in Korea made a splendid record. Their stamina, their courage and their fortitude earned them the nickname of the "Little Tigers."

In July, our Government announced its willingness to extend military assistance to Thailand. By the end of August, a military mission, which our Government had decided to send to the countries of Southeast Asia who had requested aid, arrived in Bangkok and spent almost a month. In collaboration with the Ministry of Defense and the senior officers of Army, Navy and Air Force, a careful appraisal of conditions and needs was made. Schedules of most urgently needed equipment were drawn up and a training program mapped out. In connection with this program, I again emphasized that American military personnel should be carefully selected to achieve maximum results and, in particular, to win the confidence and trust of the Thai officers with whom they would work.

Several weeks of intense negotiations culminated in the signing of a military assistance agreement on October 17, 1950, and by the end of the year considerable quantities of military supplies had arrived, which I formally turned over to the Prime Minister on January 12, 1951. "Thailand's destiny is freedom," I said on that day as many thousands crowded the Phra Mehru grounds in front of the Grand Palace to watch the ceremony and see their troops swing briskly by the reviewing stand with their new weapons, all of which were blessed by Buddhist priests sitting in a special pavilion nearby. Such conformity with ancient religious custom greatly pleased the people.

"Like grasping at three fishes with two hands," sighed Josie when I told her we were leaving the next day to open the new Consulate at Chiengmai. I knew she meant we were trying to do too much. The pace of events during the previous months had been most strenuous but we both realized how important it was to establish a Consulate and good library at Chiengmai, the second largest city in the Kingdom.

It was clear and cool in the early morning, as we left Bangkok. We followed the railway north through a gap in the mountains where air pockets bumped the plane around. Below lay a long, narrow plain well watered and rich with rice and other agricultural products. All around are blue-green mountains famous for their stately teak trees, wild orchids and wild animals. The plane taxied down a lumpy gravel runway and came to a stop.

Our new Consul, energetic young Bob Anderson and his charming wife, Thai officials, and members of the American community met us. On the way into the city, we passed ancient ruins of bygone splendor when Chiengmai was the capital of a northern kingdom. Today it is a thriving commercial city, but it has lost none of its singular charm with its hundreds of temples, markets to which the hill tribes, dressed in strange costumes, bring their produce, craftsmen beating out intricate patterns in silver, while women sit from dawn to dusk before primitive wooden looms weaving colorful skirts and scarves, gossiping the while.

In this fascinating town, American Presbyterian missionaries have labored for nearly a century and have established schools, hospitals and a leper colony which are famous throughout the country.

The day after our arrival I had the pleasure of opening the new

(257)

American Consulate and the library which had been set up in one corner of the grounds. The following morning we visited the library and were delighted to find it filled with visitors eagerly examining the magazines and reference books. In the children's corner, a young Thai girl was telling fairy stories to the youngsters who sat quietly in their little chairs, their eyes big and round. They were listening to "Little Red Riding Hood" with as much pleasure as they did to their own stories of ogres and fairies.

Back in Bangkok we greeted a new member of the Embassy staff and his wife, the Andersons. Another hardship case, we said to one another as we prepared to send them summer clothing, dishes, cutlery and kitchen utensils. He had first been ordered to a post in a cold climate and described how, after raising a loan with great difficulty, he had outfitted himself and family with winter clothes. En route to his post, he received orders transferring him to Bangkok. He and his family arrived in the hottest weather with no light-weight clothes and no money to buy anything. It was a year before their meager belongings arrived, many of them broken, damaged or ruined owing to rough handling and exposure to the elements at many strange ports as the boxes wandered around the world. They have had a very hard time.

Hardship cases of this sort are not uncommon in the Foreign Service. But unfortunately, the American public has gained the notion that the life of a Foreign Service Officer is a continuous round of pink teas and lush living. This is not the case. For the majority of the men in the Service who are without private means it is a career liberally sprinkled with hardship and discomfort and is a constant struggle to make ends meet.

We had deferred our home leave, something else a Foreign Service Officer must often do, because of pressing negotiations over economic and military aid and other matters. I was also anxious to see our economic and military missions established and functioning.

It was, therefore, not until the end of April, 1951, that we were able to leave.

Although we were only going on home leave for a bit of a rest and medical attention, the Prime Minister gave us a sumptuous farewell garden party. Our diplomatic and other friends were no less kind and hospitable, but the farewell which most deeply touched us was that of Ah Ngee, our faithful number one boy. He had been ill for a long time but had gotten up from his bed to say good-by. A thin and tottery skeleton, he placed his tribute of flowers around Josie's neck. "Madam, I no can say anything, words no come up, they go down."

It was, though we did not know it then, the last time we were ever to see him.

23

The Essential Export—
Men of Good Will

We flew to Singapore to catch the S.S. *Taronga,* a Danish freighter, which was to carry us at a leisurely pace, along with its cargo of copra, through the Indian Ocean to Genoa. Because of congestion of shipping in the Singapore harbor, there was a long delay, during which we imposed greatly on the hospitality of our young Consul General, Jack Goodyear.

This interval gave me an opportunity to meet again with Malcolm MacDonald and other British officials. Malcolm was Commissioner General of Malaya and one of those postwar British statesmen who have had the vision to see that the era of colonialism has passed, and that the Asian peoples must be given their independence with an opportunity to work out their own destinies. An attractive, dynamic individual, he possessed both the knowledge and the understanding to win the confidence and friendship of the Malayan and Chinese people. They regarded him as their friend and responded to his leadership to unite them in their efforts to achieve an autonomous and progressive government for Malaya, that verdant land, rich with tin, rubber and other products.

We sat on the terrace of the stone-turreted castle rented by the British Government from the Sultan of Johore, looking out at puffy Kelly-green islands floating on the blue-green waters of the Straits of Johore. Our conversation turned naturally to the situation in Malaya.

There was some improvement, he explained, but added it was a slow business because the guerrilla bands were so elusive and their organization, especially among the Chinese squatter population living on the fringes of the jungle, was so efficient and extensive. It had been decided, he told me, to undertake a gigantic resettlement program and move these sources of supply away from the guerrillas.

"But, Malcolm," I said, "can the flow of supplies really be stopped? Won't the result be to drive the Communists underground? At least, you know now that most of them are in the jungles; if you drive them underground, they'll be everywhere and nowhere."

There was such a danger, he conceded, but he believed they would have to risk it.

We discussed Thai-British co-operation along the frontier bordering Thailand and Malaya. As he knew, I had supplemented British efforts to persuade the Thai authorities to co-operate more fully against guerilla bands which were evading British forces when they attempted to close in on them by taking refuge in the thick jungle along the border of Thailand.

It was a long, hot and lazy voyage, with the ship calling at Penang and Colombo. When we crossed the broad Indian Ocean, millions of tiny black copra beetles appeared in the excessive heat, emerging from the copra bales deep in the bowels of the ship to bask in the hot sunshine on deck and to join the passengers. They were everywhere: in the soup, in the beds, in the folds of one's clothes, in ears and eyes and noses. They just wanted to have fun and frolic and their antics on the dining table were amusing if unappetizing. Not until the cool breezes of the Mediterranean Sea fanned our hot faces did they make up their minds to stop teasing the ship.

At first, the Italian villages seemed beautiful and serene, far from the world's clashing politics. Then I noticed an array of posters on a wall, exhorting the people to vote Communist in forthcoming elections. Was there no escape from it anywhere?

Even with a seamen's strike in full swing, the United States looked mighty good as we stepped ashore in New York to find our own luggage and carry our own bags. For a short week end we could be with our beloved people and then I went to Washington.

I was aware of a change. From the President to the Secretary of State and on down I noticed that there was much greater interest in Thailand and Southeast Asia than on my previous trips home. The war in Korea, the war in Indochina, the jungle fighting in Malaya had served to focus greater attention on that part of the world. There was an awareness of the importance of Southeast Asia in relation to global problems and of the fact that Thailand had been the first Asian nation to offer to send troops to Korea and was standing stoutly behind the action taken by the United States and the United Nations in repelling Communist aggression against South Korea.

The next two weeks were consumed by conferences. In July, Washington is hotter than tropical Bangkok and Government conferences boiled with arguments, frayed the nerves, agitated the bile and were apt to be utterly frustrating.

Problems with respect to Thailand and Southeast Asia were so numerous and so important that one longed for quick decisions.

At the same time I realized that the stresses and strains of the troubled world were so great, pleas for aid from friendly countries so numerous, that even Solomon could not have made instant decisions.

In the midst of these activities, a dramatic message came from our Embassy in Bangkok. Prime Minister Phibul had been kidnaped by his Navy.

Secretary Acheson sent for me. "Ed," he asked, "what on earth does all this mean?"

I told him I felt certain the cause stemmed, as in the past, from rivalry between Phibul and Pridi. The latter still had a considerable following, especially among elements in the Navy, and with their help he had attempted to overthrow Phibul in February, 1949. I thought the present incident was another effort on the part of the Navy either to overthrow the Government completely or to force agreement to certain demands. The outcome would depend on whether the key figures in Phibul's group came to his assistance. The men most prominent in the Thai power struggle were General Phao, Chief of Police; General Sarasdit, deputy Commander in Chief of the Army; and Air Force Marshal Ronapakas. They were known as the three tigers. Their rivalries and ambitions were causing Prime Minister Phibul increasing discomfort. They were all opposed to Pridi and to the elements in the Navy who supported him so I was inclined to believe that they would support Phibul.

They did. Later dispatches from Bangkok reported that they had conferred and presented an ultimatum to the Navy to release the Prime Minister, who was being held prisoner aboard the Navy gunboat H.M.S. *Ayuthia*. When there was no reply to the ultimatum, an Air Force plane zoomed down over the gunboat, scoring several hits, and causing it to sink. In the ensuing confusion the Prime Minister, a courageous man, dived overboard and swam ashore. An hour later, immaculately clad in a white sharkskin suit, he was back in Government House, calmly issuing orders as though nothing had happened, and in complete command of the situation.

When I had completed my official work in Washington the medical officer of the State Department popped me into the hospital for treatment of hypertension, which had developed in Bangkok eight months before. Modern medicine is, no doubt, a wonderful thing, but modern medical tests are so rigorous that the patient often leaves the hospital feeling worse rather than better. The doctors recommended a complicated operation, which had been successful in a few cases, but I had had enough and elected to go off into the woods to join Josie in our small cottage in Connecticut. Digging in the garden "cleaned my mind," as our Thai driver used to say, of political problems and worries. After a few weeks of this rustic life I was ready to tackle the job again.

The telephone rang one day way off there in the woods. It was the State Department urging me to delay departure in order to serve on the Foreign Service Selection and Promotion Board, which was to meet early in November. The work of this board is vital to the Service, involving as it does the careful reviewing of the efficiency records of Foreign Service Officers, recommending their promotion or, if necessary, separation from the Service. The board consisted of several distinguished businessmen and educators who worked together with representatives from various agencies of the Government and the State Department. Inviting individuals from outside the Government to sit on these boards was a relatively new procedure, but a sound one that resulted in greater impartiality and fairness in the promotion of career and non-career members of the Service. Every member of the board felt his responsibility and no final decision was taken until it had been thoroughly weighed and discussed.

We worked for six weeks, spending long hours poring over the records and all pertinent data concerning senior officers. First we rated them, then determined those to be promoted, and finally those unfortunates to be separated from the service for reasons of inefficiency.

We left New York on an icy January afternoon and landed in the warm humid air of Thailand, after eight months' absence. Nothing stands still and Air Marshal Ronny proudly pointed out the vast improvements at the airport, how the runway was being extended, the buildings being remodeled and new ones built. Many Thai friends and lots of the staff were there to greet us, including the new chief of the Economic Aid Mission, Austin Flegel, and Colonel Sheldon, the Chief of the Military Assistance Advisory Group.

But there was no Ah Ngee. That faithful friend had passed away three weeks after our departure, leaving his wife and nine children, all of whom he had himself delivered, unassisted. We missed him greatly.

The official family had grown from twenty in 1946 to nearly two hundred, counting families. This sudden influx of American officialdom brought in its wake problems galore. From all sides there came disheartening stories of grumbling among the newcomers, particularly among the wives, who were discontented with conditions, with the tropical climate, and enveloped in their own boredom. Because many of them were willing to pay anything for a house and a cook, prices of servants and rents rose sharply, causing criticism from other foreign residents. There was discord and jealousy caused in part by sheer ignorance of what was expected of them in their jobs and new positions. Few of the American women had ever been away from the United States before and this new experience proved to be upsetting.

It would be well for a man to pause sufficiently before entering the Foreign Service or other Government service abroad to measure thoroughly not only himself but his wife. I include the wife because it is particularly true that in faraway countries she can help him, hinder him or even totally ruin his usefulness. Carried away by pictures of a glamorous life abroad, they often fail to take stock. It is important that they should search their inner minds and characters before offering themselves and face squarely the many unusual aspects of the future. Much heartache could be avoided, many criticisms against them and their country averted if they would honestly ask themselves, "Are my wife and I sufficiently tolerant of the thoughts, customs and religious beliefs of foreign peoples?"

I never finished reading the five cartloads of books which my venerable old Chinese teacher advised me to read so many years ago. If I had, no doubt I would be a wiser man today. But fragments have come to me from the books I did dip into, and from hard knocks in the Foreign Service. I have come to know that tolerance of other men's religious beliefs, opinions and ways of life is fundamental. This way lies the formation of friendships based on mutual respect, particularly with the peoples of Asia. We can learn much from their mature wisdom, and when tolerance blends into eager desire fully to understand and fathom the mind and spirit of these peoples it is an inspiring and rewarding experience.

The East moves slowly and in its own way. Insistence on quick action in the Western way not only perplexes the Asian, to whom time is not of the essence, but also breeds irritation and resentment. And the Foreign Service Officer finds patience equally indispensable in his relations with his colleagues. He needs it to endure the "slings and arrows" thrown his way by difficult and crotchety superiors and the whims and vagaries of his own bureaucratic Government. Burned indelibly on my mind is the recollection that not a day passed in my long career when patience, above and beyond the call of duty, was not absolutely essential.

Government service abroad is not a career from which to expect monetary gain, easy living, easy promotion or public plaudits. At the risk of sounding preachy, let me say that an unusual degree of selflessness is one of the most essential requirements. It is, if you will, a kind of dedication to the service of one's country, coupled with curiosity and desire to learn how others live, and something about their customs, religions, ideas and language.

One young couple told us upon arriving at their post, "I guess it's all right here, but it would be better if there were only Americans." They never tried to like the people of the country to which they had been sent. Many were full of fears. Fearful of disease, fearful of the people and their strange customs, fearful of the native foods. And yet one simply must learn to eat the native foods, for this invariably wins the approval of people abroad, particularly the Asian people, as nothing else does. The discomforts, the fact that things are not as they are at home and the feeling of loneliness are severe tests of adaptability. How quickly the attitude of the new arrival can change from eagerness to sullen grumbling! It wasn't what he had expected. He doesn't like his job. His wife is hurt because her husband is of junior rank and in consequence they are not included in all official social life. They are dragged down in an orgy of self-pity.

Under the special stresses and strains of civil wars and tense political conditions, which are encountered in so many countries, dependability is all-important. I have known officers to crack up on the job in the face of the dangers growing out of wars and hazardous conditions. What is called for is a degree of self-control that rises to meet crises and emergencies of an unusual nature.

One needs a pretty thick skin in Government service, whether one be ambassador or a junior vice consul. A constant stream of criticism both from one's own people and from the people of the country in which one is serving must be expected. It is unpalatable and hard to take and often totally undeserved. But in the Service one must swallow hard and take it, again and again. Nor can one afford to be offended by the seeming slight. A wife rushed to Josie one day and vowed she would never enter a certain Embassy again because she had been "insulted." The fancied insult arose because no one had paid any attention to her at a reception. One must be prepared, too, for slights and insults from visitors, some important, others not, or from colleagues in other embassies. A philosophical imperviousness to slights and criticism is essential.

A man needs sound judgment in life, but in the Foreign Service of the United States it is a "must." So many crises arise which the standard instructions do not fit. One often finds oneself alone with an important and delicate decision to make. Good judgment in one case I know of meant the saving of a number of Americans in dire danger. In another case, poor judgment caused our Government acute embarrassment and impaired our friendly relations.

"We like Americans," a Thai told me, "because they smile at us." To smile seems a simple act, but time and again I have seen an interested smile win friends for the United States. In fact, more is frequently accomplished by a smile than through labored diplomacy. It has been my experience that literally everyone responds, from fierce bandits to stiff and formal Prime Ministers. I have often thought that our personnel departments in Washington when seeking good men for service abroad might well give a high rating to the candidate with a friendly personality and a warm and sympathetic smile. Like the calling card in China in the old days, it makes the difference between success and failure.

At my urging Josie, with misgivings and reluctance, called a meeting at which there were more than a hundred women. She tried to clear up for them questions of protocol, calling, housing, servants, wages, food prices, personal problems. It was, she stressed, important to respect Thai customs, traditions and religion, and to maintain a decent but not an ostentatious scale of living.

No miracle followed but there was a greater sense of belonging and unity in working toward a common purpose among the new arrivals. Periodic meetings were scheduled for the whole group, regular days for calling were organized in order that Americans could at least get acquainted with one another. Josie set aside two afternoons a week for open house at teatime, at which everyone was welcomed. For the remainder of our stay in Bangkok these "at homes" were maintained; they enabled us to meet and entertain a variety of people: our own staff, officials and business newcomers, visitors and tourists, and our friends of every nationality from every walk of life.

I was keen to find out what had happened during my absence. From Austin Flegel, head of our Economic Mission, I heard that materials and equipment were dribbling in slowly; on the other hand, a DDT campaign against malaria in the northern provinces and an anti-rinderpest campaign to save the cattle in the northeast had proved immensely popular with the country people. Rice culture research was under way and we were helping an agriculture college where young Thai were being trained as agricultural experts. The dredger for the harbor, which had been presented to the Government on the same day that the Prime Minister was dramatically kidnaped by his own Navy, was at work deepening the river channel so that large vessels might dock at Bangkok.

Colonel Sheldon reported that the Military Assistance Program was moving more slowly, partly because of non-arrival of promised equipment and partly because of the language difficulties and the necessity of translating many of our military manuals into Thai. The Air Force, whose flagging morale had been revived by the receipt of a squadron of the fastest planes they had ever flown, had made the greatest progress.

We had made a good start. I pointed out, however, that it was important for us not to be impatient, not to insist that the American way is the only way; and not only to show them how to use the new equipment but also share our knowledge as equal partners and friends. Above all, we must convince the Thai of our real interest in them, in the development of their country, and the strengthening of their defenses.

From my brilliant young political officer, Norman Hannah, I learned of disheartening developments which had taken place and had set back the slow progress being made toward a more democratic form of government. On his return in December, 1951, from Switzerland where he had gone for treatment of an eye ailment, the King was advised that the military supporters of Prime Minister Phibul had dissolved the National Assembly, thrown the constitution out of the window, and prepared a new one which greatly curtailed the powers of the King and made the Assembly an appointive, rubber-stamp organization. The King had barely set foot in Bangkok when he was met by leaders of this political move who requested him to ratify what had already been done, and to promulgate the constitution they had drafted. He replied that he would take the matter under advisement.

Such was the situation. Friends of Thailand as well as many serious-minded Thai were exceedingly unhappy over these events. However, the Prime Minister and his supporters took the position that the country was not yet ready for full democratic government and that some of the elected members of the Lower House had been obstructive. They professed to be supporters of democracy but asserted that the dangers surrounding the country called for strong leadership.

Negotiations between the King and the military group continued for some weeks, the King seeking to have included in the constitution certain provisions regarding elective government and the safeguarding of civil liberties. Finally, compromises were agreed upon, the constitution promulgated, and an Assembly appointed, packed with Government supporters. The shell of constitutional government remained but the people had little voice in the Assembly.

24

Subversion—the Insidious Weapon

In order to see for myself how our programs were progressing in that underdeveloped section of the northeast adjoining Indochina we flew there to take a look. Once again I was impressed by the desolate nature of this region. As part of our economic aid program we had bored wells and installed hand pumps in a number of villages. I found many of them broken and others not in use. "No good," the villagers claimed. But they expressed enthusiasm about the dams which we were helping them to build across streams in order to impound the precious water when the rains poured down. This was something tangible they seemed to understand, and made sound sense to them.

We visited some of the farmers' huts. By our standards there were few worldly goods: a couple of earthenware jars to store rain water, a basket of rice, some dried chilies and fish, straw mats, a few cooking pots and, prominent in the dwelling, a swinging hammock made of string for the babies. Most farmers possessed a buffalo to plow their two or three acres of land. The fact that the majority of farmers in Thailand do own their own land is a stabilizing economic and political factor.

It was subsistence living and little else, but the farmers were cheerful and happy with the prospect that the new dams would give them a bit more water for their crops. There was no doubt that an acceleration of our efforts jointly with the Thai Irrigation Department to build these small dams wherever possible would be a boon to the farmers in many ways. We also had health teams working in the area, together with the Ministry of Public Health and the World Health Organization, treating the adults and children who suffered from yaws and whose gaping wounds cried out for medical attention. A small beginning and a tremendous need.

Further south but in the same general area we held a meeting of the Fulbright Educational Board. Our group made a complete round of the schools in the town where the children were all lined up primly in their clean blue and white uniforms and the teachers smiled us a shy welcome. The latter begged us for books and reading materials for their school libraries. "We want to learn; give us the books," they pleaded. I promised to send them all we could and wished that we had trainloads of books to distribute. All through this area we found the same desire for reading material, but it must be in simple Thai and English.

The basic Thai educational system founded some fifty years ago is sound. Primary education is compulsory but at the university level facilities are inadequate. Both the United Nations and the United States are co-operating with the Ministry of Education in improving teacher-training techniques.

The hospitality extended to us, as always in this land of friendly people, was overwhelming. The affable Governor of Ubon, the City of Lotuses, gave us a banquet and ordered his officials and their wives to appear in full dress. The ladies brought out their most treasured multicolored silver-and-gold brocaded silks. This special evening was a moving demonstration of warm good will for the United States. "The friendship between Thailand and the United States is as close as the petals of the lotus," said the Governor. It was a sentiment graciously expressed and approved by all.

After an exceptionally delicious dinner, prepared by a French-trained Vietnamese, who skillfully blended European and Thai cooking, we were treated to folk dancing in which the wives of the officials, dressed in bright skirts, performed a most intricate dance between bamboo poles maneuvered in and out between the dancers' feet to a rapid syncopation thumped out on the drums.

The Governor took me into several stores on the main street to talk to the Vietnamese storekeepers. One was a medicine shop selling pickled snake, dried tiger bones and other weird remedies for various ailments. The owner was a wispy little old man, with exaggeratedly high cheekbones and a scrawny straggly beard. A large picture of Ho Chi Minh hung on the wall. Pointing to the picture I asked through an interpreter how he liked Ho. The little man, who looked rather like Ho Chi Minh himself, hesitated, looked from me to the Governor, and finally blurted out, "He is a great man. He will save my country from the French." He refused to say anything about the Communists and seemed to be scared he had already said too much. In the other stores which we visited, all of them fairly prosperous, I noticed pictures of Ho Chi Minh staring down at me. I also observed that the shops were tended by old people.

"Where are the young men?" I asked the Governor.

At first he was reluctant to reply and then admitted that many of them had gone across the river to the Communists. That was no doubt the truth and confirmed reports of heavy recruitment by the Vietminh Communist agents of the young men. They had gone to join Ho Chi Minh's armies. I asked the Governor to speak frankly to me about the Vietnamese. He told me that those who had fled from Indochina during the last world war had been permitted by the Thai authorities to settle in the northeast. They had been industrious and well behaved and had caused no trouble, he said. He did not know much about the activities of the Communist agents among them except that the Vietnamese Communists were well organized, that there was smuggling across the river into Indochina, and that many of their young men had disappeared mysteriously.

"Are you not fearful that they will cause trouble?" I asked.

He smoothed his forehead thoughtfully. "So far no trouble. In the future, who can say? But the Government at Bangkok has ordered us to watch them carefully because of the trouble going on over there," and he pointed toward Indochina.

Because these Vietnamese residents were so docile and well behaved, the Thai had not investigated their secret activities. But the French constantly complained about the smuggling of arms and supplies and the recruitment of young men for the Vietminh armies.

The Thai would now dearly love to see all fifty thousand Vietnamese returned to their homes but this is complicated and costly, since the majority of them come from Communist-controlled north Vietnam. With the steady deterioration of the situation in Indochina and the probability that the Kingdom of Laos will fall to the Communists by subversion, thus bringing the Communists right to the northeastern frontier of Thailand, the Thai now realize the danger of having the Vietnamese in their midst. The United States, too, is alive to this danger and for this reason much of our aid is being expended in the northeastern provinces, with a view to improving the people's livelihood, health, educational facilities, communications, as well as strengthening the defenses of that region.

The Bangkok press was full of outpourings on the subject of peace, which flowed in an endless stream out of Moscow and Peiping. They were not without appeal to the Thai, who are followers of the Lord Buddha's doctrine of nonviolence and who, by nature, are gentle and mild. Those of us who were anxiously watching the course of Red activities in Thailand noted with dismay the subtle efforts which had been made during the past twelve months to win over the Thai people. Buddhist priests were being told that the doctrines of Marx and the Lord Buddha had much in common. Enticing words were uttered to teachers, students and writers, and pamphlets distributed not only about intellectual and material freedom but also about the struggle for world peace. The number of Thai thus converted is difficult to estimate but the number of newspapers and magazines which repeated the Communist patter was unpleasantly disturbing. I felt that much of what was appearing in the Thai press was born not of conviction but of liberal cash distributions through the Soviet Legation in Bangkok.

The propaganda chorus swelled to crescendo as a series of well-organized meetings was held in the city, at which the theme of peace and the forthcoming world peace conference to be held at Peiping were extravagantly praised and eulogized. Well-known Thai intellectuals, teachers, students, priests and writers were present at these meetings and selected representatives to attend the Peiping conference. The Government, becoming concerned, decreed that any Thai leaving the country for Communist China would lose his citizenship. Nevertheless, a few did slip away to join the small group of Thai already in Peiping who are occasionally used as mouthpieces for propaganda directed against Prime Minister Phibul's Government and, as always, against the United States.

These events showed only too plainly that the Communist apparatus was becoming bolder, increasingly active, and furthermore proved that present efforts were being directed toward winning over the Thai. In my concern, I urged on the Prime Minister, as I had on many previous occasions, the need of trying to ferret out their plans. He sighed and said that he had instructed General Phao, the Chief of Police, to infiltrate the Communist organiza-

tion without fail. I do not believe they had much success in penetrating the hard core of the Communist machine in the country,
which is composed of Chinese.

The stage was set for more serious revelations as a result of
overindulgence in the bottle by a young Air Force officer who
became too talkative. He was a brilliant and daring young major,
the officer who dived his plane to sink the gunboat on which Prime
Minister Phibul was being held captive by the Navy in the summer
of 1951. In his cups one night he extolled the might of Soviet
Russia and the power of Communist China. The gist of his drunken
remarks was reported to senior officers who decided a change of
scene might clear his head and his ideas. He was accordingly
shipped off to London as attaché to the Thai Embassy.

British intelligence was dubious about him and his associates.
They found a sheaf of damaging documents and a diary. This was
reported to the Thai authorities, who ordered him home and
arrested him as he stepped off the plane. His diary was incrimi-
nating indeed. It showed that he had been completely won over
by the Communists and had joined a group plotting to overthrow
the Government, eliminate the King, and establish a so-called
People's Government with the aid of "liberation forces." The diary
further showed that Air Force data and defense plans had been
turned over to the Soviet Legation in Bangkok by his wife for a
cash consideration. Conveniently, the names of a number of conspirators were listed in the major's diary.

The Prime Minister ordered the Chief of Police, in conjunction
with the chiefs of the Army, Navy and Air Force, to take immediate steps to arrest all the conspirators, among them several junior
officers in the other armed services as well as a number of civilians.
The orders were carried out early in November, 1952, and for good
measure Police Chief Phao also rounded up both Chinese and Thai
who had been active in the bogus Communist peace campaign.

Subversion—the Insidious Weapon

While the public was reading avidly about the Communist plot to overthrow their King and seize the country, the Government pushed through the National Assembly a stringent anti-Communist bill, which outlawed Communism or the advocacy of Communism in any way. At the same time, a Chinese Communist publication center was closed by the police and Thai newspapers, which had recently printed pro-Communist propaganda, were sternly warned to mend their ways.

The revelation of the existence of such an extensive plot brought home to the Thai, at least those in Bangkok, in startling manner the fact that their country is a definite Communist objective. Great credit is due Prime Minister Phibul for the prompt and decisive action he took, though key Communist figures eluded the dragnet. The danger has not been eliminated by any means but the people, having felt its hot breath, have a greater awareness, while the authorities are more on the alert.

Subversion is the most insidious weapon being employed by the skillful forces seeking the engulfment of Southeast Asia. In each country subversive forces are at work. This is the danger, in my estimation, rather than from open attack, which would be risky for Communist China in view of the provisions of the Manila Pact. Furthermore, it would be so cynical a violation of the unctuous nonaggression pledges given by Communist China to the countries of Southeast Asia that they would flee from the silken web of "peaceful coexistence" being spun around them.

The Year of the Snake, 1953, was ushered in by Peiping announcing the establishment of a "Thai Autonomous Government" in south China in the province of Yunnan. The Communists had chosen the ancient homeland of the Thai people in which to set up a puppet government formed from among two hundred thousand Thai who had remained behind in China when their brothers migrated into Burma and spread into Thailand and Laos, more than a thousand years ago. It was a dramatic political move, shrewdly planned to revive the idea of a mighty federation of all Thai in Southeast Asia. It was an idea which had appealed to more than one Thai statesman and now the Communists, through their puppet Thai Government, were cleverly fostering this same vision. It was diabolically cunning. It has disturbed Thailand as nothing else has done, because the hidden danger can be seen through the sugar-coated appeal.

From the spurious Thai Government set up in South China, Bangkok turned its eyes to the northeast as Vietminh columns thrust suddenly into the Kingdom of Laos. In two weeks they were knocking at the gates of the royal city of Luang Prabang, and were within sight of the Mekong River which divides Laos and Thailand. Tense, busy days of consultation followed, but the Prime Minister took quick and sensible measures to strengthen the country's defenses along the northeastern frontier. Again in 1954 Vietminh columns sliced through Laos to the Mekong River and directly threatened Thailand. There is no doubt they could do so at any time but in future it is more likely their forces will be merged with those of dissident Laos and Cambodian guerrillas in order to maintain the fiction that these efforts to overthrow the established governments are strictly internal matters.

In general, the picture in Southeast Asia is somber, although relieved here and there by flashes of brightness. The thought of Communist successes in Vietnam is certainly sobering. In the northern half of the country is now established a hard, disciplined and efficient Communist regime under Ho Chi Minh receiving substantial material and political aid from Communist China and the Russians. It confidently expects to absorb the southern half, where political and other problems give little time to build for unity and freedom. Ho Chi Minh looks west to the Kingdom

of Laos and notes with satisfaction the growing strength of the
Pathet Laos puppet regime which he has created. He wonders
how long the legitimate Government can stand against the subversive activities of his puppet creation. He looks south to the
Kingdom of Cambodia and knows that there, too, many of his experienced agents and guerrilla leaders are seeking to make common
cause with dissident Cambodian elements in order to overthrow
the Cambodian Government. The prospects for the three states of
Indochina are not bright. We are aiding these people, but only by
a spirit of unity and resolute determination, which we cannot instill
but which must come from the people themselves, will it be possible for them to halt Communist subversion that burrows deep
like the termite.

Thailand, the oldest sovereign and independent country in Southeast Asia, is feeling external pressures from the bogus Thai Government in south China and from increasing Vietminh strength
in Indochina. Within the country itself, subversion is present
through the activities of secret Communist groups working among
the Thai, the Chinese and the Vietnamese. Bitterness among the
remnant supporters of Pridi Phanomyong, now in exile in Communist China; complaints of the people concerning widespread
corruption and nepotism among the ruling military clique; and
the beginnings of economic distress caused by declining demand
for Thai rice, are all problems or irritations which the Communists
can and are exploiting. But on the credit side of the scales may be
placed the old and strong traditions of freedom which in times
past resulted in the Thai people bending under aggression and
pressure but, like the bamboo, never breaking. Respect and reverence for Buddhism and the King, a plenitude of food, a disposition on the part of the people not to worry, are all assets which,
taken in conjunction with Thailand's satisfactory foreign relations,
her standing in the United Nations and her especially solid friend-

(279)

ship with the United States, make this little country the brightest spot in Southeast Asia. The Thai are our best friends in that part of the world and Prime Minister Phibul told the Congress, on his recent visit to the United States, "The Thai will always be by your side."

The Chinese Communist colossus sprawls along Burma's northwestern frontier. It quietly spreads the insidious poison of subversion among the hill tribes of Burma, though suave Prime Minister Chou En-lai talks of nonaggression, noninterference and peaceful coexistence. Prime Minister Nu and his Government have had considerable success in reducing the strength of the Communist guerrilla bands within Burma and in pacifying the country so that extensive plans for economic development might move forward. Communist subversive efforts continue but I believe the future of Burma is brighter. We need to remember that for several years the rulers of Burma have been combating Communism within their borders. We need also to understand that their friendly relations with Communist China spring in part from fear of the Chinese Communists and the belief that the best way to get along with this powerful neighbor is to placate him, and in part from suspicions and doubts concerning the motives of the Western powers, who as colonial rulers have left a bitter impress on the minds of many Asian nations, which only time and understanding will eradicate.

The dense, steaming jungles of Malaya still hide tough Chinese Communist guerrillas who for the past seven years have kept sizable British and Malayan forces fully occupied. Costly military operations and costly resettlement of Chinese squatters supplying food to the guerrillas have brought some success. But with the flexibility characteristic of Communist operations, their major effort is now being made through Chinese schools and labor unions. These activities jeopardize the newly established governments in the

Crown Colony of Singapore and in the Federation of Malaya. Recent events demonstrate Communist strength and underscore the fact that the struggle in Malaya has not ended.

In the fair land of Indonesia, the Communist party increases in strength and influence and stands, like the proverbial Trojan horse, ready to seize control when the opportunity arises. But hope lies in the fact that strong Moslem organizations and a number of sober political leaders realize the danger.

Such, it seems to me, are the realities of the situation in Southeast Asia, but the brightest prospects spring from the new Asian spirit which is determined to achieve freedom, progress and prosperity in its own way. It is a spirit we must seek to understand more fully as we continue our efforts to help them.

25

Words Go Down

Seven years of service in Thailand resulted in our putting down roots deep into the rich soil of the country. To pull up those roots, watered by the mellowness of its culture and arts, by the charm of its people, by the *sanuk* joyousness of its philosophy, by the baffling complexity of its politics, by the beauty of the countryside and by our own warm personal relationships with them, was exceedingly painful. But now the time had come to leave.

It hurt to part from our many friends, both high and low. It hurt to stop work on the many programs I had had the good fortune of initiating. It hurt Josie, too, to terminate her activities with the School for the Blind and other interests. It hurt to stop working with my own dependable Embassy staff and the staffs of our various missions. We were choked with emotion and bereft of words at a party given by the entire Embassy staff, including messengers and chauffeurs, when Nai Tit, the senior Thai member, spoke of their sorrow and regret at our departure. For weeks we lived in an atmosphere surcharged with emotion as we went from farewell party to farewell party, listened to kind tributes and said good-by to the many friends who came to call. There were Thai notables, princes, politicians in and out of the Government, diplomatic colleagues, businessmen, policemen and tradespeople. The house was fragrant with the flowers they left.

What could we say when a former Prime Minister handed us a little ivory Buddha, "To keep you safe on your journey," or when Li Sing the Chinese tailor brought us a silver cigarette stand with the explanation, "Sixty per cent silver, madame, good for forty years," or the watch repair man came with two pairs of silver chopsticks, or our Chinese-Thai friends from the thieves market gave us a set of miniature brass temple bells, "To make music in your house in America"? They were all our friends and we found the word "good-by" came with great difficulty.

We called on Prime Minister Phibul and his wife and on other members of the Government. For five years I had worked with the Prime Minister on a wide range of problems. He had come to realize that the United States was deeply interested in the progress and welfare of the Thai people and in their freedom and independence. He knew well my own personal esteem and affection for his people and therefore did not take it amiss when we talked freely and frankly about matters both agreeable and disagreeable. His personal charm, his sincere interest in his country, his support of the United Nations, his desire for the most friendly relations with our own country made for an unusually harmonious relationship. I was deeply touched when he said with unaffected sincerity as I was leaving, "You are like one of us, we feel at home and easy with you and Mrs. Stanton."

The day before we were to leave, His Majesty the King invited us to a private lunch with him and Queen Sirikit. It was an informal lunch such as the King likes. Conversation was not shackled by formal protocol. The lovely young Queen and Josie chatted

about feminine things, children, jewels and dresses, which seem
to offer inexhaustible material. The Queen had more than borne
out my wife's prognostication that she would go far. She was very
beautiful and charming, the mother of two children (a third child
has since been born), and had captivated the people, who followed
avidly all activities of the royal couple and particularly the little
Prince and Princess. His Majesty was unusually relaxed. He talked
seriously for several hours with me after lunch concerning the state
of the nation and the welfare of his people. He was earnest and
frank regarding the efforts of the United States to help Thailand,
and while expressing appreciation for such help, spoke of the need
for more careful selection of American personnel in order to avoid
damaging good relations between the two countries. He was wistful
when he told me he wished people abroad would not think of him
only as a frivolous saxophone player or a mere family man. So
earnestly and intelligently did he discuss the problems facing the
country that I came away from the palace pleased and impressed.
He was no longer a boy-King but a King concerned over the welfare
of his people.

Our last day. The weather was the same; hot. The sprawling,
hospitable house was the same. The view of the green garden at
breakfast that morning with its trailing crimson bougainvilleas, red
hibiscus, yellow and pink canna lilies bordering the canal, was the
same. Bangkok was the same. But it was not the same for us. The
realization that we were leaving it hung over our minds as the
morning wore on and departure time neared. The servants were
confused and distracted, rushing about. We were likewise confused, talking without making much sense and dropping the wrong
things into the wrong bags. Our mongrel dog, Mr. Nuisance,
sensing the departure, ran around aimlessly in circles and looked
anxious. People kept coming, the telephone kept ringing.

The moment came. Nai Chin drove up slowly and solemnly in

the big black Packard, cleaned and polished with extra care. His wife, daughter and sons and all the servants assembled to garland us and bid us good-by. Chin's wife and daughter fell to their knees sobbing. Josie's little maid knelt wailing and clasped her about the knees. Wash ayah bowed her head low, crying bitterly. Josie was shaking all over as she patted each one of them affectionately. Finally I pulled her away. The car drove off. Josie was crying and looked a wreck. To distract her, I said, "Your hat is terribly unbecoming. Couldn't you find anything better?" That shook her. "I know it, but I wanted to be dignified for my last appearance and I haven't any other," she said miserably.

At the airport there was a huge crowd, including the Prime Minister, Government officials and children from the Blind School, as well as the Embassy family and all my diplomatic colleagues. As faithful Ah Ngee had said, "The words, they go down, no come up." It was impossible to say anything.

The plane began slowly to taxi down the runway. Faces blurred. Uplifted waving arms seemed intertwined. But to one side, standing at attention, were four of our servants in their white uniforms, silhouetted sharply against the side of the big black Packard. In the middle stood Chin slowly waving a little American flag. One last look at the bright green fields of rice below us, the glittering spires of the beautiful temples of the city, which had been our home for so long. The land seemed to melt into the sky as the plane slipped through the clouds. Now we fully realized we were leaving these Thai with whom we had worked unsparingly but happily for seven years. A warm wish welled from our hearts—may they always enjoy peace and freedom.

Index

(287)

Index

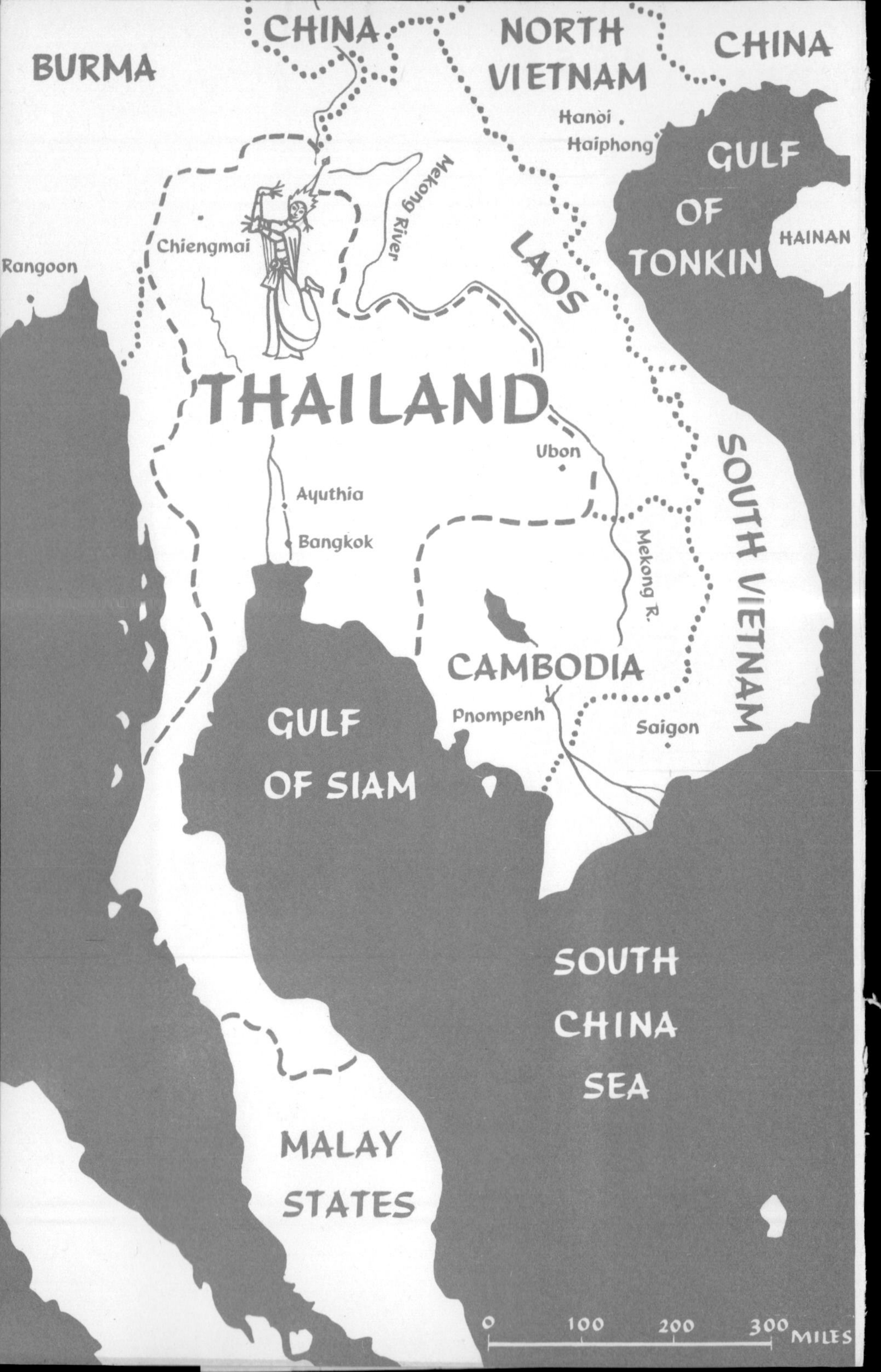
CHINA
NORTH VIETNAM
CHINA
BURMA
Hanoi
Haiphong
GULF OF TONKIN
HAINAN
Mekong River
Chiengmai
LAOS
Rangoon
THAILAND
Ubon
Ayuthia
Bangkok
SOUTH VIETNAM
Mekong R.
CAMBODIA
Pnompenh
Saigon
GULF OF SIAM
SOUTH CHINA SEA
MALAY STATES
0 100 200 300 MILES